LAST
LETTERS
from ATTU

The True Story of Etta Jones,
Alaska Pioneer and Japanese P.O.W.

Mary Breu

ALASKA
NORTHWEST
BOOKS®

Library of Congress Cataloging-in-Publication Data available upon request

ISBN 978-0-88240-810-1 (pbk.)
ISBN 978-0-88240-851-4, 978-08-88240-852-1 (e-book)
ISBN 978-0-88240-981-8 (hardbound)

Alaska Northwest Books®
An imprint of

GRAPHIC ARTS
BOOKS®
P.O. Box 56118
Portland, OR 97238-6118
(503) 254-5591
www.graphicartsbooks.com

Editor: Ellen Wheat
Interior Designer: Elizabeth Watson
Cover Design: Vicki Knapton, Elizabeth Watson

Front cover images. Top: The Montevideo Maru, *1942;*
Bottom: Etta Jones and Attu Natives, 1942.

Frontispiece. Etta Eugenie Schureman, high-school graduation photo, Vineland, New Jersey, 1898.

In memory of my great-aunt and great-uncle,

Etta and Foster Jones,

and all the victims of the Attu invasion

Etta and Foster on their dogsled, departing on their honeymoon, April 1, 1923.

Contents

RUSSIA

RUSSIA
U.S.A.

ATTU ISLAND

JAPAN

Yokohama

ATTU ISLAND

Cape
Wrangell

Holtz Bay

Attu Island

Copper Is.
Gibson Islands
Kennon Is.

Loaf Is. Chirikof
Mary Is. Point

Savage Is.

Massacre Bay

6

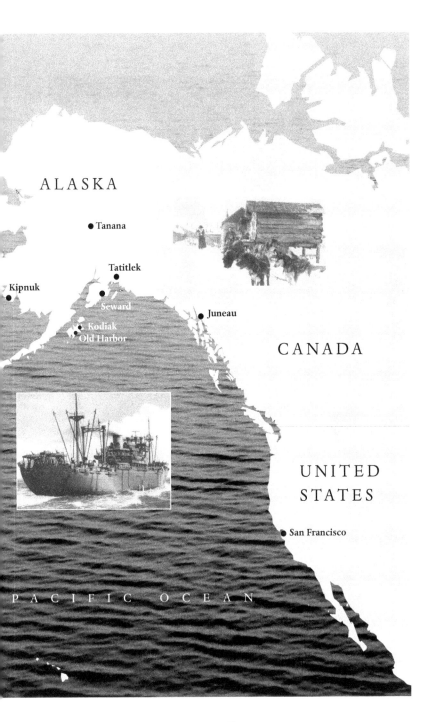

ALASKA

Tanana

Tatitlek

Kipnuk

Seward

Kodiak
Old Harbor

Juneau

CANADA

UNITED
STATES

San Francisco

PACIFIC   OCEAN

Etta Jones and her great-niece, author Mary Breu,
Bradenton, Florida, December 1952.

Preface

Etta Jones was my favorite great-aunt. For my first twenty years and her last twenty, I knew her as a compassionate, generous, genteel woman. She was short in stature, and had pure white hair and jet-black eyebrows. I always knew she had an interesting past because bits and pieces were mentioned over the years. Relatives had kept all of Etta's letters, photos, documents, and artifacts, and this private treasure was eventually handed down to me. In 2002, thirty-seven years after her death and at the end of my teaching career, I decided to put her story together to share with family members. While going through Etta's extraordinary collection, I realized that her story deserved a much wider audience, so I began to write this book.

To start, I wanted to confirm that events she wrote about in her letters were accurate in her telling, so I checked details on the Internet. Everything I read that addressed her story contradicted what Etta had written and what I knew about her. And the more research I did, the more discrepancies accumulated. I decided that I needed to do in-depth research on documents and texts located in archives in Alaska, so in 2003, I obtained a grant from the Alaska Humanities Forum to travel there. After that, I made four more trips at my own expense.

My search took me to the National Archives, the Aleutian/ Pribilof Islands Association, the Loussac Library, and the University of Alaska, all in Anchorage. I uncovered more material at the Elmer E. Rasmuson Library, University of Alaska Fairbanks. I pored over

Congressional records, Bureau of Indian Affairs records, archival documents, newspapers, and Australian and American texts. I interviewed and corresponded with key people who were involved, directly or indirectly, with Etta's story.

Etta was a prolific letter writer. Her engaging writing places the reader alongside Etta and her gold-prospector husband, Foster, when they lived, worked, and taught in remote Native communities—Athabascan, Yup'ik, Alutiiq, and Aleut—in Alaska in the 1920s, '30s, and '40s. Etta's and Foster's backgrounds were as diverse as the landscape of the Northland, but they were both conscientious and diligent workers. Hardship became part of their chosen way of life, and they embraced it. Their goal was not to change Native cultures; rather, as conveyed in her letters and other documents, it was to teach their students reading, math, and some domestic skills.

Etta's language vernacular differed somewhat from today's usage; for example, she used the word "Japs" because it was a commonly used term in the United States during World War II. I have edited her letters for clarity and relevance. Her letter writing depended on the random delivery of mail in remote Alaska villages, so sometimes she added postscripts after she had signed off and was waiting for the mail to arrive. Or, when the mailman arrived unexpectedly, she would hastily compose brief letters to be mailed immediately.

Etta also wrote a fascinating sixty-four-page manuscript in 1945 that was never published. It is full of facts and impressions that give the reader special insights into life in territorial Alaska. I have included excerpts from Etta's manuscript throughout this book's narrative. Likewise, in 1967, Foster's prospecting partner and friend Frank Lundin wrote an unpublished manuscript, in which he described their experiences during Alaska's gold rushes in the early 1900s. Excerpts from Lundin's manuscript are also woven into the narrative.

The photos in the book are primarily from Etta's collection. For the captions, I've used the information Etta wrote on the back of the photos. If there was no inscription, I gathered information from her letters and unpublished manuscript. Regarding the photos of Attu,

I've used several of Etta's pictures of the Aleut Natives to document these disappearing people.

I have created a Web site to accompany this book, where the reader may find further material on Etta's story, and a schedule of author appearances and book signings: www.lastlettersfromattu.com.

This book portrays events as they happened to Etta and Foster Jones. Qualities we often hear about, such as resolve and courage, are qualities that defined Etta Schureman Jones. She was a pioneer in Alaska Native villages. She was a remarkable woman who survived profound adversity. She played a significant role in a pivotal but less-known event in America's history.

Etta Schureman, age 4, Ellen (Nan) Schureman (Etta's sister,
and the author's maternal grandmother), age 6, Vineland, New Jersey, 1883.

To Alaska

Etta Jones stood on the deck of the ship, staring across the gray water of the Pacific. It was July 14, 1942. Years ago, she had seen that ocean with different eyes. Twenty years earlier, she and her sister Marie had embarked on the adventure of a lifetime, traveling to the Last Frontier. Impetuous Marie soon returned to the East Coast, but Etta fell in love with the untamed spirit of Alaska and a man named Foster Jones.

Etta felt her chest tighten and her breathing quicken as she again became aware of hostile voices prattling in the background. For a moment, she considered paying rapt attention to their conversation. Although she didn't know their language, she might be able to pick up on something that would tell her where the ship was going.

A curly strand of gray hair worked itself loose from the unkempt bun at the back of her head and began lapping at the side of her face. With her hands folded in front of her, Etta maintained her rigid posture. She didn't react to the hair that had begun to obscure her view. She never turned her head or acted as if she were aware of the activity behind her.

It didn't matter where they were going because there would be nothing there for her—nothing but memories of the life she had before that unthinkable day. She feared that day would be the only thing she could think of for the rest of her life. She was too numb to be concerned with whether the rest of her life would last for a few days or a few years, and she couldn't decide if she cared. The images in her head blurred as the cold mist blew across her face.

Etta was paralyzed by shock and grief, but self-pity was something she didn't spend time on. She could honestly look back on her life knowing she had lived vigorously, taking nothing for granted. She envisioned that life through the eyes of the relatives to whom she had faithfully composed so many letters over the years. Etta and Foster had made their home in some of the most remote and sparsely populated villages in the world. Yet, her correspondence was the diary of a content woman who always seemed right at home.

Etta didn't know if she would be allowed to write another letter. She knew her loved ones would worry about what had happened to her, but she couldn't see herself writing again, no matter what. Letters were about living and loving and being in that place where you knew you were meant to be. For the first time, she felt lost, like she had woken up a million miles from nowhere. How could you write a letter from "nowhere?"

Her mind drifted back to the happiest of those days, but every comforting thought was interrupted by the violence of her last few days. The sounds of the Natives' screams and the sight of human blood on the snow would haunt her for years to come. Etta was scared. Her world had changed. The whole world had changed.

The ship on which Etta stood was on course for Japan. As the sky grew darker, one of the grimy soldiers used the blunt end of his bayonet to prod her into a stifling cabin below deck. She curled up on the ragged cot that was suspended from the ceiling by two chains like a hammock. She knew she wouldn't sleep, but if she closed her eyes and concentrated on the motion of the water, she might be able to find rest in the memory of the last time she took a long voyage to an unfamiliar shore.

After high school graduation, Etta Schureman successfully completed course work at Connecticut State Normal College in New Britain, Connecticut, then taught in the primary grades for five years. While teaching, she became interested in the nursing field, so she enrolled in and graduated from the Pennsylvania Hospital Training School in Philadelphia, Pennsylvania. She had applied her nurse's training and been involved with industrial social work for fourteen years when Marie talked to her about going to Alaska.

Always adventurous, in 1922, Etta's sister Marie had already lived in the West as well as on the East Coast, something that was rare for a single woman in the 1920s. Her teaching certificate had been the ticket she needed to get to Montana, some two thousand miles from her hometown of Vineland, New Jersey. Now in Yonkers, New York, she had a comfortable position and she enjoyed her students and colleagues, but she was thirty-nine years old and still single.

Some of Marie's friends spoke to her about teaching in Alaska, and she began to think that it sounded like the perfect place for her next escapade. Alaska naturally appealed to her when she conjured up images of all that she had heard about that enchanting place: rugged beauty, thick forests, Northern lights, abundant wildlife, the highest mountains in North America, three thousand rivers, more than a hundred thousand glaciers, and three million lakes. She knew that it was larger than California, Texas, and Montana combined and had more wilderness acreage than the entire Lower 48 states. Marie was looking at what would be her greatest challenge yet— simply to survive in Alaska. This time, she would opt for the ultimate adventure.

Social standards as well as family concerns dictated that she shouldn't make a four thousand-mile trip from the East Coast to Alaska without a companion. She had the perfect person in mind, her forty-two-year-old sister, Etta, who was also single. In spite of their conventional beginnings, these two free spirits had turned their backs on the traditional roles of women. Instead of marrying and raising families, they were both driven by their careers. Perhaps they had inherited this determined independence from their father, Abram, who, at fourteen, had lied about his age so he could fight for the Union in the Civil War.

Etta had a lot to consider when trying to make her decision. She'd been working in metropolitan Pittsburgh. If Alaska's entire population of fifty-five thousand were equally distributed in the vast territory, each person would occupy more than a square mile. The city of Pittsburgh had a population of five hundred thousand. What

*Etta Eugenie Schureman, Pennsylvania Hospital Training
School for Nurses, Philadelphia, 1908.*

did Alaska have to offer besides spectacular scenery? Pittsburgh was
rich in art and culture, and it offered diverse educational opportunities, museums, libraries, shopping, and restaurants. Should she trade
this progressive, cosmopolitan city for a beautiful but boring pile
of snow? Would she be happy being far from her family and everything that was familiar? Who knew what could happen to two single
women thousands of miles away from home?

Finally, Etta decided that, yes, she could leave the city and take
a much-needed vacation, but it would be for one year only. She told

Marie that at the end of the year, regardless of what happened, Etta was going to leave Alaska and return to the East Coast.

In the spring of 1922, Etta and Marie, known to the family as Tetts and Dump, sat their elderly parents down to give them the news. Etta was the second oldest of the four children, born after another sister, Ellen (known as Nan). When her younger brother, Russ, was born, he found it difficult to pronounce Etta's name, so he called her "Tetts," and the name stuck. Their father nicknamed Marie, the baby of the family, his "Apple Dumpling." Her name was shortened to "Dump," and this was what the family called her from then on.

The sisters announced their plans to travel to a land they had only read about in books. They thought they had enough information to reassure their parents, but Esther and Abram fired off a series of questions that made it sound as if Etta and Marie had not done their homework at all. Did they have enough money to finance their adventure? How much did they need and how could they get more in case of an emergency? How long would it take them to get there? Would they go directly to Alaska, or travel at a leisurely pace,

Left: (Left to right) The Schureman sisters, Ellen (Nan) Schureman Smith, Etta Schureman, and Marie Schureman, Montague, Michigan, 1922. Right: Etta Schureman and her niece, Elinor Smith, on a boat on Lake Michigan, 1922.

stopping at landmarks and national parks? What would they do when they got there? They felt confident that with their teaching backgrounds, they would have no problem gaining employment in schools. Yes, they were facing more unknowns than guarantees, but Marie and Etta convinced their parents that they were determined to have their adventure.

Saying good-bye, they boarded a train and headed west. Their first stop was in Montague, Michigan, where they visited their older sister Nan, Nan's husband Dr. George Smith, and their daughter Elinor.

Proceeding west, Etta and Marie stopped at Glacier National Park in northwestern Montana. The million-acre park boasted turquoise-blue lakes, clear mountain streams, steep snowcapped peaks, and lush forests with trees so tall they seemed to hide the sky. This incredible landscape was home to more than 350 species of fish and wildlife including wolves, grizzly bears, and elk. They rented a cabin for a month and enjoyed the most spectacular scenery they had ever seen. At the end of the month, they reluctantly left this wonderland behind and, boarding another train, headed for Seattle, where they booked passage on a steamship bound for Juneau, Alaska.

Top: Marie Schureman on the porch of the cabin Etta and Marie
rented at Glacier National Park, Montana, 1922.

THE BOAT WAS CROWDED, the pier teeming with families and friends bidding farewell to departing passengers. Amid cheers and last-minute messages, while colored paper streamers fluttered, the ship slowly pulled away from the dock as we looked rather forlornly at each other. In all that throng, there was not a soul we knew. But what did it matter? We were adventure bound. It was thrilling!

At that time, the main business of steamship companies was to get supplies to and from salmon canneries. Passengers were of secondary consideration. Ships were tied to cannery docks whole days at a time while loading and unloading went on. Passengers amused themselves as best they could. There were such interesting fellow passengers. They enchanted us with their tales, all having something interesting to relate.

Teachers were returning to isolated schools among the Indians and Eskimos, traders from the Arctic, mining men from the Interior thrilling us with tales of gold and silver, tales of a fabulous mountain of jade known only to the Indians. There were missionaries on board— charming people, going to their lonely posts, some for the first time, some returning after a leave of absence. Salesmen who represented wholesale houses were on board. One man's story has always stayed with me. He told how the crystal clarity of the air could deceive as to distance: how on one occasion, when he was camped within sight of a mountain, he was astonished upon rising the next morning to find the mountain had moved twenty miles nearer while he slept.

After a few days, we reached Juneau, the capital of the territory. Our eyes popped at the beauty of the setting—high mountains rising almost from the water's edge, the town built on a narrow strip of land at the foot of the mountain and sprawling partway up its sides, facing calm, deep-shadowed Lynn Canal. Even a month at Glacier National Park had not prepared us for this. Here we disembarked to seek our fortune, or, Marie's job. We hired a taxi to take us to the one hotel in town, the Gastineau. After riding about two blocks over a plank street with plank sidewalks, we found ourselves at the hotel, gasping at the taxi charges—one dollar each. A dollar for two blocks! That did not seem exorbitant later when we became accustomed to Alaska prices. We learned to disregard pennies; they were not used except in the post

Juneau, Alaska, 1922.

office. Neither were nickels, and in many places in the Interior, a dime was disdained. The smallest acceptable coin was a quarter. Paper dollars were scarce. Big silver dollars were in common use. ⚜

Etta and Marie's experiences in the educational system had been in metropolitan school districts. They had no knowledge of schools in Alaska.

It wasn't until 1884 that John H. Kinkead, the first governor of the new Alaska territory, decided to address the absence of official educational opportunities in the region. Organizing a public school system in such an immense, ungoverned territory was a daunting task. In response to Kinkead's report to Washington, D.C., Sheldon Jackson, a Presbyterian missionary in Alaska who was an advocate for education, was selected to "appoint teachers, prescribe their duties, fix salaries, and make rules and regulations for the operation and administration of schools."

In a controversial move, Jackson used government funds to contract with already established Presbyterian mission schools and to encourage other Protestant denominations to open schools. The territory schools used mission school buildings, and the teachers were paid with federal subsidies, and by 1887, a school system of sorts was in place. Reflecting the population, these schools were mainly attended by Native children. However, in 1894, separation of church and state was enforced, and government contracts with church-sponsored schools were withdrawn.

The Civil Act of 1900 stated that proper provisions would be made for compulsory attendance of school-age children, regardless of race, until a permanent law was in place.

In 1903, Senator Knute Nelson of Minnesota visited the territory of Alaska and observed what he felt was a need to separate Native students from the whites. A law, bearing his name, was passed by Congress in 1905, stipulating: "Schools . . . shall be devoted to the education of white children and the children of mixed blood who lead a civilized life. The education of Eskimos and Indians shall remain under the direction and control of the Secretary of the Interior . . . and shall be provided for by an annual appropriation." Segregated schools for Natives in Alaska, and elsewhere in the United States, became law.

Curriculum in the white schools was standard: in the primary grades, students received schooling in reading, spelling, addition, subtraction, multiplication, geography, and codes of conduct, while in the fourth and fifth grades, they learned history, nature studies, and more challenging language arts and higher-level math.

IN THE OFFICE OF THE COMMISSIONER *of Education for white children of Alaska, we found a very charming young lady who told us a telegram had just come in asking for a teacher at Tanana, and she showed us on the map the spot where the Tanana River joined the Yukon just south of the Arctic Circle. We decided that Tanana would be our new home.*

In a few days, we boarded another ship for Seward. On this boat, we met a group of Shriners on one of their annual trips from Seattle to Alaska, bound for lodge work and fun in the northern cities. There was also on that boat a little bride, Mrs. Morgan, who was going to join her young sergeant husband at Fort Gibbon, in Tanana.

At Seward, we transferred to a train with a sleeper. At that time, the train went right through to Fairbanks, a distance of several hundred

Train at Curry Hotel, Curry, Alaska, located halfway
between Anchorage and Fairbanks. Both the train and hotel were
owned and operated by the Alaska Railroad. Etta and Marie
rode this train from Seward to Nenana, 1922.

ALASKA'S DIGITAL ARCHIVES, ASL-P44-06-080.

miles, traveling through the night. Old Alaskans said if people knew
the dangers of the railroad they would not sleep on the trip. In our case,
ignorance was bliss because we slept soundly.

We were glad to leave the train at Nenana, where we were to take
a boat on the Tanana River to Tanana. Making diligent inquiries we
found there was no regular passenger boat, but a trading company was
sending a boat with supplies in a few days. The boatman said, "Sure
we'll take you. Don't know when we'll leave, whenever we get loaded.
Just keep in touch with us and be ready when we are." Of course, we
haunted the riverfront and the vicinity of this boat in particular. People
laughed when we tried to find out the hour and minute of departure.
"Oh, you will get used to Alaska ways. It isn't a question of hour and
minute; it isn't even a question of what day. Just take it easy."

Eventually things were ready, and we found ourselves in a flat-
bottomed riverboat propelled by a gasoline motor. Six army cots were
arranged neatly in the open space of the boat, while crates and boxes of
foodstuffs and sacks of mail and freight were stacked around the edges,
a small cook stove near the center. The six cots were for the women

passengers because we were to spend at least one night on board. The other women were three missionaries and the little bride, Mrs. Morgan. The boat also carried six or eight male passengers who slept on the mail sacks.

The weather was ideal—beautiful, calm, warm, lazy days—and as we basked luxuriously on the tiny deck in the brilliant, soothing sunshine, we learned more about Alaskans, because besides ourselves, the young bride was the only "cheechako," or newcomer, on board. Old sourdoughs take pleasure in telling their tales to such as we. Everything was so new, so thrilling, we gulped it down and asked for more.

One man had been an undertaker in Juneau following the Princess Sophia disaster [October 25, 1918], the Canadian liner that had been wrecked on the rocks near Juneau with a total loss of all on board. This man had taken care of most of the recovered bodies, and had been so sickened with his calling that he had given it up and was then on his way to Nome to take up some other business. There were miners aboard from the Chandalar [mining] district who needed a cook, and they offered me the job. The scenery was not so stupendous as the coastal area, but it was wild, and at the same time peaceful. Occasionally a woodcutter's cabin was passed or a fish camp of tents, salmon drying in the sun and noisy malamute dogs tied to stakes for the summer. One

The gas boat Tanana, which Etta and Marie took from Nenana to Tanana, down the Tanana River, August 1922, on the final leg of their journey.

Athabascan fish camp on the Tanana River, 1922.
Alaska's Digital Archives, UAF-1985-72-142.

of the missionaries was elected cook on the boat, and from the plentiful stores provided, she prepared us a meal fit for a king. I don't remember just what we ate then, but I do remember the next morning breaking eggs into a bowl for the omelet, passing the thirty mark, and feeling stumped at frying enough bacon for so many on the tiny stove. Then the pilot came along and solved the difficulty by filling a dripping pan with sliced bacon and popping the whole thing in the oven with a scornful toss of the head in our direction and a curt, "That's the best way to cook bacon." It came out beautifully crisp and brown, and right then and there I learned a cooking lesson that I put to good use many times afterward. It was my first experience with Sourdoughs as cooks, and I can say with conviction, they are all good cooks. ❧

Although there had been a significant white population when mines were operating in the Tanana Valley during and after the gold rush of 1902, by 1922 most of the whites were gone, and the valley and the village of Tanana were once again predominantly Athabascan. Elected tribal chiefs established and enforced policies for the Natives. Traditional laws had been passed down for generations. Their spiritual beliefs, community customs, and verbal repetitions of legends, ceremonies, and survival skills were largely centered on the use of land and water resources that provided food, clothing, shelter, even transportation—boats and dogsleds. They only took what they would use. There was no waste. The resources were shared among all the villagers.

Potlatches were an important part of Athabascan social life. These were held for various occasions—weddings, naming of children, payment of debt, funerals. Outlying villagers would stay in the host villagers' homes for several days, feasting, dancing, and exchanging gifts.

Etta and Marie were accustomed to a cash-based economy

Athabascan woman in winter parka, Tanana, 1922.

Tanana Chiefs, circa 1920.

and easy access to grocery stores, department stores, banks, restaurants, and motorized transportation. The sisters had experienced cold winters and warm summers, and felt sure they were prepared for Alaska's weather. In spite of the differences between Native Alaska culture and the life they had known on the East Coast, Etta and Marie wanted to experience all that Tanana had to offer, including the extreme temperatures that were said to go from forty to sixty degrees below zero in the winter and up to three digits in the summer.

Tanana

1922-1923

It was early in the afternoon on August 20, 1922, when Etta and Marie first glimpsed their future home. The village of Tanana was situated on flats at the junction of the mighty Yukon and Tanana Rivers. Small covered fishing boats and a sternwheeler were tied to the dirt riverbank. Front Street ran along this riverbank and Second Street was parallel, one block back. These two treeless unpaved streets were dusty in dry weather and muddy when it rained.

Tanana waterfront, on Yukon River, 1922.

IT WAS NOT A VERY IMPRESSIVE sight but one that even then radiated charm. Most of the houses were of log, looking small and dingy from the outside, but how cozy and warm and hospitable on the inside, we later found out. Standing stark in the sunshine, without the benefit of shade trees, the cabins were revealed by the clear sky, which was a deep blue usually associated with a summer day.

On Front Street were the stores or trading outfits, two hotels, a pool hall, and a small church. At the extreme end of these buildings was Fort Gibbon. The fort had been abandoned, but there were still a few clearing-up personnel. As soon as they were finished with their assignment, they, too, would move away and the buildings would be left with a caretaker.

When our boat was tied to the bank, all passengers went their own way, and we realized that if we wanted our baggage moved, it was up to us to do it ourselves. It was apparent that we must find a house to live in because we could not afford hotel rates. The hotelkeeper's wife was friendly and helpful. "You're the new teacher? Well, I'm on the school board. We have been expecting you, and I can help you with a place to live." Her husband had a choice log cabin that he would rent us for $15 a month. We were enchanted with our new home, known as the Scotty Kay House, one of the few in town that had a second story. It had three rooms downstairs and two above.

Marie and unidentified child in front of Etta and Marie's home, Tanana, 1922.

28

To me, that first night in our new home was enchantment itself. I hung out the bedroom window, listening to the silence, which was so great it beat insistently on the ears. It was a living stillness. The soft velvety darkness spoke a friendly welcome, and in the distance a hoot owl added his voice. He must have been some distance away, but the clear, vibrant air brought him very near. To me, he was a friendly fellow, but not to Marie. She covered up her head, saying, "Shut the window. The silence hurts my ears." She never got used to that silence, which increased when the snow came. As poet Robert Service says, "Full of hush to the brim." There was a brooding, tangible something in that silence that sometimes seemed friendly, sometimes frightening.

The front windows of Etta and Marie's house faced another two-story cabin across the dirt road, the home of a recently married former Episcopalian missionary.

WITH FAULTLESS MANNERS, *this friendly neighbor soon called on us, inviting us to dinner. The other guest at the dinner was an old friend of her husband's, one Charles Foster Jones.*

Foster was born on May 1, 1879, in St. Paris, Ohio, to Caleb and Sarah Jones. Foster had two siblings, Mamie, 7, and Xerxes, 4. When Foster was four months old, his mother died of typhoid fever. In 1880, Dr. Jones married Julia Goodin, and they had six children: Cecil, Oasis, Caleb, Tracy, Anita, and Lowell. Foster's father was a physician and founder of Willowbark, a residential facility in St. Paris for recovering alcoholics. He owned a drug store, was involved in numerous activities in the United Methodist Church, and traveled around the state giving speeches encouraging his listeners to improve their health and lifestyles. With all of his commitments, Dr. Jones had little time for day-to-day interaction with his nine children, but he had exceptionally high standards and there was no doubt in their minds what he expected of them.

In 1897, before Foster finished high school, he had had enough of his stern father and small-town life, so he struck out for Washington state. When he arrived, word was spreading that gold had been discovered in Alaska, and Foster contracted a serious case of "gold fever." He asked his father to loan him $600 so he could outfit himself to become part of the gold rush, and Dr. Jones complied. This loan was deducted from Foster's share of the estate when his father died in 1924.

Beginning in 1898, Foster's occupations were mining and prospecting in various sections of Alaska. He never struck it rich, nor did he go broke. Images of big, strapping, bearded, gruff men are conjured up when one

Charles Foster Jones,
Tanana, circa 1920s.

thinks of mining prospectors. Foster was none of these. He stood five feet seven inches tall, weighed 150 pounds and was complacent and easygoing. Through the years, Foster corresponded with his family, but he never returned to his birthplace.

Foster met Michigan native Frank Lundin in 1911 and they became friends and were mining partners for the next several years. At one point, they were buying supplies to take to their cabin. Frank purchased the necessary staples, but Foster bought a book of poems by Robert Service. Frank commented that if they ran out of food, they couldn't eat the book, but Foster said, "When we get back to our shack on Birch Creek, look at the pleasure we will get from reading those poems."

By 1922, they had established residency in Tanana and were involved in civic and social activities in the community. Frank wrote, "In 1922, I was elected to the [Tanana] School Board. We had no teacher, so I had to arrange for one. I wrote to the Commissioner at Juneau, and he wrote back saying that he had already arranged to have a teacher sent to Tanana. The teacher who applied for the job was Marie Schureman, and when she came to Tanana, she had her sister, Etta, with her."

*BESIDES GOOD FOOD, we greedily ate up all the fascinating details of
Foster Jones and Frank Lundin's early experiences in Alaska. Both had
joined the Klondike stampede going over the Chilkoot Pass in 1898 and
had also been in the Nome, Fairbanks, and Ruby gold rushes. They
related exciting times and many thrilling experiences as though they
were commonplace occurrences. This same Foster Jones became very
helpful in preparing us for the coming winter, the intensity of which
we could not imagine. Many times that winter, when locked in by ice,
snow, and cold, we blessed his thoughtful kindness.*

*There were offers of help from everyone in town. One brought us
a gasoline stove, another cut our wood for the heater, and others fixed
storm windows and doors. We were given advice, good advice, that we
did not always follow, much to our sorrow later. It was necessary to get
the work done quickly because freezing nights and snow flurries began
sometime in September. Old-timers assured us that sixty below for a
month at a stretch was not uncommon. Watch the bottle of painkiller,
they cautioned, because it froze at seventy-two below. Marie gasped
when she found in the school register a notation by a former teacher
that school had been closed that day because the thermometer registered seventy-two below. It couldn't get that cold. Or, could it?*

Marie taught at the government school for white children who
lived in and around Tanana. The schoolhouse was about two blocks
from their home, and as she walked along Front Street she could hear
the river as it cascaded over the rocks and she felt droplets of moisture on her face as the wind blew. She passed one-story log houses
that were built close to the road and close to each other. Green plants
and bright curtains made the small-paned house windows look festive. In summer, the yards would be full of flowers. Her walk took
her past "Tower House," the town's hotel, which had a tower on
it, hence the name. There were gaps in the old board sidewalk, so
Marie had to be careful with her footing. The schoolbuilding was a
one-room, low-roofed log cabin, heated with a wood stove.

*IN OCTOBER THE LITTLE CREEKS and streams began to pour small pieces of
ice into the river, gradually filling it with slushy ice. Then larger pieces*

Tanana Public School, 1920s. PHOTO BY J.O. SHERLOCK. *NATIONAL PARK SERVICE, ALASKA.*

appeared, the current slowed up, sometimes stopping for a few hours, then moving on again. The final stoppage came early in November, and it was a topic of general interest because the river could not be crossed while ice was still running. Perhaps a friend would telephone, saying "Ice has stopped," and someone would be sure to mark it down. Mail delivery stopped until the ice was strong enough to be crossed.

Next door to the school was the Arctic Brotherhood Hall, which was the meeting place for all community gatherings. It had a hardwood maple floor that was kept polished by the soft moose-hide moccasins that everyone wore. All winter, leather shoes were not worn because it was too cold. Feet froze in leather. Tales were told of "cheechakos" who refused to listen to advice about footwear and who suffered amputation of feet as a result of ski trips in fifty-below weather wearing leather shoes. It was in the Arctic Brotherhood Hall where dances were held which everybody attended. The slightest occasion made the excuse for a dance—some strangers in town, a holiday, or just plain Saturday night. Everybody danced. We had rollicking times. I remember one dance when Foster had been out on a trip, and his friends thought he would not be back for the dance. Yet, he was there, and danced as much as anyone, but in an unguarded moment, he admitted he had almost not made it. He had snowshoed twenty-eight miles that day just so he could make it. He did not consider that unusual, snowshoeing twenty-eight miles and then dancing half the night.

This hall was also the scene of many soul-satisfying Christmas celebrations in which everyone participated. The schoolteacher practiced with the children to provide entertainment. Committees were appointed to collect money and donations from stores and others. Another committee bought presents for everyone. Young men brought in a huge spruce tree, and women worked together to decorate it with trimmings belonging to the community. Those decorations were carefully put away from year to year. Gifts exchanged by the whole town were usually put under the community tree. There was a Santa, sometimes with his reindeer. No one was forgotten. Miners, woodcutters, and trappers came in for the celebrations. It was a happy, happy time. We were amazed that first year at the extent of this giving, and overwhelmed by what we received. Nowhere have I seen a truer demonstration of the Christmas spirit. After the entertainment and distribution of gifts, a dance, and such a dance!

Drinking water was obtained in winter from the river. Ice was as thick as eighteen inches. Some people stacked cakes of this ice on platforms in their yards, bringing a cake into the house as needed, allowing it to melt in the drinking water tank. "Stacking drinking water in the yard" was a standing joke.

As the days grew shorter, artificial light was needed later in the morning and sooner at night until on the shortest day, December 22, when the sun barely made a showing above the horizon, first peeping out at about eleven and disappearing again at one. We looked forward to Saint Patrick's Day, because on that day, a six o'clock dinner could be eaten without a lamp. In midwinter, school children trooped by the house in the dark on their way to school, and often they could be seen finding their way home by moonlight, or, if there was no moon, with flashlights.

Early that first spring, we went on a hunting and trapping trip to Fish Lake, about twenty-five miles from Tanana, leaving while there was still snow to travel by dogsled, and the lakes were still frozen. It took two days, stopping one night at a roadhouse about ten miles from Tanana. At the Fish Lake Roadhouse, we found that the owner was away because he was sick, but everything was open, so in we walked and took possession. We sent word by the first traveler that we were there. The lake was full of muskrats, and as the ice gradually melted and disappeared, while Foster hunted "rats," I wandered over

*Yukon River ice breakup, Tanana, with big ice chunks
piling up on the shore, 1923.*

the countryside, gathering the early flowers. It was a lonesome place.
The few magazines it boasted were years old and well read. The old-
fashioned phonograph fascinated us. It used old cylindrical records. I
remember there were some made by Ada Jones, as far back as that.

The breaking up of the ice on the Tanana River was the big event of
the year for all persons living along its banks. Many, in all parts of the
territory, participated in the Nenana Ice Classic. They bet on the exact
date, hour, and minute the ice would break up in Nenana, paying a dollar for each bet. There were over $100,000 in this pool, one person occa-
sionally winning it all, but more often it was divided among several.
"Breakup" came most often in May when the days were long. We sometimes wandered along the bank of the Yukon most of the night, which
was daylight at this time of year, watching for this spectacular sight. It
was worth watching, the ice buckling and being thrown many feet into
the air. Noise from the grinding, huge cakes of ice was deafening, and
the danger of flood from the damming of these cakes was very real and
kept everyone on tenterhooks until the water was running smoothly.
We stood on the bank and watched this huge pageant pass by. We saw
caribou marooned on the floating cakes, perhaps too exhausted to try
for the shore. Discarded articles from villages and towns hundreds

of miles upriver went sailing jauntily by. All houses and yards were cleaned of refuse and put on the ice to be taken out.

After the ice was entirely gone, we loaded camping gear, food, and ourselves into a long poling boat and prepared to leave the village and drift on the Yukon River. In rowing through choppy water, an oar was lost, and there was no extra. It put severe strain on the ingenuity of the man of the party to keep that overloaded boat upright. With the use of a paddle, I tried to steer. Finally, with a sigh of relief, we entered the comparative quiet of a small stream that led to the river. We camped in the woods and slept under the sky. I can see and hear yet the swishing and bending of the tall birches as they thrashed in the wind high above us. The next day, the boat was reloaded, a makeshift oar was put into use, and we started again on the turbulent Yukon River with its dangerous submerged sandbars. The wind increased, bringing rain. It became necessary to camp again on a sandbar. By this time, the wind was roaring, too strong to put up a tent. The boat was turned on its side, and we crouched behind it as best we could. We could not build a fire, and what food we had was filled with sand. In fact, we were almost buried in sand. Then, to add to our miseries, the rain began. Finally, late in the day, the wind abated enough to allow us to make the return trip, and we arrived home in a drenching downpour, fur clothing soaked. The keenest memory that remains with me of that homecoming is the steady drip, drip of rain from the roof as it poured into the rain barrel at the door. ❧

Foster (left) pushes a poling boat into the Tanana River
with the help of an unidentified person, 1923.

Etta and Marie lived in a territory that was the size of 425 Rhode Islands, with wide-open spaces as far as the eye could see. A hundred thousand glaciers, some larger than entire states, had sculpted mountains, carved out valleys, and continued to flow and shape the landscape. Mountain ranges were higher, more rugged, and larger than any combined ranges in the Lower 48. Majestic Mount McKinley, the highest peak in North America at 23,320 feet, was in their back yard. Three thousand rivers, many gray in color because of glacial silt, rolled for hundreds of miles, passing through a vast wilderness. The river shoreline was punctuated by isolated villages, accessible only by boat or plane. In summer, wildflowers covered the endless valleys. Sightings of bald eagles, grizzly bears, moose, caribou, and wolves were commonplace. They had experienced temperatures that were so extreme they couldn't be registered, had taken dogsled rides and boat trips. Their meals consisted of moose, salmon, and blueberries that were the size of strawberries. Just when it couldn't get any more exciting, Foster made an announcement that would change two lives forever.

While Etta was working at the post office, Foster and his friend, Frank Lundin, walked in. Foster looked at his friend, nodded in Etta's direction, and said, "I'm going to marry that girl."

Tanana Post Office, where Etta worked in 1922.

3

Tanana

1923-1930

The weather was pleasant on Easter Sunday, April 1, 1923. Deep snow made walking difficult and the wind had blown snowdrifts several feet high, but on this particular day, the mild temperature matched the light spirits of a happy group of four people. This was the day that Charles Foster Jones married Etta Eugenie Schureman in a ceremony performed by justice of the peace Frank E. Howard. Frank Lundin remembered it this way: "On April 1, 1923, Foster married Etta Schureman. Etta's sister, Marie, and I were the witnesses. After leaving the judge's office, we went to the restaurant where I bought the wedding breakfast. Back to Etta's home we went and hooked up the dog team for their honeymoon. They went over the mail trail to Koyukuk." This was the first marriage for the bride and groom, both forty-three years old. After leaving Tanana, they had lunch at a woodcutter friend's cabin, fifteen miles away, then continued for another thirty miles until they reached their final destination, which was a cabin they jokingly nicknamed the Honeymoon Hilton.

Marie had been the most eager of the two sisters to go to Alaska the previous year. Once there, however, she encountered a lifestyle that overwhelmed her. Tanana was a tiny

Etta and Foster's marriage license, April 1, 1923.

Top: Etta and Foster's wedding photo, Tanana, Alaska, April 1, 1923..
Above: Etta and Foster's wedding party, Tanana, April 1, 1923:
(left to right) Frank Lundin, Marie Schureman, Etta Jones, Foster Jones.

Left: Etta and Foster on their dogsled, departing on their honeymoon, April 1, 1923. Below: Woodcutter Wingy Crane's cabin, where Etta and Foster stopped for lunch on their honeymoon, April 1923. Bottom: Photo inscribed by Etta (April 1923): "45 miles from Tanana, Honeymoon Hilton, end of trip."

village with a population that was mainly Athabascan. She saw the same few white people over and over again. There was no opportunity to widen her small circle of friends. She had a problem adapting to the strange regional food. The scenery consisted of hills, trees, and rivers, and the weather was intolerable to her. Marie had left her family and friends in New Jersey with a pioneer's spirit, but the tranquility of this expansive land was not what she had in mind.

> *SHE SOON DISCOVERED that she did not like Alaska; the rough life did not appeal to her. Wonderful scenery and Northern lights and the romance of the North meant nothing to her. She longed for the bright lights, theaters, "swell" dances, parties, etc.* ❧

At the end of one year, Marie returned home. Etta, on the other hand, had found more excitement and fulfillment than she ever could have expected in this peaceful place. In the fall of 1923, Etta replaced Marie at the school, thus beginning a teaching career that would span nineteen years in Alaska.

> *TIME PASSED PLEASANTLY. There were always things to do, both summer and winter, with congenial people as companions. Who were our neighbors and friends? Just like the friends we had left at home. People from Pennsylvania, Ohio, Michigan, New York, from the South, the North, East, and West, from Canada and England and Scotland. Just people, like ourselves.*
>
> *Around June 21, the sun hardly left the sky. We used to go to Bridge parties about nine or ten in the evening when the sun was still shining, and we went home soon after midnight. There was always much laughter and joking. Happy memories! Early in June, we planted our flowerbeds. Soon we had huge pansies, mignonette, sweet william, mallows, hollyhocks, nasturtiums, daisies, asters, marigolds, almost any flower that grew in the States, and the wildflowers—lupines and wild roses. One vivid memory of these early days remains with me—of the gorgeous fragrant wild roses that grew in great profusion in the yard of an abandoned cabin across the street from our first little home after marriage. These brilliant beautiful things covered old fences, they*

surrounded doorways, they almost covered the old ruins. I looked for them every spring. They were like old friends who came back to tell of the warm weather coming. They are associated in my mind with spectacularly inspiring cloud effects, brilliant sunshine, and soft breezes.

The gardens grew incredibly fast. With the hot sun above for almost twenty-four hours and with frozen ground a few feet underground supplying moisture to be drawn up by the sun, they raced along. One could almost see them grow, and vegetables grown under these conditions were unusually sweet and tender. Gardens were started early in June as soon as the ice was well out of the river, and in a few weeks harvesting began. Some things, like string beans, were risky because they would not stand frost, and often there were frosts in July or August. Tomatoes and cucumbers were grown under glass. Highbush and lowbush cranberries, strawberries, raspberries, blueberries, currants, and gooseberries all grew wild and in profusion. There were jelly and jam-making times. The Alaskan cranberries were especially good—much sweeter than those in the States. They also kept beautifully fresh. There was always plenty of cranberry sauce to be served later with wild duck or goose, ptarmigan, grouse, moose, or caribou.

Blueberries were put up in a way that was a forerunner of the modern deep-freeze method. As they were picked fresh, gallons and gallons of them, they were put into a wooden keg. A layer of berries, a layer of sugar, and the keg was put into a hold in a deep thicket where the sun did not penetrate. The hold was covered with moss, and the berries kept perfectly until we wanted them. Also like the deep freeze was the method of keeping cakes, cookies, pies, rolls, and bread. Late in the fall, after the cold weather was a settled thing, there would be a grand baking day, perhaps pies one day. I have made as many as eighteen—apple, mince, or berry—taking them directly from the oven to a forty-below temperature out of doors. They froze so quickly the steam inside seemed to be frozen right there. When wanted, they only needed to be allowed to stand in a warm room. Parker House rolls were made in quantities, put into a clean sugar bag, and hung up in the cache. When eaten, they were just like fresh rolls. While frozen, all these things could hardly be broken with an axe. They kept as long as the weather remained cold, until March or April.

Ice cream was also made by mixing the ingredients, putting them into a tin lard pail, hanging the pail on a line, and beating it a little from time to time. This was only in subzero weather, however. Along the same line was the way travelers prepared beans for a trip into the wilderness. White navy beans were parboiled in salt water, drained into a sugar sack, and hung on the line to freeze, rubbing them from time to time to prevent them from freezing in a mass. They froze as individual little pellets, harder than in their natural state. These were kept frozen, being hung outside a cabin. When needed, a cup or two were brought in and dumped into a skillet in which bacon had been fried. In the deep, hot fat they fried like doughnuts, a delicious, crisp brown, soft on the inside. I have also made huge quantities of soup, freezing it, and bringing a small hunk into the house as needed.

In June, along with wild roses and other beauties, came the pests of the North—mosquitoes. No part of Alaska is free from them. One would think that a region lying under ice and snow, mostly with subzero temperatures for six months, would be free from such things, yet they thrived. As snow melted from one side of a road, mosquitoes appeared while there was still snow on the other side. No one went out without protection from them—head nets, gloves, high-laced walking shoes, even citronella.

In the summer, there were berrying and fishing parties.

We had a houseboat and so did our friends, the Cooks. Loading the boat with people and good things to eat, leaving early in the morning, we went up the Yukon River for picnics. At a convenient spot there was a beach fire, dinner around it, bathing in the river, exploring trips into the wild hills, and home late at night. Or if it happened to be too windy, or a little rain should come up, we ate in the dining room of the boat. It was a little crowded but everybody was happy.

Drifting slowly with the current on the broad Yukon one sunny summer day with the engine quiet, Foster brought forth from his remarkable memory some of his favorite poetry by Robert Browning and Robert Service. Hour after hour, the beautiful words synchronized with the lovely hills and woods along the banks, the mighty river about which Service wrote so much, and the man himself, Foster, typifying the best of the early settlers. The water was calm and deep, leaping

Etta, Foster, their houseboat Esther, *and friends, 1926.*
Foster is second from right; Etta has her arm around a child.

fish once in awhile made a faint splash, but there was no other sign
of life. While drifting on the quiet river, a deserted cabin occasionally
came into view. There were beautiful clouds floating lazily in the blue
sky. There was no sense of hurry, no pressing worries or immediate
demands. This was the true Alaskans' life at its best. For this, they
shunned cities.

One summer day we had gone up the river in our houseboat, the
Esther [named after Etta's mother], and while tied to the bank, Foster
was cleaning salmon for our dinner. A man in a poling boat passed close
to the shore. "Hi, Charlie," said one. "Hi, Jim," said the other. No other
greeting. After the friend had passed, Foster remarked, "Knew that
man in the Klondike. Haven't seen him for twenty years." I wondered
why they didn't stop for a chat. He said, "It isn't considered polite in
this country to inquire into another man's business."

We had many good trips on the Esther. One fall, Foster suggested
that we go on a caribou hunt. At that time of year, caribou often crossed
the Yukon on their migration to other feeding grounds. It was beautiful weather in early October. We took our time, tying the Esther to
the banks when something attracted us on shore, perhaps good fishing places, or likely caribou country, or special fall flowers. Slowly, the
wind began to rise, and it became apparent that we would have to seek
a better anchorage because this bank was rocky. Foster turned back and

started for home. The wind increased in fury, whipping the water into high spray that froze as it hit the boat. Soon, we were ice-covered and listing. Steering became increasingly difficult, and darkness descended upon us.

Foster knew what I did not realize at the time—the river was full of sand bars that the waves and spray hid from sight, and the shore was too rocky to anchor. He knew this part of the river pretty well, and there was only one sandy beach that he remembered where old Abe Royal had his trapping cabin. It grew pitch-dark, and we had no other light except a flashlight. When he thought he was at about the right place, I threw the feeble light of this flashlight on as much of the beach as it would reach. We gritted our teeth, hoping it would be sand and not rocks we were going to strike, and then it was all over. We were safe and high on a sandy beach. The wind howled with ever increasing vigor. It was patently not safe to remain in the boat, and as we jumped to the beach, I was bowled right over by the wind. It was all I could do to stand against it. Foster felt around until he found some big boulders, then brought fur robes, and we crouched behind the rocks, trying to get a little shelter.

In spite of the fact that I wore corduroy trousers, a fur coat, fur cap, fur boots, and was covered by a fur robe, I believe I was never so cold in my life. We shivered in misery until it began to get daylight. Foster then scouted around until he found Abe's deserted cabin. It was high on a hillside, some distance from where we were, but how gratefully we carried everything to it and took possession. Abe had been dead for some years, and no one else had used the cabin. We found the roof partially fallen in, but in a corner was a big pile of clean, dry hay and, best of all, we were out of that terrific wind. It was quiet and peaceful, and, gratefully, we dropped to the clean hay and slept for hours.

In some neighboring woods, Foster found some wood for a fire, and we feasted on bacon and eggs, hot coffee, and biscuits. By this time, the wind had brought a drizzling rain, but we were comfortable, warm, and dry. We stayed there for three days. On the third day, a Native, who was paddling down the river, saw the Esther on the riverbank and no sign of us. He took the news to Tanana. "I think the Jones lost like hell. Their boat there. I no see them."

We had quite a time getting that boat floated again. It had been driven onto the sand with such force, and the wind had helped keep it there.

Our friends were glad to see us again because in that same storm, on Fish Lake, where Foster had lost an oar and had difficulty getting across the lake, two young men drowned when their boat capsized. Although the lake was dragged, their bodies were not recovered until the following spring. They had remained under the ice all winter.

Because of the rugged terrain, transportation in the summer was limited to boats, and Etta didn't take trips on the *Esther* by herself. At one point, she wanted to visit a friend, but reaching her destination posed a problem. In typical Alaska fashion, the problem was solved.

I WANTED TO VISIT MY GOOD FRIEND at Rampart, which was about twenty-five miles upriver. The regular steamer was not convenient, so how could I get there? I made arrangements to go with an Indian family who were members of the congregation of a missionary friend. It was midsummer, hardly any darkness, and the Indian seemed to prefer traveling at night, so it was early evening before we got started. He had a large flat-bottomed boat with a gas engine. Quilts and blankets were provided so his wife, children, and I could lie down. It was pleasant looking up at the stars, listening to the chug of the engine. At about 2 A.M., we stopped for tea. It was chilly on the water, and as we climbed out on the bank, the fire he had built felt good as we sipped our tea. I can still get the feeling of that early morning meal on the bank, not as one would imagine a chilly 2 A.M. morning would be outside with the sun already high in the sky.

Arriving about noon, I sat down to a good hearty meal, because my friend kept a roadhouse. It became very hot during my visit, and I went with her to her icebox to get provisions. Her frozen meat was delivered by the river steamer, and was put immediately into the icebox, and such an icebox! It was a cave hollowed out under a hill with supporting timbers, and there were convenient tables and shelves. One reached the innermost room through a series of outer rooms. Entering from the glaring, blazing summer heat of the outside into a cool entry, one went through a door into a much cooler room, and finally into a real icebox. I did not see the temperature, but it was too cold to stay in comfortably, and things remained frozen until they were removed— meat, fish, berries, etc. There was nothing to induce freezing except the natural temperature of the earth.

As pleasant as summer was, winter was the most enjoyable. I think without exception our friends said, "We like winter best." We still went out on trips, taking dinners and suppers, but traveling by dogsled or walking instead. Woodcutters' camps were our objectives. There, usually in a tent, we warmed up the stew or potpie, made coffee on the woodcutter's tiny stove, brought out the sandwiches, salads, cakes, and pies, and amidst jovial, gay talk, ate good things while sitting on boxes or on the man's bed. As always when a few old-timers, the Sourdoughs, were gathered together, there were fascinating tales of adventure, of daring and sometimes rash, hazardous experiences that they or their friends had experienced and about which they could tell so well.

A gold miner who operated a nearby placer mine used to come to see us and visit. It was a great relief to him to be able to talk to someone.

Winter picnic, circa 1920s. Etta is in front without a hat;
Foster is in the back wearing a fur hat.

He said he had been alone all winter and was so lonely that he had tamed a weasel, spending hours talking to it. These old-timers seemed to have imbibed the bigness and freedom of the country; there was no place or time for petty remembrances. The more alone and familiar with this immense country a man was, the more gentle and understanding of the other man.

In the house, we dressed for summer weather with no extra warm underclothing, no wool dresses. But to go out in the cold, I prepared by taking off my housedress and slip. I donned wool tights that reached to the ankles, two pairs of home-knit-

Etta in her Native fur parka and mukluks with snowshoes, circa 1920s.

ted, four-ply, heavy wool stockings, corduroy trousers that had a cuff that buttoned below the knee, a wool jumper, insoles that were really ankle-high slippers of wolf skin with fur on the inside, and over those I put boots with moose-hide soles. Then I put on a fur parka, which is a short coat put on over the head with a fur hood attached. I wore a knitted woolen cap or a fur cap with earflaps and woolen gloves covered with fur-lined moose-hide mittens. These were attached to a cord about the neck, and were not used until after the dogs were hitched up.

When driving the dogs, one did not sit comfortably in the basket sled; rather, one stood on the runners at the back of the sled where a foot brake was of some help in slowing the dogs and guiding them entirely by voice. The lead dog, if he was a good one, understood "gee" and "haw" and could swing the team his way. Once as I was being whirled out of my yard while standing on the runners and holding on for dear life, the brake fell off and I was left helpless to manage the dogs. The leader soon realized my plight and he paid no attention to my "gees" and "haws." He had a grand time going his own way at top speed. His impish grin could almost be seen on his happy face. When someone finally came to *my aid and stopped them, he should have been whipped. A good trainer would have done that, because he knew what he was doing, but I was a softie with dogs, not a good trainer, so they were not obedient.*

Many women had their own dog teams. I had three dogs that I hitched to a sled and took out. They were small dogs and very dear to me, but Foster would not have them on his team. He said they were absolutely no good, but we had many good times together. On a sunny day in midwinter, when the temperature was not too low, perhaps my neighbor would telephone: "Would you like to go for a ride today?" "Yes. Where shall we go?" A route would be settled on and a time for leaving. The sled was tied to a stake while the frantic dogs were being put into the harness. They were wild to get out, being kept tied all the time they were not being used. Then, as my friend sailed out of her yard with dogs yelping, not barking, for malamutes do not bark, we flew behind and raced away down the trail, hoping to goodness that we would not meet any other teams until the dogs had tired themselves somewhat and quieted down. This they did in time, and we were able to enjoy the fresh, keen air, the evergreens, and beautiful winter landscape. Usually we followed a well-broken trail, a trapper's or woodcutter's trail. Sometimes we brought cameras and took snapshots, and sometimes we just tied the dogs and wandered around in the woods.

Another favorite ride was to the Episcopalian mission, Saint James, in a village about three miles from town, where there was a government school for Indians, and the mission church with housing for missionaries. Some of my fondest memories are connected with this grand place. On a sunny winter day, a ride behind the dogs to the village was not without some trepidation, for Indian dogs were fierce and always ready to fight our dogs. However, having safely arrived at our destination and the dogs safely tied, we were welcomed to a cheerful living room. Off came the parkas and outer wraps. Tea and cake were accepted gratefully, and after an hour or two of pleasant chatter, the dogs were hitched up again and we returned home. These missionaries were wonderful people. They also kept a little church running in Tanana, the bright spots being the visits of Bishop Rowe or the archdeacon.

One time, Foster and a prospecting partner were getting ready for a long trip. Supplies were carefully considered for the time they

Foster and his dog team, Tanana, circa 1920s.

expected to be away. Everything they needed had to be carried on their sleds—dog food, their own food, their clothing and equipment, even a lightweight Yukon stove. They had enormous loads. My dogs and I were to accompany them for about ten miles, and, of course, we had an empty sled. We begged a load for as far as we went to help balance the sled and slow up the dogs. A case of eggs was put on my sled. I brought up the rear, and my dogs were wild with excitement. I bore down hard on that brake with seemingly little effect. As we slid around curves, bumping stumps and trees and sliding off the trail, I thought about those eggs, wondering how many would be left whole. When it came time to turn over my precious freight, I expressed the hope that not too many eggs would be broken. I can still see those men laughing at the silly cheechako. "Why," they said, "you could not break one of those eggs if you tried. They are frozen solid. Just try sometime to break a frozen egg." After handling a few later, I realized how impossible it would have been for me to injure those eggs.

　　Another occasion stands out in my memory, typical of the Alaskan's love of his country. It was winter, a sparkling, brilliant moonlit night. "Let's take a ride," we said. Foster's dog team went first, and mine followed. We went miles out into the "silence that bludgeons you dumb" [Robert Service] along a good trail. Miles out on the trail, we picked up a load of firewood. There were two loads because my sled carried some, too. On the way back, jogging along in the moonlight, Foster was whistling contentedly, and the whole world was at peace. Cold fear found me that night because eventually we came to the top of a long, steep, winding hill. Trees had been cut on either side, leaving jagged stumps close to the trail. Down that hill went the team ahead, soon getting out of sight, and with yelps of joy my dogs raced after. We banged around curves, hitting the jagged stumps. However hard I stood on the brakes, there was no slowing those little brutes. I envisioned myself upset, and impaled on a stump with no help near. I had to do something. Suddenly I broke into song, of all things. "Oh say, can you see, by the dawn's early light." Somehow it brought courage. I never admitted how scared I had been.

In February, when the land was locked in with ice and snow, I went for a bath in the bathhouse at the springs. Escaping steam formed huge stalactites around the door. I undressed in an inner room and then went into a shed enclosing the pool into which hot and cold water were piped from the spring. At the time of my visit, something had gone wrong with the cold water supply, and the pool was almost too hot to be borne. We came out scalded a bright pink, but our skin was soft and smooth from the effects of the minerals in the water.

The hospitality of Alaskans was proverbial. When unexpected guests suddenly drove into the yard with their dog team, the greeting was always the same: "Come in! Come in! Glad to see you." We brought in some moose or reindeer, got a roast in the oven, brought out some of our home-grown potatoes, opened a cabbage or turnips, opened cans of vegetables, brought in rolls and pies from the cache, opened jellies and jams, and a feast was soon in progress. Our Christmas and Thanksgiving and other holiday feasts were something to talk about. We wanted for nothing.

Foster once filled a tooth cavity for a miner who was working with him. After first cleansing the cavity with painkiller, almost pure alcohol, Foster then used a filling made by filing a dime to fill the cavity. Another time some dry [prohibition] agents asked us if we could help a bootlegger whom they had arrested. When starting the uncovered engine of his open boat, the man's sleeve had become caught in the belt *and he had dislocated his shoulder. He was past seventy years old, they were 100 miles from a doctor, and if they brought the man to us, could we do something? At first, I said no, I was not strong enough for such a task, even if I had the strength. Foster, however, whose father had been a doctor, said, "Why, yes. Bring him. I remember seeing my father successfully treating such a case by laying the patient on the floor, putting his foot in the man's armpit, while he worked the shoulder joint into place." It was hours before they could get to us, and by that time the man's muscles were stiff. We had nothing to relax him, he was almost fainting with pain, but Foster made a good job of it. I then applied a shoulder pad and bandage, and we sent him off, making him promise to go to the hospital in Fairbanks at once. Several years later, we saw this old man and, raising his arm above his head, he said, "See? Good as ever. Never had any trouble and never did go to Fairbanks."*

The village of Nome, located on the shores of the Bering Sea, was threatened in January 1925 with a deadly diphtheria epidemic. The village needed one million units of antitoxin and, due to weather conditions, the only way possible to have it delivered was by dogsled. A relay team of twenty mushers and 150 sled dogs was organized, and the mail route from Nenana to Nome, a distance of 674 miles, was chosen as the fastest route to transport the serum. Also known as the "Great Race of Mercy," the serum run was successfully completed in a record-breaking five and a half days.

In his book *Eskimo Medicine Man*, Dr. Otto George wrote about Foster's role in the historic run. "[Foster] told me details of a diphtheria epidemic in Nome, to which he carried serum along with the mail. With the thermometer at 60 degrees below, or colder (the alcohol in the thermometer froze, and that should not occur until 72 below), Jones's problem was to keep the serum from freezing. He modestly explained that he was only one of many who relayed the serum—thirty-five miles in his case—to Nome, and the man who was supposed to have the next-to-last leg of the journey passed his relief carrier (who was waiting his turn) and also made the last leg with the serum into Nome, to be acclaimed a hero." Foster had a certificate designating him as a carrier of the serum to Nome.

Etta and Foster's house on the Yukon River, purchased for $40 in the late 1920s.

REAL ESTATE WAS CHEAP. *Our first little home was a four-roomed log cabin, warm in winter, cool in summer, very cozy, and attractive inside. The initial cost was $100. Later we bought a charming summer home just out of town on the banks of the Yukon, where we could have a garden and we could fish for salmon. Its cost was all of $40. A few years later someone wanted to buy it. The selling price was $40. Later we bought a larger house, a more pretentious place that boasted six rooms and bath on two floors. The price was $600. We lived there one summer and sold it for $1,000.*

In March 1922, Foster petitioned for membership in Tanana's Masonic Lodge, listing his occupation as "miner and prospector." On July 16 of that same year, he was raised to Master Mason. The fraternity of Masons is one of community and charity service activities. Membership is sometimes composed of those living or working in a given town and/or sharing a particular interest or profession. Wives of Masons are eligible for membership in the auxiliary organization, Order of the Eastern Star, and on September 14, 1925, Etta became an active member in Tanana's Midnight Sun Chapter Six.

Tanana, Tatitlek, and Old Harbor

1928–1932

After Vitus Bering led a Russian expedition to Alaska in 1741, the vast populations of sea otter, seal, and fox in the Aleutian Islands region were perceived as commodities that were available for the taking. As competing companies strove to dominate the fur business, Alaska's indigenous islanders, the Aleuts, were exploited because of their legendary hunting abilities. Forced labor, massacres, captivity, disease, and starvation diminished the Aleutian Islands Native population by half.

Grigory Shelikov established a Russian settlement at Three Saints Bay on Kodiak Island in 1784. Ten years later, a school was built, and Russian Orthodox missionaries arrived and began teaching Native children reading and writing in Russian. Local languages were also recognized, and eventually alphabets for these were developed. Literacy in Russian and the Native language became goals of the schools. Recognizing that the Natives had thrived under difficult circumstances for a very long time, the priests were pragmatic in their approach. Instead of attempting to abolish the Native culture, they lived their Christian lives by setting an example—simple, humble living while practicing their religious doctrine.

A monopoly in the Alaska fur trade was created when the Russian American Company was established in 1799. Schools continued under the company, and promising students were sometimes sent to Russia for further training. The sea otter, seal, and fox populations were not limitless, and the company imposed conservation measures. Nevertheless, the fur trade declined. Hunting expeditions could last from two to four years, and the cost was prohibitive. With decreasing monetary returns, Russia started to lose interest in Alaska. The Crimean War and other external pressures added to the concerns of the government. American whalers and fur dealers had started to make their presence felt in the territory, and on March 30, 1867, Russia sold Alaska to the United States for $7.2 million. Russia continued to subsidize church schools for Native children until 1917. With the outbreak of the Russian Revolution, all funding for Alaska missions was terminated.

The Nelson Act of 1905 established a segregated system in which schools for Native children would remain under the control of the Department of the Interior. The goals for Native schools were twofold: integrate Natives into the white culture, and preserve the Native culture. Students in these schools were taught the most rudimentary reading and math, but the emphasis was on domestic skills for girls and woodworking and mechanical trades for boys. The Native children were provided with an unsuitable patchwork of American textbooks.

Having observed this educational disparity, in 1928, Etta decided to change the focus of her teaching. On her application for appointment in the Alaska Indian Service, she was very specific. "I wish to be more actively associated with the Natives." Her wish came true when her application was accepted and she was assigned to teach twenty-four Athabaskan students in Tanana.

Foster gained employment with the Alaska Indian Service in 1930. He listed his experience as, "Clerked in a drug store and studied under a pharmacist and physician" [his father]. His skills were listed as "drawing, carpentry, operating gas and steam engines, cooking, and washing clothes." He also stated that he was qualified to teach "arithmetic, history, geography, hygiene, and first aid."

Transfers within the Alaska Indian Service happened frequently for several reasons: the teachers requested a transfer; the teachers met the needs of a different Native village; new schools were built and teachers were hired; unsatisfactory performance by a teacher required a replacement; or, when teachers left the Alaska Indian Service, the vacated positions needed to be filled. In the 1930s, in addition to teaching certification, employees of the Alaska Indian Service were required to successfully pass a Civil Service examination. Those who didn't qualify were dismissed, creating open teaching positions.

When transfers occurred, expenses for the move were subsidized in one of two ways. If the Alaska Indian Service made the recommendation, it was deemed "not for the convenience of the employee," and the Alaska Indian Service covered the cost of the move. If an employee requested a transfer, the employee had to pay his or her own expenses.

In 1930, Foster was assigned to Kaltag, an Inupiat Eskimo village located 327 miles west of Fairbanks, while Etta was transferred to Tatitlek, twenty-one miles south of Valdez and 450 miles southeast of Kaltag. In a letter dated June 19, 1930, the Commissioner of Education stated, "This transfer is not for the convenience of the employee." There was no post office in Kaltag until three years later, so correspondence between Etta and Foster during that year was infrequent at best.

Tatitlek is an Alutiiq Indian village on Prince William Sound in Southcentral Alaska. In 1930 it had a Native population of sixty-two; Etta was the only white person in the village. Describing her new location, Etta wrote, "Tatitlek is a small fishing village between Valdez and Cordova, twenty-eight miles from Valdez, fifty-five miles from Cordova. The ground is wet and swampy at all times. No wells can be driven. The water supply comes from a spring on the hillside. The Natives do a little trapping in the winter, but their main occupation is fishing for the canneries of Prince William Sound. They are industrious and thrifty, and make a fairly good living. The village is gradually growing smaller as families move to Valdez or Cordova." The length of the school year was 159 school days, enrollment was twenty-two students, and the average daily attendance was eleven.

In 1937, villager Paul Vlassof wrote about his community: "Tatitlek is a little village located halfway between Valdez and Cordova. I think it is the nicest little place in Prince William Sound.

*A view toward the Alutiiq village of Tatitlek,
on Prince William Sound, from McDonald's Island, 1930.*

Tatitlek School, 1930. Historical Album of (Bureau of Education,
Bureau of Indian Affairs) Schools in Alaska, 1924–1931, Vol. 2 National
Archives and Records Administration Pacific Alaska Region, Anchorage, Alaska,
Record Group 75, Bureau of Indian Affairs Box #234, Folder 05/04/08(2).

My home is halfway surrounded by trees, while out in front is the
water and an island about a mile and a half long. There are about
sixteen houses and about eighty-five people living there. My people
make their living by hunting, fishing, and trapping. In the winter,
we have dances every Friday and Saturday, and quite often we have
our school programs. In the summer, it gets so warm that most of
the people do their cooking outside their houses. The government
schoolteacher governs the village with some help from a person from
the village. There are no electric lights here, so we use gas lamps for
light. Most of the houses have radios, which we listen to to pass the
time in the evenings. So whenever you get to Tatitlek, drop in to one
of the houses and see what kind of entertainment you get."

In spite of the fact that Etta was in Tatitlek without her husband at her side, she had a successful year. In her Teacher's Efficiency Record, her "success as a village worker" and her "ability to overcome difficulties" were rated "very good." This report was issued on her eighth wedding anniversary.

At the end of the school year, Etta was transferred to Old Harbor on Kodiak Island.

On June 11, 1931, a radiogram was sent from the Office of Indian Affairs in Juneau to the Commissioner of Indian Affairs in Washington, D.C.: "Request transfer George S. Wilson present salary from Old Harbor to Kaltag with transportation effective entrance on duty and transfer of C. Foster Jones from Kaltag to Old Harbor same salary with transportation effective entrance on duty. Also transfer of Mrs. Etta E. Jones from Tatitlek to Old Harbor transportation effective September first at salary of $1,620 per annum less $240 for school term. These transfers requested in order to place two teachers at Old Harbor as scheduled, retaining only one at Kaltag. As Wilson is unaccompanied, we can place him at Kaltag making it possible to place Mr. and Mrs. Jones together at a two-teacher school."

A letter to Etta soon followed.

June 17, 1931
United States Department of the Interior
Office of the Secretary
Washington
Mrs. Etta E. Jones of Alaska
Madam:
     You have been appointed by the Secretary of the Interior, upon the recommendation of the Commissioner of Indian Affairs, an Assistant Teacher, Grade 6d-g, in the Alaska School Service of the Indian Service, at a salary of $1,620 per annum less $240 per annum for quarters, fuel, and light, effective on the date of entrance on duty, but not earlier than September 1, 1931, by transfer from Teacher, Grade 7d-g, at $1,800 per annum less $240 per annum for quarters, fuel, and light. New position. Employment and payment limited to the period of the school

year. You are still subject to the provisions of the Retirement Act.

The Secretary has also approved the allowance of traveling expenses in accordance with existing orders and regulations, from Tatitlek, Alaska, to Old Harbor, Alaska. This transfer is not for the convenience of the employee.

Respectfully,

J. Atwood Maulding

Chief, Division of Appointments, Mails and Files

Through the Commissioner of Indian Affairs

Order No. 2472

Etta and Foster were reunited after a year's separation and would be together for the next eleven years. Before going to Old Harbor on Kodiak Island, Etta and Foster spent time with friends in Tanana, Fairbanks, Anchorage, and Seward. From Seward, Etta wrote to her mother and her sister, Marie, to share news of their reunion and express hopes for a long, happy life together.

Seward, Alaska

July 20, 1931

Dear Mother and Dump:

Well, here we are at Seward. It is a dull, rainy Sunday and I seem to have no ideas at all. We came in on the train from Anchorage Friday evening, and our boat does not leave until Tuesday night or Wednesday morning. But time goes quickly. There are many little affairs of business to be attended to.

Seward is much like Valdez in its setting, with high snow-capped mountains all around. The little town is on an apparently land-locked bay. The rain seems quite natural. It doesn't seem to inconvenience very much, like Juneau. One doesn't get very wet in it. This cool moist climate is a relief after the dry, hot, dusty Interior. Tanana was very hot before I left, and we almost suffered from the heat in Fairbanks and Anchorage. Nellie Grandison took us for rides in her car in Fairbanks, and in Anchorage friends took us over all the automobile roads of which the town boasts, about thirty miles.

We both like Anchorage. It wouldn't surprise me to find myself living there sometime. Foster liked the town well enough to patronize the bank, which surprised me. He opened an account there, and bought U.S. Steel through them.

Most of our fellow travelers on the Yukon River steamer came with us as far as Seward, and there we parted. The Los Angeles school marm and her sister from Nome stopped off at McKinley Park for a week. They had intended to stop only overnight and join us again at Anchorage, but the fascination of the park was too much for them (at $15 per day each for living in a tent).

It takes about three days to go from here to Kodiak, and there we shall probably have to take a small boat to get to Old Harbor. As you say, Mother, I am seeing something of Alaska. I missed a good chance to see more of it. I have always wanted to go over the Richardson Highway by automobile from Fairbanks to Valdez, but as the stage fare is $100 and I couldn't connect with any private cars going over, I had given up the idea. The night before we left Fairbanks, I learned that Jack Coats was in town, husband of Dump's friend in Chitina. I had just received a letter from Mrs. Coats, forwarded from Valdez, in which she said she had made arrangements for her husband to drive me from Valdez to Chitina if I would only visit her for a week or two. So in Fairbanks, when I learned he was there, my plan was suddenly made to go with him to Chitina, from there to Cordova over the Copper River Railroad, the most beautiful of them all, and join Foster again either in Seward or Kodiak. It would have cost much less, and there would have been over 300 miles of superb scenic highway. Of course, that was not considering his plans, but, drat the man, I could not locate him anywhere. Nellie helped me look for him. We found his car and his hotel and his friends, but we could not find him, and our train left at eight the next morning. So the Richardson Highway, Chitina, and the Copper River Railroad I still have to look forward to.

We bought an Underwood portable typewriter in Anchorage, so from now on you will not have to strain your eyesight trying to read my scrawl. I may get time to write in Kodiak or on the boat. They tell us we get mail only once a month in Old Harbor, but I think it may be as it was in Tatitlek, which was whenever a small boat goes to the town of Kodiak. There is also a government radio station at Kodiak town.

Love to all,

Tetts

Dump: From Anchorage I mailed you Mary Lee Davis's latest book on Alaska. Hope you enjoy it as much as I have. Are you still wanting a silver fox? I saw some good ones today and can get you one if you wish.

ONE SUMMER DAY, *we landed late in the afternoon at Old Harbor. As the* Starr *dropped anchor in the cool clear depths of the strait, we seemed to be in Paradise. The green hills were deep and smooth and luscious. From a distance it appeared like a well-kept lawn. "Wouldn't think that foliage is shoulder high, would you?" said a fellow traveler. Later, we discovered that to be true. The silence after the noisy engine was soothing, and the shadows of the hills crept out over the smooth water. We landed at the rickety dock, with its unfinished dock house and barnacle-covered pilings. Although it was midsummer, it was fairly cool. The town was situated along the water's edge, on a low bank, so low that at high tide sometimes it seemed as if the town would be flooded. The storekeeper welcomed us. He was practically the only one in the town. All the Natives were working at the salmon cannery at Shearwater Bay, about twenty-five miles distant. Their little toy wooden houses and tiny yards were neat and clean. The hills across the strait, within sight of the village, were snow covered most of the year. On part of another island there was a glacier that glistened all the year round.* ❄

While in Pittsburgh, Etta had embraced the tenets of Christian Science. She believed that God and creation are good and that spiritual thought would bring a person closer to God. She also believed that healing was possible through the power of prayer, and she prayed on a regular basis. Her doctrines allowed her to accept other

religious sects that she encountered, including the Moravians and
Alaska Natives' Russian orthodoxy.

THE ALUTIIQ NATIVES *of Kodiak were friendly and likable. Being very
devout members of the Russian Orthodox Church, they steadfastly
refused to drink during Lent. I loved to go to special services in their
church, be it Easter or Christmas. They had good singing voices and
good ears for music. In the beautiful chants of the Orthodox Church,
without instrumental accompaniment, they sang four parts in perfect
harmony.*

*The memory of their funeral services remains strong. There were
solemn words in the church followed by the slow procession going up
the stony path to the burying ground on the hilltop. They chanted the
hymns as they carried the coffin. An emotional service was held at the
gravesite. Artificial flowers, expertly made, were always in evidence
when there were no real ones.*

*The hills of Sitkalidak Island, across the strait, were just as green,
with bare gray crags above them and many turbulent streams running
down the sides. Later, in exploring these hills, we found deep gullies
where the streams came down, covered with luxuriant bushes, mostly
salmonberries. It was fun to pick them, mostly from bushes over my
head and berries as big as large strawberries. It seemed almost like picking cherries. We picked gallons and gallons, eating the fresh, and making jelly of some. They were too seedy and too watery to can whole.*

The school was built to accommodate twenty-eight students.
Stoves heated the building, and coal oil and gas lamps were used for
lighting. In the summer of 1930, a play yard was cleared. Bookcases,
a schoolroom cabinet, medicine cabinet, workshop, storeroom, and
coal bin were built. In 1931, playground equipment was constructed
and sewer connections were installed.

December 27, 1931
Dear Mother and Dump:
    **We are expecting a boat soon with mail, so I will have a
letter ready to go back on her. I hope there will be lots of good**

61

news for us, my usual hope.

I have been wondering about your Christmas. It must
have been a very quiet one for you, Mother, if you and Russ
were alone. I suppose Dump had her new family with her, and
Nan, too. Christmas tree 'n everything. [Marie had married
Frank Wiley, a friend from her church. Frank had two grown
daughters, Helen and Betty.]

We had a nice, quiet Christmas. It looked like Christmas,
too. More snow than they have had here for years, several inches.
There was bright sunshine during the day, and a brilliant moon
at night, so the snow sparkled all the time in true Christmas
style. The day before Christmas we had our little tree in the
school. It lasted well, and looked quite gay with its decorations.
The children did their little pieces. Much of the English could
not be understood, but listeners did not know the difference.
Everyone in the village came except one woman who was in bed
with a new baby.

I was surprised by the gifts I received. This was the first tree
and school entertainment they had ever had here, and I didn't
think they would know about gifts, but two of the women had
been raised in a Baptist orphanage, and they got the rest of them
started. They knew what was what. I got: four bags of bear
gut—two trimmed with eagle feathers, one with bits of colored
yarn, one with beads; a little basket woven of Native grasses,
beautifully done; a homemade necklace; some kind of ring;
an ermine skin; a very much worn fancy comb for the hair; a
washed handkerchief; and a much worn "boughten" necklace.

The eagle feathers make the best trimming. Foster got a
ladies new handkerchief. That night there was a dance in the
schoolhouse, which everybody attended. There was a dance also
the next night, but few came to that. Two dances in succession
seemed too much.

Well, I'll sign off until I get your letters, and then I'll write
again.

Lots of love,

Tetts

January 17, 1932

Dear Mother and Dump:

We are just finishing up the Christmas holidays. After our regular Christmas, there were all the Russian celebrations. Tonight the whole village masks and goes around from house to house to mystify each other. There can't be anyone at home in most of the places except children and old folks, because everyone else is on the road. There is a continual procession of them in here and some of them are good. We are supposed to guess who they are, and we usually guess everyone in the village, beginning at one end and going right through. In that way, we are sure to hit the right one sooner or later. Some of them are so funny, I have laughed till my sides ached. They get a lot of fun out of it. They have done this masking every night now for over a week. Usually there was a dance, where different masked ones danced the Weasel dance, but tonight being Sunday, we will not let them dance in the schoolhouse, and last night being Saturday, and part of their Sabbath, they would not dance. As one of them expressed it, "The priest might give us hell."

The first three days of their Christmas were strictly religious, church twice a day, and carol singers going from house to house with the Christmas star. That is a very pretty custom, and the singing is beautiful. I went around with them for two nights, and when they came here, I treated them to cake. It kept me busy baking, because I used three cakes each of the three nights, nine cakes, all iced, too. Tonight's masking is different from the other nights. There is something about not seeing their shadows, so they back in, all wrapped up in sheets or blankets, and stand very solemnly until we guess who they are. Tomorrow there is a church service in the afternoon, and that ends their holidays. What tickles us is that the U.S. flag has been hoisted over their church at this time, and no other so far as we can find out, and the explanation is simply "holiday."

We are more than anxiously looking for a boat from Kodiak tonight, because it has been more than a month since the last one was here, and we have been looking for it almost every day since New Year's Day. The weather has been pretty cold and stormy for ocean travel, so I suppose that is the reason for the delay. The last few days have been delightful, warm and quiet, and a boat from Seattle was expected in Kodiak two days ago, so surely one must be on the way here. A trader's boat stopped in here a few days ago on its way to Kodiak, and they took the mail for us, but they may not have connected with the Seattle boat. In that case, it will be a long time before you get my letters. I hope they did make connections. The next two months will be just about as bad, because they are stormy months, but after that, mail will be more regular.

Although we have had some cold and stormy weather so far, the winter, as a whole, has been a mild one. We hear over the radio of fifty below temperatures around Fairbanks and other places, but here, except for two nights, it hasn't gone below zero. The radioman tells us of the queer freaks played by the weather in Alaska. At Takotna, there were seven feet of snow, and twenty-eight miles from there only seven inches. The temperature in one place rose over seventy-five degrees in twenty-four hours, from around fifty below to thirty above.

I'll send this off, and answer your letters when they come. I hope there will be many to answer.

With love,

Tetts

February 6, 1932

Dear Dump:

Yesterday your letter of January 12 came. That was pretty quick for this time of year. Last week we got mail that was almost two months overdue.

Mother's letters sound so much better than they did, more natural. She did enjoy all the Wileys so much at New Year's. Her letters were full of it!

I wonder if you have any old shoes with low heels that you want to pass on to me. It seems a shame to get new ones for this place. You get the new ones (joint account), and pass on the old ones. You know I am not "hard" on shoes. Last summer I bought a pair of shoes, the first I have had since I was home.

It is a gorgeous day, like May on the Yukon. Wish you could be here for a hike, the only form of entertainment we have to offer. But when we get our boat, we shall be kings of all we survey.

Love,
Tetts

April 2, 1932
Dear Dump:

Your letter with the bank statement, Book-of-the-Month News, and four books all came yesterday. Needless to say, I am delighted. Thanks for all your trouble. I don't know what I would do without you. The Sherlock Holmes books are splendid. I have always wanted to read all of his, and I hoped they would send me *Mr. and Mrs. Pennington*. You see, I have time to read the book reviews, and so am able to keep up fairly well. I have read parts of *Mary's Neck* and like it, so that is OK. However, I do not want all the novels. We are both rather serious readers. It isn't often that Foster will even attempt a novel. He says it is a waste of time, but I would like *Finch's Fortune*. I love the Whiteoaks books. And if you can get it, Kristin Lavrandsdatter, *Then, Only Yesterday, The Doctor Explains,* and *Strange Animals I Have Known.* I think that will do until the next bulletin comes. The trouble is, I want them all.

Sorry to hear of your neuritis, and I do hope it is entirely gone. Couldn't you get a substitute for a time and come up here for a rest? I am sure this wonderful air and scenery would smooth out all the pains. There are absolutely no distractions here, the calm and peace are unsurpassed, and the stillness would not hurt your ears as at Tanana. There is the wash of the surf, the call of wild ducks and seagulls, the whistle of the winds through mountain draws, and the tinkle of streams down mountainsides.

I am sending you some film for printing, for yourself and the family. Of course, that means Mother and Nan, and be sure to pay for them out of the joint account. Three are taken from the mountain in back of us. The land opposite is Sitkalidak Island but doesn't show the snow-capped mountains. Two pictures are of a bearskin hanging over a pole in a neighbor's yard. In one, I didn't get much of the head but the other seems to be all head. And one is of the beautiful little stream where we fished and berried last summer. These make good postcard-size enlargements, and I would get the enlargements if I were you, because they are too small to be seen well otherwise.

Take the *Admiral Evans*, Pacific Steamship Company. It sails every two weeks from Seattle. Please send me a set of postcard enlargements, but only one from the mountaintop. The more I think of your coming up here, the more I see that you *must*. Not only because you would like to, but because you *should*. I am convinced this can get you well as nothing else can, and you probably will spend the money for doctors, anyway. I'll wager Frank agrees with me. I am writing the steamship agent to send

Two Alutiiq girls and a bearskin, Old Harbor, circa 1930s.

you a folder. The *Watson*, too, probably comes to Kodiak in the summer. Let us know in plenty of time and we'll meet you in Kodiak.

Come *now.*

Tetts

May 24, 1932

Dear Dump:

Foster came home from Kodiak last night bringing, not you as we had hoped, but your letter of April 25th. I told him to open that in Kodiak to make sure about you. We were delighted with its news, except, of course, the BIG DISAPPOINTMENT. I noted that you were to send the cancelled checks and new bulletin, but there were other things to read and see about, so I did not bother about it until later today, and there, oh joy, another letter from you. So we feel that we have had a feast.

Your two books have not come yet, but I shall look for them eagerly. I have wanted to read both of them, especially Willa Cather's. I must have been very vague about last month's books. I DID get *Mr. and Mrs. Pennington*, long ago, and all the others right up to date. I take it Warden Lawes's book is on the way, and you are right about that. I would not want to miss it. Sometimes the books are pretty wet, but that isn't their fault. It is the sloppy seas on the way down from Kodiak.

Yes, the shoes came, and I put them right on and have worn them steadily ever since. They are just right for the house, and will last me for years, so don't bother with any more.

No, my psychology did not work this time, not even with myself, because all along I have not once felt that you would be here, much as I would like to have you. We will concentrate now on you and Frank coming together sometime, and hope it will be soon. It is such good news that you are feeling like yourself again, and your letters sound like it.

Many thanks for all your trouble with my affairs.

Love,

Tetts

Etta and Foster's success at their posts came to the attention of their supervisor at the Alaska Indian Service. In June, 1932, plans were made to transfer them to the isolated village of Kipnuk, 414 miles to the northwest on the Bering Sea. Commissioner of Indian Affairs, C. J. Rhodes, wrote: "Kipnuk is a new station being opened this fall. The building is in the process of construction at present. With reference to filling this position, Superintendent Garber wired, 'Teachers for Kipnuk should sail via *Tupper* about August tenth. Please bear in mind complete isolation, difficult water supply, great destitution of Natives, and necessary Native health program in making your selection. Practical man whose wife is a nurse is the best combination for this place.'

Mr. Jones has lived many years in Alaska and is familiar with the isolation and hardships which exist at such a village as Kipnuk. He has had some pharmacy training, he has a great deal of experience in the operation of gas engines and gas boats, and is a practical carpenter. Mrs. Jones is a graduate nurse as well as a teacher. She has taught successfully in our Service for several years. It is believed that Mr. and Mrs. Jones will be an admirable combination for this new school, and it is therefore recommended that they be transferred as recommended above. It would not be desirable to send to this station persons unfamiliar with Alaskan conditions and whose training and experience have been largely academic."

In a Letter of Justification from the Department of the Interior, Mr. Thomas wrote:

"For the proposed transfer of Foster Jones from the position of teacher at Old Harbor to the position of teacher at Kipnuk, Alaska.

The appropriation for Education of Natives of Alaska, 1931–1932, provided funds for the erection of a school building and teacherage at Cheechingamute, Alaska. The building material was purchased in Seattle and shipped with Cheechingamute as its destination. Due to difficulties of transportation it was not possible to get this material any farther than Kipnuk, at which point the material was landed. Kipnuk is a large Native village, and estimates had been submitted for the establishment of a school there for several years. Authority was therefore granted to erect the building at Kipnuk. The building is in the process of construction.

The salaries of two teachers were provided for Cheechingamute in the appropriation act for 1932, but the positions have not hitherto been filled due to delay in endeavoring to get the building material to its original destination and in its construction at Kipnuk.

There are at present thirty-four children at Kipnuk of school age and, with the establishment of the school, it is expected that other families will move to the village and that there will be additional children enrolled."

In July, Etta received a letter from the Department of the Interior, Office of Indian Affairs, informing her that she was being transferred from Old Harbor to Kipnuk, a Yup'ik Eskimo village located on Kuskokwim Bay, one hundred miles southwest of Bethel.

Unaware that they would be leaving Old Harbor, Etta and Foster had made all the necessary arrangements to spend another year, including ordering a year's supply of food. Careful planning was required when generating a list of food items that would be required for one year: thousands of cans, cases, barrels, and crates. Foster made the decision to leave the food supply in Old Harbor for the new teacher, and when they arrived in Bethel, just north of the mouth of the Kuskokwim River, forty miles upriver from the Bering Sea, Foster would pick up supplies there.

5

From Kodiak to Kipnuk

1932

In their six-week journey to Kipnuk, Etta and Foster would have interesting experiences, but they had a schedule and were anxious to reach their destination. Their house and school were not completed, and with winter fast approaching, it was urgent that both structures were built and furnished before snowfall. Etta and Foster looked forward to helping with the projects.

Kodiak
August 5, 1932
Dear Everybody:

We are still waiting for the *Starr*. It may leave Seward today, as we were informed in a telegram that it would, or it may not leave until the 8th, its regular day. Whenever it gets here, it will find us waiting. We have been here about a week now, and it is getting pretty tiresome.

We pine for the *Starr*, because we want to get settled. It will be much colder where we are going, but not as cold as the Yukon. However, we are going back to the land of the dog teams, and I think we are both glad. If the mail is more regular, we can stand a lot.

Well, I will keep you informed as to our adventures.

Lots of love to all,

Tetts

Nushagak, Alaska
August 30, 1932
Dear Everybody:

There will be an airplane here in a few days which will take this, and if I get a chance to write from Bethel, I will. Otherwise, don't look for letters too often. I hope to goodness we find letters from you at Bethel. We left orders at Kodiak to have them forwarded. They will go by way of Anchorage and should have reached there long before we do. You can imagine how hungry I am for letters.

Lots of love to all,
Tetts

Bethel, Alaska
September 5, 1932
Dear Mother and Dump:

We are still a week from our journey's end. The mail leaves tomorrow and I must get this in because it will be the last letter you will get from me for many months. The question of mail service is rather discouraging. They tell us it will be perhaps twice in the winter when the dog teams travel, and less in the summer, only when an occasional boat happens by. Incidentally, we haven't had any letters since leaving Old Harbor, and unless a plane comes before we leave in three or four days, we won't have any until after Christmas. It is a lesson in patience, isn't it?

Bethel reminds me of Tanana—similar river, similar surroundings, and similar houses and people. There is a Moravian mission here, and as the Moravians originate in Bethlehem, Pennsylvania, they seem rather familiar. We went to church last night and might have been in any little church in any little town in the States. I counted twenty-five white people there and twice as many Eskimos. They are the one strange note, entirely different from the Indians of the Yukon and the Aleuts of Kodiak.

The Eskimos of Kipnuk are among the most primitive Natives of Alaska. They live in igloos that are little better than

SS Tupper, *1930s. From Jeremy S. Snapp,* Northwest Legacy:
Sail, Steam and Motorships, *page 202.*

dugouts, just holes in the ground, and are extremely destitute
and squalid. We are not expected to have school the first year,
just get acquainted and do what we can in the homes. In fact,
there could not be school because the building is not yet finished,
hardly more than the walls and roof so far. It will be a wonderful
building when finished, a duplicate of the one here in Bethel,
and that is the finest school building in Alaska that I have seen
so far, and I have seen a great many of them. We have met many
who envy us the opportunity of going into a new community
and building it up. Certainly there is the opportunity of making
it what we will. There are no religious organizations working
there now, but the Moravians are reaching out that way from
this side, and the Roman Catholics from the other.

Our nearest neighbors, eighty to one hundred miles away,
are a Moravian missionary and his wife at Kwigillingok. We met
him last night, and he is a splendid fellow. They say his wife is
just as fine. She is the government teacher. We may stop at their
place on the way to Kipnuk. It will take us at least six days in a
small boat.

Most of the teachers in this section have shortwave radio
sets, have learned Morse code, and talk to each other over the
radio. The superintendent broadcasts each day, by voice and by
code. We are being fixed up with something suitable and will
learn the code. Also, the army radio operator here broadcasts

each day. Therefore, we are not really out of touch with the world. I suppose if you want to get a message to me, you could wire to the operator at Bethel to be relayed to me. He is very accommodating.

We have met some lovely people here. Many teachers are in from surrounding communities to meet the *Tupper* and get their freight [annual supplies]. We have been entertained at dinners, luncheons, and suppers. Last night after church we had a wild goose buffet supper. Such a jolly crowd. Tonight there is to be a Bridge party. The *Tupper* is still here, and this noon the captain invited all the white people of the town to lunch on board. It will be three or four days yet before we get away, and already the nights are frosty.

Don't try to send any packages for Christmas. They will be held up in the Seattle post office, but do write as often as you can, and I will do the same.

Lots of love to all,

Tetts

THROUGH A TRADER, *transportation was arranged to use a Columbia River boat. It was an open, wide-bottomed boat that had a gasoline engine. It also had a sail just in case anything happened to the engine. The freight was loaded onto the front of the palatial carrier, freight that included our clothing and personal belongings, school freight and supplies, and food supplies for a year.*

When leaving Bethel, our friends had said, "You are going by water. Dress for it, just as you would in the winter." We had plenty of fur clothing for the cold—fur boots, coats, caps, and mittens. I thought it was foolish to start in these outlandish getups from the hot town where everyone wore thin summer clothes. However, as soon as we were well started, I realized the wisdom of our good advisors.

The scenery was flat and uninteresting, there was nothing for me to do but sleep most of the time. Starting early in the morning when the tide was right, we ran smoothly down the winding, muddy Kuskokwim, sometimes passing Eskimo villages, fish camps, and tent villages. At the mouth of the river, the boat anchored to "wait for tide." Everyone slept. I woke once to find that everything was dark, there was a pale moon, there was nothing to be seen but water, and no sound except the gentle lap, lap of waves against the sides of the boat. Later, I woke again because I seemed to be standing on my head. Sure enough, the boat was tilted over on its side to what seemed to me a very dangerous angle. I looked out to find no water around us. We were on a dry riverbed. I could have climbed out and walked all around the boat with dry feet. That was what was meant by "waiting for tide." Soon the gentle lap, lap of the water began again, the boat righted itself, the anchor was lifted, and we were once again on our way. This process was repeated again and again at every turn of the tide for the six days it took us to reach our destination.

It took Eskimos who were familiar with the locality and its peculiarities to successfully steer a boat through the shallows of the Kuskokwim Delta. We were never very far from shore. Many times we grated over sandbars, and when the boat stuck, they just threw the anchor out and "waited for tide." We would float as long as the tide lasted, and then had another stop. I wondered how these Eskimos knew anything was there, but they felt around with poles until they found the river current. We would twist and turn down a narrow, muddy stream that had low mud banks. There were no trees or bushes or anything to relieve the monotony for hours and miles.

When we reached Kwigillingok, it happened to be low tide, so they turned in there to anchor. That suited us because we had a fine visit with Mrs. Martin, the teacher.

We left Kwigillingok that afternoon "on the tide," and followed the same dreary pattern of landscape for eighty to one hundred miles. We came to the mouth of another muddy stream, the Kipnuk River, where we again "waited for the tide." As we followed its twisting course, I strained my eyes for the first view of our new home. It was a very desolate area. The riverbanks were not a foot or more above the high tide, there were no trees, not even a bush. Sedges around the numerous small lakes were the highest form of vegetation. The ground was covered with a deep moss, which was disastrous to try to walk on without rubber boots. Overshoes would be inadequate because one's ankles were covered with the water.

Aerial view of the Kuskokwim Delta, 1930s.

As our boat felt its way up the muddy stream that day, we could see for miles around because there was nothing to obstruct our view. In the distance, we saw our future home, or part of it because it was in the process of being built. The village consisted of a few sod huts near the riverbank. Kwigillingok was a modern town by comparison.

The few people there met us at the bank. The first question asked by the one white man present, the builder, was, "Did you bring our tobacco and matches?" A gangplank was put out from the boat because the boat could not get close enough to tie up. Unloading proceeded rapidly, because when the tide went out, any chance of working from the boat was gone until the next tide.

Only the shell of the house was finished. There was no place for us to live. The builder and his Native assistant were living in the coal house. On one of the fairly dry raised spots, a tent was put up for us, and this is where we slept and kept our personal belongings. We ate in the coal house with the other two people. I did the cooking. There were cases of eggs, sacks of potatoes, hams and bacon, canned vegetables and fruits—plenty of food. Every morning I made "sourdough hotcakes" which are much better than any other kind. They are made from a soured sponge of eggs, milk, shortening, a little sugar, and enough soda to make it foamy and light. When eaten with plenty of butter and syrup, they are hard to resist. As hard as I tried, I could never make them as good as any of the real Sourdoughs.

In the tent, the ladies of the village made social calls on me. They were very friendly and curious. They came before I was out of bed in the *morning, smiling and jabbering happily as they handled me and all my things that they could reach. Once, an elderly lady sat on the floor and ate what was left in the cat's food dish. Most of them had never seen a white woman before, and while many things amused them and there were many shrieks of laughter, they were never overwhelmed or awed by my material possessions.* ☸

In the following letter, Etta describes Foster's introduction to, and fascination with, a transmitter radio—a skill that would become significant.

Kipnuk, Via Bethel, Alaska
September 12, 1932
Dear Everybody:

Again I must write to you all at once to save time and paper. This is the last piece I have until millions of boxes are unpacked, and the boat which brought us returns soon, so I must get off a few words to you. We were six days on the trip, an open boat about forty-five feet long and twelve feet wide. A canvas top was put over the engine in the stern under which we lived and slept. The rest of the boat was filled with freight, about six tons. A canvas tent was stretched over that, and somewhere in the bow the three Eskimo boatmen slept. One night we struck a bar about 9 P.M. They cast anchor and everyone went to bed. Our bed was made of blankets spread over life preservers. We towed three Eskimo sailboats, one after the other. It must have made quite a picture. When we stopped, there was visiting back and forth between the boats, then everyone went to his own bed. It was a queer feeling, anchored in mud and no sign of life anywhere.

The only social call we made on that long trip—indeed, the only village we saw—was Kwigillingok. It could not be seen from the shore. The tiny village had wood houses, a schoolhouse, and a small wood church. I wondered how anyone could be content in such a place. We tied up in front of the teacher's residence, and pounded on the door to wake her up.

A charming and pretty young girl appeared and welcomed us in. She not only wholeheartedly extended full hospitality to us, she put all the accommodations of the house at our disposal. She prepared her spare bedroom, taking it for granted, as people of the North do, that we were there for an extended stay. The house was cheerful and homey. We had arrived at seven in the morning, and she prepared breakfast, one that I will never forget. After the dirty boat and living for days in the same clothing, the dainty table appointments and marvelous food were wonderful.

It was in this remote village that we first came in contact with the shortwave radio set. Bess Martin, our hostess, talked while we were there with her husband, Gus, who was 200 miles away in Bethel. They have a shortwave sending set, and while we were there she held her daily conversations with the missionaries at Quinhagak, across Kuskokwim Bay, and at Bethel. She talked into a mike and when ready to listen to them, switched the thing over to a receiving set and their answers came through the loud speaker. It was like a wireless telephone. She told them about the Joneses, and we made arrangements to buy some canned reindeer meat from them. I thought how nice it would be to talk to you that way. Later, she ticked off messages to the army operator in Bethel in code. He talks with a number of stations in the district that way, and then broadcasts all the local news he gathers. We listened to the news about ourselves and others. Incidentally, the news that we were coming here was known to everyone in these parts a full month before we knew it ourselves.

Foster became interested in this radio and soon built his own set. It worked so well, better than many expensive sets, that other people wanted his help with their own sets. He was flooded with orders for the "Jones Special," as it was jokingly called. Foster realized he had better call a halt to the requests because he did not have a license to manufacture and sell radios.

I will tell you about Kipnuk later. I am quite sure all of you would be filled with horror at the thought of a winter here. It is bleak, desolate country, worse than Nome, everyone says. Not a tree, not a hill except a low one about ten miles away. There is nothing but monotonous tundra, but we like it. I am sure the winter will be an interesting one. Just now there are thousands of geese and ducks everywhere, big fat ones, making the tundra look like a chicken ranch. One of the Eskimos said there are reindeer tracks on a creek not far away, so we may have some reindeer meat.

The building isn't finished enough for us to live in yet, so we are in a tent, and so happy to be there after our six weeks of traveling. We left Old Harbor July 29 and landed here September 11. Just before we left Bethel, a plane came with mail and there was a letter from Nan enclosing one of Dump's. I devoured them over and over. I suppose the rest of your letters are on the way from Kodiak. I'll get them about Christmas. I am sorry to hear of Uncle Tom's passing. Mother will feel very much alone now.

I will write occasionally and keep a letter handy in case I have a chance to send it, but I don't see any hope of sending until Christmas anyway. Very soon now the Bering Sea freezes, and the tundra freezes, and traveling will be by dog team.

Please send me a package or two of stamped envelopes. The first boat to bring packages from Seattle leaves early in May. If I send for things, try to get it on that boat.

I might as well say Merry Christmas now.

Lots of love to all,

Tetts

6

Kipnuk Culture

1932

In Kipnuk, Etta and Foster settled into what would be their home for the next five years. There were new people to meet and customs to learn. They shared with the villagers some of their own protocol as well.

THE ESKIMOS WERE PEACEFUL, *friendly, and full of fun. One wondered sometimes what they had to be happy about, they were so poverty-stricken. They were the warmest blooded people I ever met, and their fat cheeks, particularly the women, were so red, visitors usually asked what they used to paint their cheeks. Their black eyes sparkled with health and good spirits, their black hair glistened with natural oil, their whole bodies seemed to ooze oil.*

The villagers did not live under tribal rule. There was no chief. They seemed to be just a group of people who happened to live near each other, and they were constantly moving from village to village. While the village held about two hundred people when the school was built, traders familiar with this locality said there was a possibility that all might have taken up residence somewhere else, and the village site left empty. This was easy enough for them to do because they were in this spot only during the winter months.

In the fall, they chose a spot for a house, made a sort of framework of driftwood by fastening longer poles together, tent fashion, then covered it with sod and moss, leaving a square opening in the roof for smoke to escape, but making a wooden covering for the opening to keep out storms. The entrance was dug, slanting down, so the dirt floor was below the level of the ground. Wooden platforms were built for their fur robes used as beds.

They trapped fox and mink, which they exchanged with the traders for gingham, summer parkas, and a little underwear. They fished for food, and hunted walrus, seal, ducks, and geese for food and clothing. Their main article of diet was the needlefish, so called because of its sharp needle-like spines. The whole fish did not exceed an inch in length, and were eaten raw. In the fall, we noticed them putting little nets in tiny running streams to catch these fish. Children finding these nets would sit down on the ground and greedily munch the wriggling fish like our children eat peanuts. In the winter, holes were cut in the ice, and these fish were scooped up by a net attached to a long handle. Needlefish seemed to run in schools, and if the schools were running another way, there was no food that day, but usually they were lucky. The fish were dumped in heaps on the ice where they soon froze. Gunnysacks were filled with the frozen fish and stored for future use. As fishing continued, I have seen children run from pile to pile, choosing from the freshest pile, which were the most wriggly, then eating rapidly with grins of satisfaction. There was a particular way of swallowing them so the spines did not stick them going down. Two fish were put into the mouth at once, head first, and, with a crack of the strong teeth and a few crunches, the deed was done, grinding the backbone, making it harmless. White men have lost dogs that ate these fish. Evidently, the dogs did not know the correct way to eat them.

Babies too young to walk sucked contentedly on hunks of raw seal fat. They never had more than two weeks' food supply at one time. If storms came up that kept them housebound for more than a week, it was just too bad. They went hungry.

Duck skins, especially loon, were made into warm parkas, but most of their parkas were made from reindeer skins, and a very few from the mountain squirrel, or ick-sick-buck. Only the most affluent could afford those. The women carried their babies on their back, and in cold weather under the parka. Their foot covering consisted of a piece of dirty rag wrapped around the foot, and then carefully covered with dry grass, over which was drawn the skin boot. The boot soles were made of moisture-proof sealskin, and the tops were reindeer hide or fish skin.

The tundra was as flat as the ocean, dotted here and there with numerous small lakes. Nowhere could anything be seen except toward the west where there was the outline of a distant hill. In winter, this was a sea of driven snow. The frozen lakes made good skating before there was too much snow covering. The Eskimos were good skaters, often going the distance to the next village, eighty miles, entirely on skates. The skates were made from old pieces of iron or steel that were picked up perhaps on the beach. They filed the metal down and attached the metal to pieces of driftwood. The driftwood was cleverly shaped to fit the sole of the foot. This was then strapped with strips of raw hide to the soft mukluks.

Whatever their midwife customs were, they were very careful not to let us see any of it. They never notified us of a birth until everything was all over. The mother was around again immediately with a healthy baby. There never seemed to be any difficulty, and their delivery records were perfect. Though infant mortality was high, most deaths occurred after the baby was near the year-old mark. They believed that the soul of the last old man or woman who died entered the body of the new infant. Thus, a willful child was made so by the soul of the old wise one who ruled the child.

Their dead were buried on top of the ground. Put in a small box, the body was bent double as much as possible and tied to get it into the smallest space. The box was put on the tundra, on a raised spot, if possible, and sometimes large driftwood logs were placed on top of the box to keep it from being blown away by the wind. Here the custom still prevailed of putting personal belongings on the grave or beside the box. We have seen hand sewing machines, kerosene lamps, cooking utensils, valuable necklaces, guns, spears, etc., at gravesites. There were several deaths that first winter, and we looked forward to the summer with some horror, because many of these new graves were very near our house. There was no marked place for them. They were put anywhere that seemed feasible to the family. But by spring, there was no indication of decaying flesh. The wind, rain, and snow elements had done their work. No one ever went near the burial places to molest them in

Gravesite at Kipnuk, ca. 1930s. Etta inscribed on the back
of the photo: "Grave near us. Remains in box on top of ground.
Must have been a woman because of cups, pans, etc., left for her use.
A man's grave has paddles, guns, etc."

any way. Some of the very old burial boxes had rotted with the years, and bones were scattered about, but no one seemed concerned.

We learned how their seal oil, the Eskimo's wealth, was stored in sealskins. The seal's legs and other openings were securely tied off, thus making skin bottles. These were placed in high spots on the tundra, where holes could be dug, and the cache was covered to protect it from storms and animals. Although these storage spots were sometimes miles and miles from their winter dwellings and others were aware of their locations, they were perfectly safe and were never disturbed.

Before we had been in Kipnuk more than a week, while still living in the tent, the men, boys, and some women found out that old things were good for trade with us, and they began to bring their treasures. Some of them indeed were rare treasures, and we were happy to have them, such as: old primitive knives fashioned by skillful hands from scraps of steel and tied with hide to a wood or ivory handle; ceremonial masks; ancient drills used probably for generations by their forebears; tobacco boxes made of driftwood; walrus ivory inlaid boxes with hinged lids cunningly attached with wooden pins; ancient dolls with ivory heads and hay-stuffed bodies; ivory story knives; arrowheads of ivory and flint; and old Russian beads made into earrings and necklaces.

There were many other things of no value whatever to us for which we gave tea, soap, coffee, and chewing gum. Some did not seem to know the difference, or if they did, tried a trade anyway, and if refused, they retreated with a broad grin as if to say, "No harm in trying."

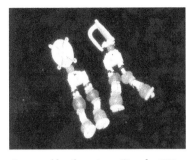

Ivory and bead earrings, Kipnuk, 1930s.
Courtesy of Jean Kline, Douglas, Alaska.

Their word for trade was kapoosak, and one of the first and most persistent traders was a fat, greasy, ragged, dirty, inefficient but perpetually smiling man. Where he dug up all the things he brought for exchange was a mystery. He must have spent his days so doing, for he was at the door at all hours, and many times a day, holding out his offering with a hopeful, "Kapoosak?" His smile never failed, even when refused, and refusals never discouraged him. We soon nicknamed him "Fatty Kapoosak," the name clinging to him all through the five years we knew him. In fact, his real name has been lost to me, and that is the only name I can now associate with him.

The rapidity with which they learned enough English to make themselves usually understood was gratifying. Their natural aptitude for details was amazing. While standing at a door talking, apparently looking anywhere but at the other person or his house, they could later recount in astonishing detail everything they saw during that interview. White traders who spoke Eskimo told us we would be astounded if we knew of the complete, detailed descriptions they gave of us, our dress, habits, house furnishings, even after the most cursory glances.

Although these people were so poor that they had hardly enough food and clothing for themselves, they gave potlatches like other Natives of Alaska.

Lavish and extravagant gifts were given to the visitors one night that the visitors returned the next night. Gifts—bolts of cloth, furs, guns, spears, and beads—were thrown on the floor as each group finished its dance. One man gave his boat, but, obviously, he could not

83

bring the boat into that small space so he drew a picture of the boat and threw that in. Three key men before whom the gifts were piled seemed to be the masters of ceremony. They were bare to the waist, wearing a headdress of feathers and beads and a necklace of ivory carvings. They led the chanting. In spite of the severe weather outside, little rivulets of sweat ran down their chests and backs. Then refreshments were passed around. Each person had a wooden dish. Distributors passed around delicacies, throwing into each dish a handful—whale meat, fish cooked, raw, and dried, and a special delicacy I think they called titmuk. It was seal meat, cut into hunks and stored in the sealskin which was buried underground for a certain length of time. It was about the consistency of cheese and smelled to high heaven, but was the favorite of all the foods.

At the dance, the feet are not moved from one spot. All movements are made by the head, trunk, and hands to the rhythm of drums. Hands especially receive much attention. Some of the little schoolgirls were being trained as dancers. We persuaded them to practice sometimes in the schoolhouse, and such training! Over and over they were made to repeat what seemed to us to be very simple movements, but perhaps one little finger would spoil the perfection of the performance. They were stopped and made to repeat. The dance orchestra consisted entirely of drums—sealskin stretched tightly over a flat wooden ring about twenty-five inches in diameter. The drum was flat, round, and hollow underneath. They held the drum in one hand and beat it with the other, using a stick that had a padded end. The least touch of the drumstick on these drums made them sing with overtones too fine for the white ear. As many as eleven drums were used at once, led by a leader who sometimes stopped the whole performance when something displeased him, and a new start was made.

Over one hundred people crowded into a tiny hut, eleven drums accompanied to the clapping of hands and the rhythmic swaying of bodies and the singing or chanting in their peculiar minor key. The odors in that close place probably had their effect, too—seal oil, which is more smelly than cod liver oil, sweating bodies, and parkas that had been washed in urine. It more nearly approached hypnotism than anything else I have ever experienced. In spite of all my efforts to resist the influence, I felt myself slipping into a region I had no desire to explore, and so my evening was terminated by an ignominious retreat.

Their names gave us a little trouble at first because they all had Eskimo names, but they would not give them to us. We had to name them in many cases. The missionaries who worked with them gave them Christian names for baptism, but even these were hard to get from them. One of the first of the "city fathers" who came to see us displayed his knowledge of English as he grinned and said, "Me Jim Mute." Thankfully, we put that down as a beginning. Then, we discovered that Jim had several brothers, all were married and had big families, so we soon had a long list of Mutes. Long after, when all the Mutes had been registered, we learned that "mute" is their word for "people" or "persons." Jim was trying to tell us that he was a person named Jim. Kipnuk was the village, meaning "bend in the river," Kipnukamute were the people of that village. Cheeching was another village. Cheechingamute were the people of that village.

Getting the ages of these people was another task that was required by Uncle Sam. I tackled that job while the interpreter was still with us. Even the most advanced had no idea of birthdays, so it was my duty to give each one a birthday and teach it to him for future use. I tried to find out from the mothers if a child was born when snow was on the ground, when the ducks came, or when berries were ripe, then gave a wild guess at the year. We found that these people, living hard lives in their efforts to survive the rigors of the country, had short lives and aged quickly. Traders who had known them for many years doubted that more than twenty-five percent were over forty years old. Some looked eighty. We could see the rapid change in some. For instance, one young, smiling, happy, unconcerned fellow in the beginning became a bent, old man with trembling hands and a feeble step in three or four years.

As soon as possible, the men got enough flooring on the second floor finished to hold a bed, and, thankfully, sometime in October, the day came when we could move out of the tent and into the new house. I had to climb a ladder to reach it, but at least it was private. Men, women, and children were warned to not climb that ladder. Warning was hard to enforce at first.

Etta at Kipnuk, circa 1930s.

It was a well-constructed, cold-resistant building with five thicknesses in the walls and five layers of flooring. Storm sheds at all the doors on the lower level helped keep out the cold. There was no basement because any holes dug would immediately fill with water, and the water would stay frozen all winter. By this time, snow was beginning to fly and the nights were freezing. All birds, ducks, and geese had gone to warmer places and the Eskimos were digging in for the winter.

At first, the Natives barged right into our house without knocking.

86

To teach the white man's queer custom of first knocking on a door, Foster took a free-minded visitor in hand for a lesson. Going outside the door, he knocked, and after waiting a suitable length of time, Foster said, "Now, all right. You try again." Then going inside, he closed the door, waited for the knock, and then opened it up to the beaming visitor. A few days later, he had occasion to visit the same man's house. The Eskimo, seeing him coming, hurried into the house, closed the opening, almost in Foster's face, and waited for the knock, then opened to his beaming guest, no doubt pitying the poor crazy white man for his foolish ways.

The summers were very pleasant, never getting very warm. Between forty and fifty degrees was normal, and when it reached seventy, we felt the heat because the humidity was high, I suppose. A coat or sweater was always comfortable to wear.

The bird life all over this region was fascinating to watch. It seemed that every variety of bird came there to nest, from the white swans and sandhill cranes, down to the tiniest warblers. We found seven varieties of duck eggs, many of geese, loons, all the waders, gulls and terns, barn swallows, robins, sparrows, and some I could not identify. All made nests on the ground except the swallows, which utilized our roofs. I wonder what they did when there were no buildings. We always had to be careful where we placed our feet when walking over the tundra, or we would step right into a nest.

Finding a loon nest one day on the edge of a lake, I made daily visits so I could see the newborn birds. The nest was so tipped, the eggs seemed sure to fall into the water. They did not, but evidently the newborn chicks did, because the eggshells were still wet when I got there, and two balls of black puff were sitting on the water right under the nest. The mother circled overhead and cried to those babies. They seemed to understand because instantly they dove out of sight to come up again out in the middle of the lake. They could not have been more than a day old.

We found many crane nests. The nest was a slight depression in the ground, holding two large eggs. After the young birds were hatched, it was interesting to watch their gatherings. They were in groups of twenty or more, but at such a distance from the window, it was difficult to see what they were doing. One day, Foster was hidden behind a blind he had fixed for shooting ducks, and he saw one of their dances, called the mating dance, though this was in late summer. He said they formed in a circle and then did a sort of buck and wing, bowing and swaying to each other, raising and lowering their wings.

There were many kinds of geese that summered there. At molting time, when they could not fly, the Natives slaughtered them by the hundreds. They visited the breeding grounds, killing them with sticks, clubbing them to death. In the fall, when it was just about time for them to fly south, the geese gathered on a sandbar just across the slough from our place. They seemed almost too heavy to fly. Day after day, the number increased until there were thousands of them—snow geese, Emperors, Canada geese—all kinds. Some were literally stepping on each other's toes. We wondered if they were selecting their leaders and appointing their companies for the long trip. Then, suddenly, they were all gone.

The ptarmigan, especially, were almost impossible to see, so completely did the bird sitting on the nest, as well as the nest itself, blend into the surroundings. Once, from the window, I saw a mother ptarmigan, really a grouse, leading a brood of twelve chicks right by the house. I went out carefully, but she gave the warning and by the time I reached the spot, although I knew they were there because they could not fly, there wasn't a bird to be seen, search as I might. I was afraid to stay around too much for fear of stepping on the little things. These birds, which turn white in winter, were expert in blending with their surroundings in winter as well as in summer. A vast sea of frozen white, nowhere to hide, but going out hunting them, it was almost impossible to spot them until they moved. Their little red eyes were the only touch of color on them. Sometimes, they would rise almost from our very feet. Shooting them on the wing was the only way to get them. They were too small to pluck, so the skin was just peeled off, feathers and all. The feet were also covered with feathers, and no matter how cold it was when they were killed, the bodies were very hot, far above our body temperature. I used to think how cold they must be, sitting out in those biting winds without shelter, but nature provided for them. They were splendid eating. We liked them best drawn and cut in half, dipped in *eggs and cracker crumbs, browned in hot fat, and then steamed slowly in a Dutch oven for several hours. We did six or eight at a time. Except for the breast, there was very little meat on them.*

The nearest lake was perhaps forty feet from our front door. From the window, we watched many interesting things on that lake. Mother ducks appeared, then, followed by their broods that were too young to fly, waddled off over the tundra with them to reach another lake. One such family we had watched for several days, when an Eskimo came along, killed the mother, and took her away for food. The babies were left alone until another mother duck appeared with ten ducklings. The orphaned twelve immediately attached themselves to her. Her looks were very expressive as she looked behind her at this long file of twenty-two ducks following with military precision. Finally, she decided she did not like it, and she made many vicious attempts to kill the strangers, but they managed to evade her. After a few days, she was killed, and we watched twenty-two orphans until another mother duck, followed by ten offspring, appeared on the lake. The twenty-two immediately attached themselves to her train, and she looked back in amazement at her following of thirty-two. Apparently, she found a satisfactory explanation because she sailed proudly around, leading her small army. I told Foster, "Now, we must see the end of this because it will be a great sight when she waddles off, followed by that gang." However, they disappeared one morning before we got up.

Late in the afternoon one sunny winter day, we saw from our living room window an arctic hare hopping leisurely over the snow. These hares were like rabbits, but much larger and pure white in the winter. They were good eating, if caught young enough. As we watched Mr. Hare, he was soon joined by a large arctic owl, also pure white in winter. All birds and most animals put on Nature's white protective coat in winter, changing to darker colors in summer. The owl had not come to play with the hare, but to prey on him. There were no clumps of grass or bushes, no trees or holes where the hare could hide. The owl swooped down at the hare again and again with extended claws ready to grasp, but the hare, pursuing a zigzag course, was not where he should have been when the owl poised over a spot with his clutching claws. What intrigued us most was the unconcerned manner of the hare. Nibbling away at things in the snow that we could not see, he meandered from side to side, seemingly paying not the slightest attention to the owl, except to keep zigzagging. After fully an hour of futile trying, the owl flew disgustedly off. Long after, we could see the hare, still leisurely hopping along in the distance.

A Native once brought us a leg of hare, almost the size of the hind leg of a fair-sized dog. It was big enough to roast. Thinking that would be a good way to cook it, I put it in the oven, giving it the baking any such roast would call for. No amount of roasting would make it fit for the table. Finding it too tough to eat, we were forced to throw it away.

7

Letters from Kipnuk

1932-1933

E tta and Foster were very effective in their roles and enjoyed their work. Letters they wrote and received, however, were a mainstay in their lives. Etta often reflected on how much letters meant to her as well as pondering how her family members spent special holidays. Geographically, she was thousands of miles from home, but her thoughts were often centered on her family.

November 8, 1932
Dear Mother:

It did seem so good to get your many letters. There were seven or eight, most of them long and full of news. We also received your pretty Christmas card. It had been mailed to somewhere in Washington, but it did get here with the other mail.

Thanks for Skeets's picture. He is a good-looking little fellow and I know just how attached you all are to him. Dogs have a way of worming their way into our affections. How many times have I promised myself that I won't get attached to this dog, and, before I know it, he is a member of the family. Our dogs are not allowed in the house. It is just that much worse when they are living in the house with the family. For some time, Foster has wanted a wirehaired terrier, but one couldn't be kept in a place like this. We almost got a hunting dog in Seward

Etta and one of her dogs, at Kipnuk, circa 1930s.

last year when we went through there. It's just as well we did
not because we could not have brought him here.

I wonder if you can put a few head lettuce seeds and a
few parsley seeds in an envelope and send them to me when

you write. We are thinking of starting a little hot bed near the house a little later, but we have no seeds. By the time we get a catalogue and place an order, it will be too late. I hope a letter from you will get through before late spring.

We hope these letters will go out soon. We are expecting a fur trader through here who is going to Bethel, and he will take our letters for us. There is always this question of the mail. I wonder what it would feel like to have daily mail service for a change.

Lots of love,

Tetts

December 1, 1932

Dear Mother:

Merry Christmas and Happy New Year.

I wonder and wonder how you are getting on this winter. Do you have someone with you and do you have plenty of coal?

How do you manage the furnace when Russ is away?

I shall be glad when I get some letters from you. I don't like this lack of mail service. It makes me feel so very far away. Otherwise, this is an interesting place and I am glad we came.

Lots of love,

Tetts

Dec. 24:

Still waiting for that plane and just now, 1:00 P.M., we listened to the Bethel broadcast. For Mrs. Foster Jones there was a message via Western Union from Yonkers. Christmas wishes and love from the family. Gee, that made us feel good! We have been hoping that sacks of mail would get here so we could celebrate Christmas properly. Well, we must just make the best of it. I'd better change my Christmas wishes to Fourth of July wishes. I think we will have wild duck (for Foster) and canned reindeer (for me) for Christmas dinner.

Love,

Tetts

January 8, 1933

Dear Everybody:

This is the Sunday after New Year's Day, so we dined sumptuously on turkey. We felt very grand when we two sat down alone in front of a twelve pound turkey. You will surmise from this that the plane came at last. The day after New Year's, when everyone had about given up, it swooped down suddenly, stayed half an hour, and took off again. The pilot took with him the two carpenters and twenty gallons of our gasoline; however, he left us a sixty pound sack of mail, a turkey, and a loin of pork. That pilot also took away with him a check for $20 for those things: $7 for bringing the mail, $4 for the pork, and $9 for the turkey. We were glad to get all three at almost any price. First we feasted on the letters, of course. I forgot to count them, but there was a stack. Everyone had contributed: Mother, Dump, Nan, Elinor, Mother Jones, and all our friends. There were enough magazines and papers to last us several months.

The weather has been extremely cold. I have not poked my nose out of doors for weeks and weeks. Several nights, we have taken turns sitting up all night to keep the fires booming so that potatoes and apples and other things will not freeze. Most of my plants have frozen. I have two miserable little geraniums left and I am trying desperately to tide those over. It surprises us that these people don't seem to mind it. Very few of the children wear underwear, no mittens and no socks. Their mukluks are stuffed with dried grass and gunnysack. Some of them painstakingly rip up the gunnysacks and crochet a kind of half sock with the twine. It doesn't sound very warm to me, but they never seem to be conscious of their feet. And the little cotton garments they wear under their parkas barely cover their bodies. They do have warm parkas. In their igloos, they usually don't take those off, day or night.

The first day in school, they intended to sit with their parkas on, and when I insisted they remove them, the results were startling. One little girl stood revealed in part of a man's undershirt which covered her about as much as a bathing suit would. I had to send her home until I could make her a suit of underwear out of an old one of Foster's. I also made her bloomers and dresses. She has worn them steadily ever since, two months, without once being washed. An older girl, about eighteen, clutched wildly at her parka and shrilled, *"Pe-tie-tuk,"* which means "all gone" or nothing left. An older boy also clutched his parka with a wild *"pe-tie-tuk."* I suspect that in their cases there really was nothing underneath. Most of them merrily show part of their tummies or backs.

One afternoon I had a sewing class for the women and older girls. It was a cold, windy day, and the room, which was on the windy side of the building, was hard to heat. Twenty came, and with their parkas off and their scanty clothing, I was afraid they would be cold. However, it was not long before some of them began to wipe the perspiration from their faces. As I began to put more coal on the fire, I suddenly realized that the room was very warm. I think that the heat of their bodies warmed it more than the stove did. They have very little fire in their igloos, and yet they seem to always be warm. Foster says, "These women are so husky they could butt a bull off a bridge." I believe they could. They are Amazons, yet I doubt if there is a sack of flour in the whole village. They use no sugar, salt, milk, or vegetables. Their diet consists of a little tea, fish, seal meat, seal oil, and whale when they can get it.

On Christmas Day, the radio was coming in unusually strong, so we decided to give the villagers a concert. Foster has made an opening large enough for the radio between the living room and the schoolroom. About once a week, we invite them to listen to the radio, and they are fascinated by it. They have very carefully examined the ground wire and antenna outside, trying to find out the secret of the voices, I suppose. They sit in the schoolroom. We could not possibly have them all in here. When the bell rang Christmas Day, about sixty or more rushed in, and for two hours, with complete silence and hardly a movement, they listened, spellbound. We did not try to have any other celebration for them. There was no use. They have no English for "pieces," and we could get no tree or other decorations. We had brought about fifty pounds of hard candy for their Christmas, so on the Friday before, each one got a bag of candy. Some of them did not know what to do with it. The government had sent a good many bandana handkerchiefs among the supplies, so we put a handkerchief in each bag. Everyone knew at once what to do with that. It was promptly folded corner-wise and tied about the neck. Then each one learned to say "Merry Christmas!" They soon got the idea, and for a week they kept coming with gifts, baskets, pieces of ivory, old spear heads, rings, all offered with a "Merry Christmas!" Each one got a handful of candy in return and I suspect the candy had a lot to do with the continuance of the gifts. Finally, we had to refuse any further offerings. Besides, the candy gave out.

We thought when the plane came there would be signs of fear because most of them had never seen one, but that was not so. Everyone went out—men, women, and children. When the skis began to move, that was usual because they have sleds, and it looked just like a big sled. The engine did not matter. When the skis left the ice and slid off through the air, that was a huge joke. How they laughed!

Mail sled, Kipnuk, circa 1930s.

January 19

A fur trader who is passing through is spending the night with us and will be on his way toward Bethel in the morning, so I am getting my letters ready. It is bad weather to be traveling. The snow is swishing around the house now, and it is blinding. Yesterday one could not see twenty feet away, and last night I don't see how anyone could stand against it. The fur trader has a big compass on his sled, and he goes entirely by that. He did not travel yesterday; instead, he lay low in a cabin near here. He says the most important thing to carry on trips in these parts is a shovel to dig oneself out in the morning. The snow drifts so high sometimes that in a night one can be packed in an igloo so tight there is no possibility of getting out without a shovel.

Lots of love to all,

Tetts

January 25, 1933

Dear Everybody:

We heard over the radio today that Mr. Gus Martin, the missionary from Kwigillingok, left by dog team this morning for these parts. I think after this trip, he goes to Bethel, so I must have letters ready for him to take.

The Natives are having a potlatch and have invited the whole village of Chofoganik. There will be about 100, I guess. I don't know where they will put them all because they are packed in like sardines now. I think there may be some weddings. They want Mr. Martin for something. I hope they do want him to perform their marriages. Until now, their marriages have been by tribal rites. Every night there is a dance in the *kashim*, which is a community igloo. Only the women dance. I think they act out various episodes in their daily lives such as hunting and fishing. They have seal oil lamps hanging from the ceiling and a place on the dirt floor in the center for an open fire. There are no windows. Foster went one night and he said the air was so thick, it was like a wall pressing against one. I can't stand the odors, so I stay away. I wonder what Dump, who is so sensitive to odors, would do in our schoolroom. Faint, I imagine, because it gets pretty fragrant, even though we have good ventilation. I never cared for perfumes and such, but now I am sending for the smelliest kind and sachet and toilet water.

February 13, 1933
Dear Everybody:

We heard over the Bethel broadcast this noon that Pilot Brown of Fairbanks was headed down the coast and had mail for Kipnuk. Then *Zoom*! We heard an airplane motor, and there he was circling around. Soon he and a Mr. McDonald were in our house with a huge sack of mail. Twelve books were in that sack, besides the usual number of magazines and papers. There were also packages we have been expecting since last summer. All the things sent to Old Harbor, including Dump's books, have come. Wasn't I glad to see them!

We have only your latest letters. A few days ago we heard over the radio that the Bethel missionary had taken letters for the Joneses to a certain roadhouse, about halfway between here and Bethel. I suppose the pictures and bank statements are among those. They will be along in time. I am getting this ready in case they leave tomorrow.

No, the Christmas night radio greetings from the Joneses of Alaska did not come from us, though I would have liked to have sent a message had it been possible. Next year, we are fixing up a sending apparatus and then we will be in direct communication with Bethel.

Glad to hear you are all well. More next time.

Lots of love,
Tetts

February 21, 1933
Dear Everybody:

This morning a man arrived from Kwigillingok with a few letters for us. They were written before the ones we had by the plane last week, but these have come over the trail from Bethel and have therefore been on the way a long time. However, they are just as welcome.

Our "constituents," as Foster calls them, have settled themselves back to normal life after their big potlatch. In a few weeks they will all be gone for the summer. They go closer to the coast where they can get plenty of seals, and then they feast. Seal oil is like honey to them. It is much more odorous and nauseous than cod liver oil, and, therefore, more precious. We have about twenty gallons of cod liver oil, and some of the sickly ones get it regularly. The bottles are emptied so quickly by other members of the families that it is necessary to call a halt. Twenty gallons would soon be gobbled up. Castor oil is almost as popular. They come and ask for it. They have a name for it that means "oil like water." They also have a name that describes its effect. Sometimes they pantomime its effect. They lick their lips with pleasure after a dose.

Love,
Tetts

March 3, 1933
Dear Everybody:

Last week we had a chance to send our letters with a Native who was going to Kwigillingok. There is more travel from that village than from this one; therefore, there is a better chance of the mail getting to Bethel. We were fortunate because the very next day Pilot Brown stopped there with a Catholic priest. Our letters were taken off and must be on their way by this time. Now we have more visitors from Kwigillingok. Several Native church helpers for the Moravian mission came last night, have gone on to another village today, and will be back tomorrow. One of them goes beyond Bethel on his way home, so our letters will go with him. We have had more opportunities to send mail this winter than we expected, but this may be the last until after the river opens. I think no planes come this way during April because of the soft ice.

Foster has been having quite a time with a castor oil bottle this afternoon. About an hour ago, a man brought a bottle for *okoke*—their word for oil—for the baby. It was refused. "Baby has had too much castor oil. It's not good for him." Then a woman brought the same bottle for *okoke*. It was refused with a little lecture. Just now a man brought the same bottle. Foster has his mark on it. This man is from another family, and he is wise. He said it was for himself. He was offered pills, which he volubly refused, then a dose of salts. The conversation was funny. I sat in here snickering. The English side. "Now you take this. It will physic you good." Then the other side energetically, *"Okoke susutuk tsalit,"* and much more, then some more English about physic, and much more Eskimo. It was to no avail. He refused a physic. Then Foster thought he had better go down into the village to see who really wanted castor oil, and found it was the wife of another man not represented at all. She got pills, but she may not take them. I laugh many times a day at our funny experiences.

Time for "Amos 'n Andy" now. I may get a chance to add more later, if there is anymore to add. News is scarce. You might ask questions if there are things you want to know.

Love,

Tetts

Dear Dump:

Will you please send Mother flowers for Mother's Day for me? Make it enough for both of us and let me pay. You have done it every year.

Tetts

March 13, 1933
Dear Everybody:

Again I have an unexpected chance to send mail. A few days ago a fur trader came by, had dinner with us, and said he would be back this way again in a few days on his way to Bethel. Not only that, but he will come this way again after his Bethel

100

trip, and will bring our mail. That is surely good news. Also, a few days ago, we heard that someone going to Kwigillingok is bringing our mail from Bethel. I hoped that would be here in time to answer before the trader gets here, but, so far, there is no sign of it.

Our bean dinner tasted good. Foster was the cook, as he often is, and he uses what he calls a fifty-fifty recipe. That means half beans and half salt pork cut fine. Usually he makes it part pork and part bacon, but all the grease has to be there. Then two good onions are boiled with it, and just before it is taken from the fire, a good handful of chopped garlic is added. Maybe that does not sound good, but I cannot leave it alone. I don't eat pork or bacon, but I lap up the beans and garlic. Today he used lima beans, and I feel that I have had my allotted number of calories. Usually we eat only once a day. After such a meal you can understand why we feel satisfied with just one.

I am reminded that this is a month of birthdays in our family. I send my wishes for many more happy birthdays.

Love,
Tetts

March 15
Dear Dump:
Our mail has just come, and the trader not yet returned. He may be along today. There were letters from home but none from Yonkers. Is there a problem? Perhaps your letter has shared the fate of four Christmas cards we just received, two from Alaska. One was from Cassie Roy and one from Frank Lundin, all mailed in November, early, so we would be sure to get them by Christmas. Some of our mail has been as far as Nome, so yours may be floating around this land somewhere.

Frank Lundin is interested in a gold mining company in Ishpeming, Michigan. He is vice president and treasurer, and he is offering stock for sale. It may be a good thing. I hope for his sake it is.

I shall continue to look for your letter. It must be somewhere, even perhaps in Yonkers.

Lots of love,

Tetts

March 29, 1933

Dear Everybody:

Luck again. I think there will be another opportunity to send letters because our fur trader expects to make another trip. He may be here tomorrow, on his way to Nelson Island, and then back this way.

Saturday will be our tenth wedding anniversary. We want to celebrate, but how? I suggested making a cake, but Foster said he would rather have a pie. Dried apples are the only things we have to make a pie, so dried apple it will be. They are really good apples, and, when properly soaked, make a pie that is hard to tell from fresh. What the rest of the menu will be is hard to say, but I am quite certain that we shall not overeat.

April 2, Sunday

This is just about as bad a day as we have had this winter. It isn't cold, but it is so very, very windy and stormy. The air is so thick with flying snow that we cannot see the coal shed from the house, and that is only a few feet. This morning we heard over the radio from Mr. Martin at Kwigillingok that Mr. Hall, the Northern Commercial Company manager from Bethel, and Mr. Dull, his trader at Quillingok, left that place for Kipnuk, expecting to get here tonight. This morning the sun was shining, but the wind has been gradually getting worse. I don't see how they can possibly get here. They might pass within a few feet of the village and not know it, even if they get this far. We think they will hole up somewhere if there is the least opportunity. I wish they could get through. We would feel better about them if they spent the night here. Besides, they have our mail, and every day counts. I have a good supper prepared in case they do come. They will be pretty tired and hungry.

There haven't been any children playing around here today as there usually are. They get behind the building, out of the wind, and play with their story knives. Almost every girl has one. These knives are made of walrus ivory, about the size of butcher knives, usually twelve inches long and decorated with carvings. Males carved the knives and gave them to female relatives. The girls smooth off the snow with them and draw pictures in the snow, all the time telling a story. Usually one girl at a time talks and talks while illustrating with the pictures. A large circle of children will sit spellbound while one does the picturing, with intense interest on all the faces. Sometimes it ends with shouts of laughter. Then, another girl will tell her story, drawing as she talks. This goes on for hours. I would like to know what their stories are about. The pictures do not mean anything to me. Sometimes they look like conventional designs.

Story knife, owned by the author, similar to those used by the Yup'iks in the Kuskokwim Delta.

April 7, Friday

Mr. Hall and Mr. Dull did not get here Sunday night after all, but they came dragging in at about ten o'clock the next morning, wet to the skin, and very, very tired. They had slept out in the storm because there was nothing else to do. They brought our mail, which was not as much as we had expected, but we were thankful to get it. There is still more in Bethel waiting to be brought here, and we may get that before summer because Mr. Dull expects to go to Bethel and back as far as Kwigillingok. We can send over by dog team for it. He is also bringing us batteries for the radio. Ours are down, and will soon be gone altogether. We cannot think of being here without a radio.

Love to all,

Tetts

Easter Day
April 16, 1933
Dear Everybody:

This is an Easter greeting, although you may not get it until the Fourth of July. It is a very wintry-looking day, though not so very cold. There are heaps and heaps of snowdrifts around the house. It is even snowing some more, occasionally. We are getting tired of looking for spring.

This is another anniversary for us, so we had a special dinner: canned reindeer sausage, baked potatoes, corn on the cob, native salmonberry jelly sent to us by our neighbors, the Martins, fresh hot-cross buns without the currants and the cross, dried apple pie and cheese. We had that at about 11:00 A.M., our one meal of the day. At about four we have coffee, made and served by Foster. Every day we do that. To miss the coffee is like missing a meal. While we ate, we talked of that other Easter Day ten years ago, how warm and sunny it was. We had our noon meal that day with "Wingy Crane," a woodcutter who lived about fifteen miles from Tanana.

We are looking forward to more mail, glory be, perhaps tomorrow. Some of my letters were not even written, and yours were not finished. Now we cannot count on any more Bethel trips until after the boats run. This delayed spring gives us a chance, though. Someone may be going through.

I wonder how the Easter parades on the Boardwalk are faring this year. There will always be some to look on, if not to parade.

Love,
Tetts

Sunday, May 7, 1933
Dear Everybody:

Yesterday was a gala day for us because we received another load of mail. Spring has been so delayed that the crust on the snow is still firm and hard, and it makes a good trail. Mr. Martin and Mr. Dull at Kwigillingok took advantage of the weather to send another dog team to Bethel. They were kind enough to bring back new batteries for our radio and our mail. One of our villagers happened to be in Kwigillingok when they returned, so they loaded him with our things and sent him on here. After traveling all night, he arrived at six in the morning before we were up. It is light almost all night now and it is a good time for travel. All our people are at their seal camps, and he was on his way there. Foster invited him in and gave him breakfast, while I gobbled my letters in bed.

June 4, 1933

Just two days ago the ice on our little river, or slough, went out, and now we are looking for boats and hoping for a chance to send letters.

We heard over the radio that the government boat, *North Star*, gets to Bethel June 8th, and the *Tupper* on June 12th. Soon after that, we can expect a boat here bringing all our freight and mail. I hope Dump was able to get the books mailed in time to land with one of them.

I am going to send you each a few Eskimo curios. With Mother's, there will be something for Bea and for Mrs. Barnes. She sent me an anniversary present and a card. She never forgets.

Love,

Tetts

June 24, 1933

Dear Dump:

The camera came, and it is a dandy. I have not tried it yet because it has rained every day since it came, but I will try it out at the first opportunity. I wonder how they can sell them at that price. With things going up, I think we must have bought it at the very best time. The books and Mother's picture were not with the other things, but I am hoping they will come with the *Moravian*, which we are expecting any day. Evidently they did not make the *Tupper* in Seattle, and I wonder how that is since the camera did.

The mail boat Moravian, *which traveled between
Bethel and Kipnuk on Kuskokwim Bay, Alaska, circa 1930s.*

Thanks for all the maneuvering with the bank account, etc.
I knew things were rather ticklish, but did not realize they were
quite so bad. I do hope your salary knot gets straightened out.
Thank you for the snapshots. I thought I sent you several rolls
from Bethel last summer, but perhaps I sent them to Anchorage.
I am rather hazy as to what I did exactly in that hectic time.
Anyway, I have seen nothing of them, so they are probably lost.
The stamps came okay, and thanks a lot for them.

I'll enclose a few more films for printing. One is of Luke,
one of the outstanding figures in our school, and in the other is
Molly, the gypsy-like beauty, and Lillian, one of our brightest
and sweetest. There is also a picture of our building. The door
shown leads into our living room. The schoolroom is on the
right, or left, as you see it in the picture.

I was so glad to get all your letters, and they sounded
natural, too. I could not understand why I had not heard from
you because in Mother's letters, she always said you looked and
felt well. [Etta is not aware that Marie has been diagnosed with
breast cancer.] Anyhow, I hope you can find time to write more
often. Please send Mother and Nan prints of the pictures, too.

Love,

Tetts

August 23, 1933

Dear Everybody:

Just a few lines to go with the individual letters. Everybody speaks of the heat, and it was worth speaking about, I know, but we had none of it here, although Nan was kind enough to want to send us some. Today it is forty-eight, and that is the usual temperature except for a few occasions. However, we have enjoyed the summer. There has been plenty to keep us occupied and interested. Every decent day I have tried to take a walk. That meant putting on rubber boots, heavy ones, and most of the time pants and a sweater. Skirts make the walking harder and it was hard enough as it was. Walking over the tundra is like walking over a deep feather bed. One sinks down, down, down with every step in the soft moss. Water is usually at the bottom. Lifting heavy boots out of deep places with every step does not make for easy walking. Usually after half a mile or so, I was puffing like a porpoise. Sometimes there were dry hummocks where one could sit down and rest, and on fine days we did that. When I got back to the house, I felt that I had done my daily dozen. I knew it did me good to get out, and a little strenuous exercise would not hurt me. The cat went with us whenever he got the chance. The formation was Foster in front with his gun, the cat right behind him with his tail in the air like a banner, and I brought up the rear. I took some pictures of what was in front of me on one occasion. Foster does not know yet that I snapped him from behind. They are good, and I will send you some.

The May issue of *National Geographic* has an article on New Jersey, as I suppose you know. I read every word and studied all the pictures and maps until it made me rather homesick. The July issue has an article and pictures of Southeast Alaska and I am thrilled and proud of Alaska.

We are hearing about bad storms along the Atlantic Coast. Conditions have not been good for our radio reception lately, because of so many electrical disturbances, I suppose, and we got only snatches of the details. When Atlantic City was mentioned, I naturally pricked up my ears. That and Cape May are pretty close to home. I hope everything is all right in Pleasantville [New Jersey].

We are getting splendid lettuce and parsley from our "garden." The sweet alyssum and mignonette are spreading all over, and there are lots of blossoms.

Now I have dishes to do. That happens only every other day, once, and they must be done.

Lots of love,

Tetts

Christmas 1933

Dear Everybody:

This is a beautiful Christmas Day, but cold. I think it's about ten below. There has been a stiff wind, but that seems to have died down. The sunshine is very bright. It dazzles the eyes to look out over the tundra. The hard-packed snow sparkles like millions of diamonds. We are very cozy and peaceful by the fire, surrounded by stacks of magazines and books. All the books Dump has sent must be here. There are seven, one of which is from Mrs. Adams. The package forwarded from Chitina is here. How good they all look to us. It is rather bewildering with so much reading all at once. Foster is already deep into *British Agent*.

Our friend Pilot Brown came just in time. We have had so much extremely cold, stormy weather that we began to despair that he might not be able to get here. Mr. Martin at Kwigillingok said he thought he would have to go to Bethel himself with his buzz wagon if Pilot Brown did not show up soon. Then one morning last week, we heard over the shortwave set from Bethel that Pilot Brown was there, ready to start for Kwigillingok and several other Bering Sea towns. Foster got an Eskimo with a big dog team to start early the next morning for Quillingok. Kipnuk was not included on the itinerary, but Kipnuk mail was part of his load. In the morning, Mr. Martin told us over the radio to send a big team because there was an enormous sack of mail for us, weighing seventy-five pounds or more, but the big team was

108

already on its way. The next morning, Friday, he told us that the big load had started on its return trip a little before eight o'clock. It was hard traveling for the dogs, and we made up our minds not to begin to look for them before six, maybe later. It would not have surprised us if he had taken two days for the trip.

Around noon I was looking out over the white ocean of snow and saw two teams several miles in the distance, but coming from the direction of Quillingok. There were also two other teams coming from another direction, but they did not interest us. Even the ones from Quillingok did not excite us because we did not think they could be the important ones. When they got right outside the window, we recognized our messenger. There was some excitement! We forgot about the second team, which was some distance behind. With all these enticing things tumbling out of the sack, including letters with longed-for news such as Dump and her improvement, we found we had visitors. The son of the Quillingok trader and an Eskimo from Nelson Island had come forty miles that cold day and were on their way to Nelson Island, so we had to stop and get a meal for them. They did not stay long, however. Instead, they went on to a place six miles beyond here. Then we were free to proceed to our letters and packages. Of course, you know how happy we were to know that Dump was better. Yes, Nan, the jewelry came, all in good condition except two strings of beads. The strings had broken, but the beads were all there. Such a gorgeous lot!

While I was unpacking them, the man who had brought them from Quillingok came in. He had been well paid for his trip, but I gave him a string of beads for his wife. He saw more of the rest than he was supposed to see and about ten minutes after he went home, the news was out. The first to arrive was a tiny girl with a basket-like object woven in the shape of a saucer. She said she had done it herself, and it was a "Merry Christmas." I gave her a "Merry Christmas" in the shape of a necklace. That afternoon, we had had a sort of Christmas celebration, singing of songs followed by a radio concert, and all the school children, fifty of them, and some in the village, cripples and sick, had received bags of candy, nuts, and cookies. There they heard again the "Merry Christmas" they learned so readily last year. The tiny girl was immediately followed by her sister, who offered as her "Merry Christmas" an ivory crochet hook and a pair of earrings. She received a pair of earrings in return. By that time it was pitch dark, but we knew they would continue to come, so the next to arrive was told to come tomorrow. She was wise enough to ask for Mrs. Jones. Foster gets up at six in the morning. It is very dark at that time but not a bit too early for our "constituents." They had to wait, though, until I got up. There was a steady stream all day. "Merry Christmas" with carved ivory, story knives, arrowheads, buttons, pipe bowls, baskets, all sorts of things. Some of them tried it two or three times. Old women sent notes with little boys: "Please give me Merry Christmas, tea, me, Minnie." The note wasn't spelled that way, but we knew what was meant. Here are two notes verbatim. "HaIIov Mr. Junes brris kiff my Boking Sood Christmas Ms Nellie Slim Doday." Nellie wanted baking powder for Christmas. "Allu Ms. J Blease gave me Lewis Tea Christmas." They all can spell Christmas. It would never do to have that magic word misunderstood. This morning they started in again, but we had to tell them *"Pischeegatok"* (impossible).

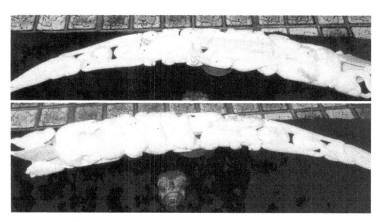

Two views of carved ivory cribbage board and stone mask, Kipnuk, circa 1930s.
COURTESY OF JEAN KLINE, DOUGLAS, ALASKA.

Christmas was over as far as gifts were concerned, so today has been comparatively quiet. For dinner, we had canned whole chicken, corn on the cob, native berry jelly from Mrs. Martin, and ice cream with chopped nuts and red cherry preserves, which was a cherry sundae, I suppose. It was good, and the chicken was good, too. It browned in the oven very nicely.

Lately, we have had good radio reception. We heard about the cold snaps in the East and West, and hope you have not suffered. I have thought a great deal about all of you today, wondering about your Christmas. It will be an unusually happy one for all if only Dump is herself again.

Mr. Martin told us over the shortwave that he expects to be in Kipnuk sometime this week immediately after Christmas. He will come in his auto-sled. He has overhauled it, made some improvements, and expects to use it more this winter. We shall have mail ready for him, because he will go to Bethel later.

With lots of love to all,

Tetts

Gus Martin's auto-sled, circa 1930s.

8

Kipnuk School

1932-1934

When Etta and Foster taught in Tanana, Kaltag, Tatitlek, and Old Harbor, the Native schools had been operating for several years. Prior to their arrival in Kipnuk, however, no school had ever been built and no formal educational program existed. Etta and Foster were the first white teachers to establish an instructional program. Although the school was meant for the children, adults also attended, and Etta and Foster created a curriculum that addressed the needs of the Natives. To them, it seemed the most logical approach to effective teaching.

When the school building was in the process of construction, some of the men, being skillful with hammer and saw, were employed as carpenters' assistants. Vassily, however, one of the "city fathers" and eager to work, was considered too slow to work with the others. He was given the job of painting the windows. He did this under a separate canvas by himself. On rainy days, he did not work, but each day he did work, he reported to the builder when he started and when he stopped, his time being put down in the time book with the others. He was paid by the hour. When payday came at the end of the month and his time was figured, deductions were made for rainy and partly rainy days, and he was very angry with the result. He said through the interpreter that it was not correct. To prove his statement, he produced his own system of bookkeeping, which was a paper covered with moons, half moons, quarter moons, and hieroglyphics significant only to him. Quite a problem in higher mathematics he had to figure out, a flat rate per hour, days of differing length, and he got a result that differed from the white man's. Another careful checkup on the white man's part showed him his error. The unschooled Eskimo was right, and corrections were made. Where did he learn computation? They surprised us with many abilities we took for granted they could not possibly possess.

As for the safety of our belongings, there was no danger of theft. No more honest people exist than these people. With scrap building material lying all around the new house, no one took home the tiniest piece without first asking permission. The temptation must have been great because driftwood was the only wood they had, and they had to go great distances to procure it.

Those first days of school were rather trying, and looking back I wonder now how we managed. Adults were encouraged to come as well as children. At that time, we still had the interpreter with us. There were sixty-four students when school opened and no one had ever attended school before. Not one spoke one word of English, and my Eskimo vocabulary was limited to perhaps three words.

A fair amount of sewing materials, some yarn and knitting needles, and some carpentry tools had been sent with the school supplies. We put them to work with these as much as possible, the boys making food boxes, the girls clothing. The very young ones were put at a play table, and gradually we built up a vocabulary. With these names of familiar things, we made our own textbooks, broadening it as time went on, with customs and happenings of village life. They were amazingly quick at understanding, showing great pride and delight when they were able to read about themselves. Their bubbling good humor was constantly in evidence. They had no inhibitions, and how they did enjoy each other's mistakes and discomfiture. They would double over with noisy laughter, even rolling on the floor in their glee. It was impossible not to enjoy their fun with them.

With sixty-four enrolled and thirty-three seats, it was necessary to divide them. The younger ones came in the morning, the older ones in the afternoon. Most of them had unpronounceable names or no names at all. I believe it was the custom to name only the firstborn. We had great fun naming them, and they were proud of their English names. When a new pupil came, they all gathered around and listened breathlessly for his English name, then they all repeated it over and over, laughing and rejoicing with him.

I got into the schoolroom about nine. It was not hard there. I really enjoyed it. The children were so happy, so intelligent, and so good. Most of them were already in the room when I got there, and they all shouted, "Good morning, Mrs. Jones!" and kept on with their greetings until each one had been answered individually. They knew about twenty-five kindergarten and primary songs and they loved to sing them. The words were not always terribly distinct, but it sufficed.

Then I noted the absentees and we proceeded something like this: "Where is Nunak?" Answer, "Iuktut" (gone). "Where?" "Pemukbuk." "What for?" Answer, jabbering from which I gathered he had gone for wood. "Where is Annie?" Answer, "Tchmai" (home). "Why doesn't she come to school?" Answer, more jabbering until a brave one ventured an English word, "Eat." Then there might be more jabbering and delighted motions toward the hall, by which I understood that Annie had arrived, and soon she appeared. "Where is Adam?" Answer, "No bell" (he had not heard the bell). Sometimes the answer was, "Nom-e-keeko" (I don't know). Then we went over the questions again, and they were drilled, answering in English.

Questions and answers were written on the board and served as a reading lesson. They were copied as a writing lesson, and later parts of them were given as a dictated spelling lesson. They understood almost everything I said (I found myself using all kinds of gestures with my talk), and I understood many things they said. Everything was used for conversation and reading and writing English, because, after all, that was what we were supposed to teach them. We talked and wrote about a new dress, a new pupil, a sunny day, a cold or windy day, everything. They walked about the room, chattered to each other softly, played at the table, wrote on the board, and were altogether natural, but never obnoxious. They subsided at once when told, and they did have to be told sometimes. Twenty-five white children moving about a room make plenty of noise, scuffling shoes, but these, in their soft mukluks, made no noise as they walked. They never quarreled and their soft chatter was only about their work. They had colored blocks, colored sticks, wooden beads, etc., to play with after their work was done, and it was interesting to watch the use they made of them. A white child would build houses. These children were altogether absorbed making beautiful designs, using various color combinations.

Sometimes a little seven-year-old crippled girl came. She was feeble-minded and could not use her right hand and arm. She should not have been in school, but I didn't feel like refusing her when she felt like coming. At first, I just gave her playthings, but the others wanted her to have pencil and paper like the rest, so I gave them to her. All the little girls and boys took turns doing her writing for her. Sometimes her paper was filled with six or eight different samples of handwriting. They were delighted when I marked it perfect, and they gave the little girl all the credit.

They were wonderfully deft with their hands, and they learned to write beautifully in no time. They were very good in weaving and paper cutting. After Mr. Martin's last visit on his motor sled, I gave them black paper and scissors and told them to cut his sled. In a jiffy, every one of them had a good paper model, some of them perfect to the last detail, even the crank handle on his engine.

They were whizzes in numbers. In the beginning, they could not only not read a figure but had no concept of numbers beyond their ten fingers and toes. In ten months, half of it half-day sessions, they learned to do long division rapidly and accurately. I don't know what good it will do them, and we didn't emphasize that work, but they simply ate it up. There was no use holding them to "two and two" when they leaped ahead by themselves. Foster had about twenty in his room, not all of them advanced, some of them beginners, but too big to fit into the small seats in my room. I had twenty-five, all small and all regular. Even the youngest pupils knew all the combinations of addition and subtraction to twenty. Some of the slightly older ones mastered multiplication and short division, even though some of them had no more than five months of school and had to guess what the teacher was talking about most of the time.

Life was a merry one in our school. One day there was a disturbance about Lena, and a little drama was enacted. Lena was about eight and was one of the really clean ones. Her parents were about the most intelligent, clean, and thrifty. She wore underwear, clean dresses, and a neat little sweater. She was a serious, matter-of-fact little thing, with neatly parted hair braided in two pigtails. In front of her sat Luke, who came from about the dirtiest home. He was about twelve. We had to guess at all the ages. He had a round, fat face with dimples, and his eyes crinkled into mere slits when he laughed, which was most of the time. His dirty rags barely covered him and his torn boots shed the dried grass stuffing, but, to Luke, life was merry. However, this particular morning, he was frowning and indignant, because Lena was evidently blaming him for the two large "gray backs"—bugs—which she deftly pushed around on her desk with the point of her pencil. She scolded until her precise pigtails shook, and Luke steadily denied fault. The children were laughing in glee, enjoying it immensely. Lena kept the "gray backs" corralled with her pencil all the time. Finally, in a business-like manner, she killed them with her thumbnail and swept them from her desk. School life again resumed the even tenor of its way.

The students found many things to laugh at, but I think the funniest happened during a reading lesson. Everything had to be demonstrated because they did not know the meaning of any words. I showed them the picture of a bird, told them it was a bird and he could sing. The next day when I asked the name, it was a sing and he could bird. Eventually, they got it.

In their primers, when they had words like "walk," "run," "hop," "jump," they did all those things to show they understood the meaning. That was great fun. We came to the word "fly." It was Molly's turn, and Molly could fly about like a cow. She was about fifteen, overweight, and slow in movement. She dragged her feet when she walked, was very deliberate in getting out of her seat, and moved her hand slowly when she wrote. She looked like a Gypsy because she had dark, slanted eyes, thick, silky black hair, and red cheeks. She wore about ten strings of heavy beads around her neck, long dangling earrings and several rings and bracelets. Though Molly's body was slow, her mind was very nimble. She easily kept ahead of everybody, and she understood instantly what "fly" meant. She illustrated while the others almost had hysterics. They doubled up and held their sides, they shouted until the

116

tears came. Molly joined in because she could see the funny side, too. The sight of Molly flying about that room was too much for my gravity. The next time we came to "fly," it was Palookta's turn. Palookta was a twin, about fourteen, and was much bigger than his twin. He was clean and neatly dressed, but he was at the gangly age, and his clothes were too small for him. He came to school irregularly because he was a hustler. Sometimes we saw Palookta before daybreak going off with a gun to hunt, or with dogs going for wood, or going fishing. Besides, he was quite deaf. I doubt if he got the word "fly," but he got the meaning, and he was willing to be the goat for the amusement of the school. His demonstration was terribly funny to all of them, himself included. He good-naturedly joined in the laughter. The next to "fly" was Paul. He was small, light on his feet, and quick. He flew so gracefully around the room that it was not funny at all to anyone.

The little ones learned how to read with less difficulty than the older ones because the pronunciation came easier to them. They all had difficulty in pronouncing "r." They said it like "l," so that Robert became Lobbet. It was funny to hear them sing the song "Merrily we roll along, roll along." Try it, substituting "l" for "r." They whooped it up.

A two-hour session was enough, and at eleven o'clock, I was back in the house, preparing myself a light lunch, usually tomato soup, crackers, and tea. Foster got whatever he fancied, sometimes ham and eggs, sometimes reindeer steak, sometimes fish. He liked to cook.

At noon we began again so as to utilize the maximum hours of daylight, especially in the winter when it was dark at 3:00 P.M. Foster had the higher branches of learning. We called his room the "Academy." His English classes were really funny, but they did wonderfully well, considering everything. They never heard an English word outside of school.

When compared with white standards, they were still dirty, but much, much better than they were at first. The crawling things could no longer be seen on their persons, except occasionally. It became a disgrace to have insect powder used on one, and little girls cried from shame when it had to be done. Some ears and necks were still dirty, but faces were clean. If one happened to be conspicuously dirty, the others told him about it and he rushed out to the steps, washed in the snow and returned, beaming. There was still a thick odor in the room, but one got used to that.

With the iron roof, rain gutters, and spouts on the coal shed, Foster had arranged a rain-catching system. One day when it was above freezing, the snow was melting and running down those spouts. We were amused when we saw a boy take advantage of a chance for a shower bath. It was cold and blowing, but off came the parka and cap, and his head went under the spout for a thorough soaking and rubbing, neck and arms too. I expected to see him take off the rest of his clothes, but he let it go at that, sauntering off happily in the cold wind with his wet head.

9

Letters from Kipnuk

1934-1937

January 30, 1934
The President's Birthday
Dear Everybody:

   The cold weather has not interfered with the potlatches, feasting, and dancing. A village between here and Nelson Island is entertaining the people of Quillingok, and a village between here and Quillingok is entertaining the people of Kipnuk. Our village entertained last winter. The Quillingok men took all the dogs for their trip, and that left the women and children in the village without any wood. They were burning up storm sheds and caches. Meanwhile, the men got this far on their way and were held here almost a week by the weather. This village had to feed them and their dogs when they could barely feed themselves. It is a wonder some of the travelers did not freeze on the way. Some of them could not get here before dark and had to sleep out in the blizzard and intense cold. There is absolutely no protection from the wind on this tundra, and they are poorly equipped without blankets and sleeping bags. Some dogs were lost, but the men all got here, though all were frostbitten on hands and face. One man had a terribly frozen cheek. His parka must have frozen to his face, and when he removed his parka, part of the flesh came off, too. Foster tried to persuade him to stay here or go back home, but he grinned and went on with the party. They are tough. Our men have not yet started on their party, and we are glad to see them getting in plenty of wood before they do start.

We heard the president's speech on his birthday very plainly. There was absolutely no static. We enjoyed all the rest of the program, too. One evening, I was amazed to hear a half-hour program from our local station at Anchorage dedicated to Mrs. Foster Jones of Kipnuk, because of a lovely letter she had written, and part of the letter was read to prove it. It will make me careful of how I write letters.

February 3
Dear Dump:

No news should be good news. It has been a long time since the last word about you and your hard luck. I have been wishing a speedy recovery and the very best of health for you.

Lots of love,

Tetts

March 11, 1934
Dear Dump:

It looks and feels like spring here, at least it feels hopeful. There is still plenty of snow, but there is also a warm south wind, what they call a "chinook" wind. I hope it does mean an early spring. Our villagers must think so. They are already getting ready to move to their spring seal camps. By the first of April there may be no one left here. This is a nice short school year, October to April. I don't see how the city teachers stand it going into May and June.

I am sending Nan some more film for prints. She will send some to you. There are groups of the school children taken in the fall. The boys have their shaven and shorn heads. We thought we would compare some of our 170-pound first graders with "teacher," but for some reason they all look small. There are groups of little girls playing with their story knives, and there is one of a very snippy and sour me. Also, there is a picture of what seems to be nothing but tiny white dots, hundreds of them. They are snow geese asleep on the bar across the river. They are out of reach of the gun and always keep a weather eye open for danger. The minute Foster ventured too near the edge of our bank with his gun, they rose in clouds and drifted away.

Foster and I are practicing Morse code. We have a tiny transmitter that doesn't work yet, but it will in time. Anyway, it works better with a key than a mike. He is getting ready to apply for an amateur license.

Mother said she hoped you would be home for Easter. I hope you are. My, oh, my! Easter on the Boardwalk! Wouldn't I love it! But from all accounts, it is not what it used to be. I will think of you all there, anyway.

> Lots of love,
> Tetts

Sunday, March 18, 1934

Dear Everybody:

We have just been reminiscing about our coming wedding anniversary. It comes on Easter Sunday again, the first time since the wedding day. Today is just such a day as that was, brilliant, quiet sunshine, but perhaps a little colder. It doesn't seem possible that it was eleven years ago. We wonder how we can celebrate. There doesn't seem to be any way but just by being thankful. It is too blindingly bright today to look out of the window without snow glasses. I have been thinking about the little cubbyholes all over the world where very little, if any, sunshine ever penetrates, and I think I prefer too much to too little.

Yesterday was very, very windy and warm. It was impossible to see more than a few feet because of the drifting snow. We hardly expected anyone from Quillingok, but about five o'clock, the trader's son and his dog team suddenly emerged from the flying snow just beyond our window. He travels by compass, but even so, got off his course a little. We cooked supper for him and made up a bed so he could stay all night.

Mr. Martin had said there would be mail for us, and the trader's son brought it. We are so glad to hear that Dump is still improving. Of course, the cold weather has been hard on all of you.

Mother wants to know what we do with our time. Well, there is plenty of time for everything but it passes quickly. The days slip by smoothly. Foster gets up early, between five and six, gets his own breakfast, which is usually coffee. I get up between seven and eight, sweep up a little, make the bed, and go into the schoolroom.

School is over about 2:00 P.M. By that time in the winter, the radio is coming in fine and we sit down and listen. There is a steady procession of programs we like from New York, Chicago, Denver, Salt Lake City, San Francisco, Seattle, Mexico, Hawaii, and last, our own station at Anchorage. There we hear all the local news, often about people we know, and that gives us something to talk about the next morning. We listen to the radio and the shortwave conversations with Quillingok. We can hear Bethel, too, but so far have not talked directly with them. The shortwave neighborly visits come between 7:30 and 8:30 every morning. Now that the long days are here, the outside radio does not come in until 4:00 P.M. and later.

After school I get sewing done and more reading. Every other Saturday, I wash and hang the laundry up to dry in the living room. Soon now I'll be able to hang it outdoors. On Sunday morning I do the ironing.

I do very little cooking, thank goodness. Foster never eats cake or pudding, and seems to be losing his taste for pie. We have oodles of canned fruit and that serves as dessert.

Once in a great while I can get out for a walk, but usually it is too cold, too windy, or too wet.

Foster is a perfect companion—never sick, never worried, never irritated. He is always sane and even-tempered and wholesome. When things do not turn out as he expected, his usual comment is, "Well, I suppose it is really better this way." He has an unusually successful manner of dealing with the Natives. They accord him respect, accepting his leadership without question. He has been asked to settle disputes, and both sides abided by his decision. A visiting scientist remarked that when Foster accompanied him in his visits among the Natives, all eyes turned to Foster with smiles of welcome, and whatever he recommended was done.

The people are getting their kayaks and sleds ready for the spring move. They won't actually get under way until the weather gets warmer. They are like the birds and the animals in that the seasons give them the impulse to move. In two or three weeks however, we expect to be alone.

Dear Dump:

By this time your cold spells are over and I know how relieved you must be. I do hope you can go to Mother's for Easter. Perhaps you have daffodils in bloom and lily-of-the-valley and lilacs getting ready. Our California broadcasters urge us to drive through there and see their millions of fruit trees in bloom. Wish we could.

I still can see you in robust health again very soon. Wouldn't you like to try your hand with the little Eskimos? You would love them—except for the smell.

Lots of love,
Tetts

Etta's mother, a victim of diabetes, required surgery, so that summer, Etta went to New Jersey for five months to care for her. Foster remained in Alaska. She returned to Kipnuk on October 20, 1934.

December 13, 1934
Dear Helen [Marie's stepdaughter]:

This is your copy of the family letter, and here's a special Hello and How are you and Good-bye and more personal things next time for you.

I have been home from the States about two months and haven't had any mail yet. One of our "constituents," as Foster

calls them, is contemplating a trip to Bethel in a few days, and
I am looking forward to what he will bring back. Of course,
I know everything is all right with "you-all," but it will be
so good to have a letter or two or three. I wrote you a couple
of weeks ago when an Eskimo from a neighboring village,
euphoniously called "Cheechingamute," stopped in to say he
was making a trip to Bethel in a day or two. That was fully two
weeks ago and we heard yesterday that he had not gone yet. I
hope the letters we gave him won't be too highly scented with
seal oil and other delightful odors. I wonder where he has kept
them all this time. He isn't to be blamed for not going, however,
because Alaska has been in the grip of the strangest December
in its known history. Warm rains, thunderstorms, "chinook"
winds, melting ice in rivers and lakes, all causing snow to vanish
from the land and from the Arctic Ocean to the southernmost
shore of the territory. All the coasts, river valleys, everywhere, it
was too warm. Airplanes could not use skis, dog teams could not
travel, vessels could not discharge cargoes because of storms on
the coast, and our Eskimo friend could not travel to Bethel.

Well, about ten days until Christmas! How many shopping
days? None for us, and our few Christmas preparations were
finished very quickly. The sight of an evergreen tree or a sprig of
holly would help wonderfully to capture the Christmas spirit. I
have decided to have a plum pudding, anyway. To be sure, I have
no suet, which does seem rather a poser, but I will use butter,
and steam the stuff in tins. I never would dare to attempt a
pudding cloth. Suet is the only ingredient we lack, so why not be
festive and have plum pudding? We are to have both foamy sauce
and hard sauce. This has already been decided. The fowl will be
canned chicken.

Our villagers have already been asking about Christmas.
They know it means gifts. All the school children know the
exact date, and that is something when one considers that time
means nothing to them. They have no months or weeks or hours
or minutes. The sun regulates their days and their seasons, too.
When the snow and ice begin to melt in the spring, it means

move to another locality where they can get seal and walrus. When the sea and lakes begin to freeze, it means come back here where there are needlefish to eat, and mink and fox to trap. We have about fifty pounds of candy to distribute for a Christmas treat, and that will be the extent of our Christmas celebration—with a few songs. They cannot command enough English yet to "speak pieces" or perform plays. Even if they did, no one in the village could understand them, so what is the use?

Lots of love to all,

Aunt Tetts

June 20, 1935

Dear Family:

It was one week ago today at 3:30 A.M. that Foster left for Bethel. Oscar [a Native] came at about three and banged on the door. The tide was right. All boating here is done by the tide. You go out with the tide and come in with the tide. There are many sandbars along this coast, and to escape the rough seas out in deep water, they usually sail between these bars and the mainland. At low tide there is not enough water to float a boat, so they drop anchor and wait for the tide. Time is no object here. Men do not count how many days it takes to go to a certain place; rather, how many tides. So figuring tides and stops, I set today as the earliest he could be back. I promised to listen at 5:30 every day over the shortwave radio. He could let me know when he arrived and left Bethel. The radio has not been good, and I have heard nothing. I really have not looked for him until today. Can you imagine how it feels to be all alone in a village, with the nearest Eskimos about fifteen or twenty miles away, and the whites about sixty miles and no way to get there if I wanted to? I can't even walk because of the marsh, lakes, rivers and sloughs. I had made up my mind it could only be as bad as I made it. I took up *Kristen Lavransdatter*, a book I have wanted to read for two years, but have lacked the courage to start so ponderous a volume. I have been fascinated, enthralled, hardly able to lay the book down. For hours and hours I read, forgetting all about my surroundings while I lived in the stirring times of the Vikings. I came to myself occasionally to find the fire was out, or it was bedtime. Sometimes I was brought back suddenly by a knock on the door, and there would be an Eskimo or two or three, who had come silently in their kayaks to "*kapoosak*," or trade. They wanted a goose, a few geese eggs or duck eggs, tea, soap, crackers, coffee, spear heads, even "smoke" (tobacco), anything they could get.

Etta Jones in front of her house and garden, circa 1930s.

I wish Foster were home. At first I fixed my thought on the mail he would bring, the letters and magazines, the news of our friends and business that concern us, of the fresh fruits we have longed for, especially lemons, but now I don't care about any of those things except letters and him. If only he would bring himself home. I'm beginning to understand some of what he went through last summer, five months of it, and only lately have I known of what he suffered with his arm when he fell into the hold of a boat. The shoulder muscle was torn from its place on his right arm, and he had no one to do things for him. He has never uttered a word of complaint, but little by little I have wormed out of him small details and have completed the picture for myself.

July 1
Kwigillingok

Foster came home just a week after I wrote this much of my letter. It isn't necessary to say how glad I was to see him. I grew sick of watching the water for signs of him, and when he did come I was fast asleep and did not see him coming at all. I was awakened at six in the morning by a familiar voice in the living room shouting greetings. He had been delayed by telegrams, sending and waiting for answers. He brought the news that he was to help with the new school building at Kwigillingok. He told the powers that be that it would cost at least $200 for a boat to bring us and our things down here, but they wired back authorized money, so we packed up some belongings, food, the cat, stowed ourselves in a Columbia River sailboat, and sailed merrily away.

We had an Eskimo for a pilot. They are marvelous sailors, and know this coast as well as we know the streets in our hometown. There was an engine in the boat, but it did not want to work. The weather was fine, just enough wind to go along smoothly, and as we had all the time in the world, why should we worry? The first night we pulled into a little slough to wait for the tide. At about four the next morning, we went out with the tide, and enjoyed a long, beautiful day of sailing. We stopped once at their seal camp, called Pozeckbuk, where we changed pilots, took on some fresh white fish, and sailed on. We got here at about 7:00 P.M. Our pilot was not sure we would get in that night, but that did not worry us.

We stayed that night with the teacher, Ralph Magee. His wife is away just now, but will be back soon. The next day we cleaned out the old schoolhouse, moved in a cook stove, a bed, some dishes, and here we are as snug as can be, right at home, including the cat. I will tell you about the Magees later. They are very interesting people. She has taught in Mexico and China, as well as in our own West. He was in the Marines and has seen service in all parts of the world. This place brings back memories of the Martins to us because this is where they were. They went out to the States, tried the West, and the East, and are now back in Anchorage. Their baby was born there a short time ago. I think he has opened some kind of shop. He is so efficient and resourceful that he could make almost any kind of shop hum. [Bess and Gus Martin were the Moravian missionaries, staying at Kwigillingok where Foster was introduced to the

transmitter radio. Ralph Magee and his wife, Ruby, like Etta and
Foster, were employed by the Alaska Indian Service, and the two
couples became good friends.]

I have a lot of official mail to get ready, so I will write again
a little later. Several boats will be going to Bethel from here. We
think we will be here possibly a month, but when the mission
boat comes with our freight for Kipnuk, they will stop for us and
we will go back regardless of this school building. I do hope it
will not come too soon because this is a nice change.

> Much love to you and the family,
> Tetts

In 1935, Etta and Foster requested a transfer from Kipnuk to
Quinhagak, seventy-five miles southeast of Kipnuk on Kuskokwim
Bay. Their request was denied.

Kipnuk
August 23, 1935
Dear Dump:

A few days ago, I sent a family letter in such a hurry
that there was no time to add a personal note. Yesterday the
messenger came back from Kwigillingok with a large gunnysack
full of mail. There were at least thirty-eight letters. Almost
everyone we know had a letter in that batch. We were terribly
excited. There were three long, newsy ones from you, and I want
you to know how much I appreciate those letters because I know
how much of a task it is for you to write, feeling as exhausted
and nervous as you have felt, and with the terrific summer heat,
too. I hope both you and Frank get well rested and built up. Only
one of you needs the building up, I take it. Yes, I wish you could
both come here. You know, just being in Alaska fattens most
people. Poor Mrs. Martin has found that out. You remember Mrs.
Matthews, too. She weighed something like 110 when she came,
and in a few years it was 210, and then 220 and more. So after
Frank put on twenty or thirty pounds on the way up here, he
could feast on walrus and seal and fish until his pores oozed oil,

just like the Eskimos. Also, at this time of year, there would be plenty of ducks and geese. I am tired of them, but Foster never seems to get tired of them.

Mother's picture came and I love it. It is a marvelous picture. I could not talk about it for a long time after I opened it because I was all choked up. I never tire of looking at it. There was also a picture of Elinor that was very sweet. She has done wonderfully well, hasn't she? Nan is so proud of her, and she has cause to be proud. She is a great comfort to Nan and I am so glad. While on the subject of pictures, there was also one of Naomi and her husband. She has also done well, and I am proud of her. I hope you have time and energy enough to take a few snaps yourself while you are resting.

I suppose Mother's pension was cut like all the others. I am going to ask her to accept $40 instead of $30 to make up for that. I have been thinking of giving her her winter's coal supply for Christmas. Is it about eight tons that she burns? Whatever it is, will you arrange to have it delivered as she wants it? I don't suppose she has room in the cellar for it all at once.

If you must send me something, I might suggest a fountain pen. I have been thinking for some time of getting one. Mine is about worn out. Just an ordinary one will do.

You must be like the absent-minded professor, sending books to Chitina. I think they will be here before winter closes in. Two packages of books came from you and two from Mrs. Adams, so I have lots to read at the present time. When the other two packages arrive, I will feel well fortified. Books have meant so much to me here, and I have been happy to have so much leisure to read them. Here are some for future sending if you have not already included them: Van Loon's *Geography* (I love his History of Mankind), *The Good Earth* (I already have *Sons*), *As the Earth Turns*, *Ann Vickers*, *The House of Exile*. Nan says Elinor will teach this year, so she will not need the money I was going to send her. (Nan did not say that about the money.) However, I wish you would send Nan $25 for Christmas for me, and $10 for Elinor. I wish I could think of something you really want to send you, but will you buy it yourself and take it out of my account? I have a feeling that you don't charge some things to me that you should. You know I was never good at figures, and I do not keep very close tabs on my accounts. Please send Elinor $10 for her birthday, too. Also, please get me a dozen linen handkerchiefs. January white sales will be soon enough, to be paid from my account.

Thanks for the books and picture.

Lots of love,

Tetts

With irregular mail service, Etta could not have known when she wrote this letter that her sister had died one month earlier, a victim of breast cancer. Regardless of the miles that separated them, Etta and Marie had enjoyed a very special sibling relationship. Marie was the only member of Etta's family who met Foster. When Marie returned to the Lower 48 in 1923, she took care of all of Etta's holiday shopping for family members as well as her banking accounts until her death on July 16, 1935. Marie and Frank Wiley were married seven short years. She died at her mother's home in Pleasantville, New Jersey, and was buried in Yonkers, New York.

After four years at Kipnuk, Etta and Foster desired a change, and Foster submitted his request for a transfer.

February 14, 1936

Dear Mr. Dale,

When you were here last fall, you said you would recommend our transfer to any other available station. Friends in Old Harbor are asking us to return there. They say the Noninis do not intend to remain there another year. This would suit us admirably, as we like it there. So if you can see your way clear to have us changed to Kodiak Island, either to Old Harbor or Karluk, we shall be properly grateful. This is a very interesting place, and we have enjoyed working with the people here, but four years in so isolated a place, without mail service, makes us ready for a change.

Although we have no mail service, we are in daily communication through shortwave radio with Mr. Snow at Akiak, and also with Mr. MacDonald at Akiachuk. Any message sent to us through either of them will reach us quickly.

We hope you will keep your promise and visit us again this spring, bringing Mrs. Dale.

Very truly yours,

C. Foster Jones

Four months later, Etta and Foster were informed that there were no vacancies at Old Harbor, but they could be transferred to Noorvik, located approximately 500 miles north of Kipnuk, inside the Arctic Circle. Noorvik boasted a "cooperative store, reindeer interests, and excellent possibilities." Etta and Foster declined the offer and remained in Kipnuk another year.

In 1937, they again requested a transfer to Old Harbor.

Juneau, Alaska
April 22, 1937
Mr. and Mrs. C. Foster Jones
Kipnuk via Bethel, Alaska
Dear Mr. and Mrs. Jones,

No doubt you are anxious to hear if your request for transfer to Old Harbor will be granted. This is to inform you that we are recommending you for this transfer. We feel that people who have done the kind of work that you have at Kipnuk the past four years should be recognized in a request of this kind. However, there may be a slight disappointment in this when you learn that Old Harbor is only a teacher and special assistant station. As a result of the reallocation under Civil Service requirements, one of you will be changed in status from teacher to special assistant. That would also be true if you remained at Kipnuk. Ever so many stations formerly rated as two-teacher schools will this year become teacher and special assistant setups.

As you undoubtedly realize by now, Mr. Jones would be unable to meet the educational requirements for teacher in community school. Neither can Mrs. Jones qualify under the Civil Service. But because of the superior service that both of you have rendered at Kipnuk, we are wanting to retain you in the Service. Hence, we are recommending that Mrs. Jones, who has had more of the training in education and experience in teaching, be given the status of teacher in community school, 12 months at $1,800, less $20 per month for quarters. Mr. Jones would be retained as special assistant at $600, less $60 per annum for quarters. This is in keeping with all teacher and special assistant stations.

Since you have requested the transfer, it will be necessary for the travel to be at your personal expense. However, this will not be so great since you will be able to make your trip on a government boat, the *Boxer*, no doubt.

We trust that in spite of the automatic reduction in your combined salary, as a result of the reallocation under way, you will still want to go to Old Harbor. Please acknowledge receipt of this letter and advise this office of your reactions to this proposed plan.

Yours very truly,

Claude M. Hirst, Director of Education,

Alaska Indian Service

U.S. Bureau of Education ship Boxer, *which delivered annual school supplies, circa 1930s. From Eva Alvey Richards,* Arctic Mood, *page 161.*

Foster and two of his dogs, at Kipnuk, circa 1930s.

Etta and Foster accepted the positions, and in August 1937, they were back in Old Harbor on Kodiak Island.

HAVING COME FROM FIFTY- *and sixty-below weather on the Yukon, we thought we knew the ultimate in cold weather, but we had never experienced such weather as we lived through in the succeeding five winters. Although the lowest temperature was about thirty below zero, the terrific winds with their clean sweeps across that frozen ocean made thirty below much harder to endure than sixty below in the calm, dry climate of the Yukon. In those days, we burned coal, and no matter how the dampers were fixed, the appalling draft drew the fire right up the chimney. Sometimes, during the worst storms, we took turns sitting up* all night, keeping enough coal in the stove to prevent our freezing. At other times, when wet snow accompanied the wind, whose force kept it moving almost horizontally, it acted like a damper and put the fire out completely.

In spite of these exceptional times, we were very comfortable and happy in our work at Kipnuk. Their ways were not our ways, but who were we to say their ways were not best for the life they were forced to lead in that barren, inhospitable land? White men could not survive the conditions under which they lived so happily. They were intelligent and ingenious. They made the best of what they had. I think they were always sure their ways and things were best, and, for them, their ways were best. It was a matter of the survival of the fittest, and their long residence on these barren shores and struggles with or against the elements had hardened and fitted them for their struggle. ❧

10

Old Harbor

1937-1941

No physician resided in Old Harbor, but Etta's nursing skills enabled her to assist with minor illnesses and injuries. There was no community store, and, as in Kipnuk, the villagers in Old Harbor relied on boats and planes to deliver mail and supplies. Still, Etta and Foster were glad to be back.

I DON'T KNOW OF ANY MORE fascinating spot than the site of this village. It faced south, and there was a high range of craggy mountains on Sitkalidak Island across the strait. In the winter, it was fascinating to watch for the sun to peep over the tops of the peaks. They seemed to rise almost from the water's edge. In the spring, leaping streams fell down the sides like waterfalls. The noise of these falls could be heard outside our door on a still night, and with the moon shining down on them, the view was breathtaking. While working at the kitchen sink, I had a grand view through the window. About twenty-five miles away, a two-headed mountain arose, apparently right from the water. A blue mist hovered around its towering peaks. Sometimes it was snow covered, but it was always incredibly beautiful.

On the shimmering expanse of water between my window and this mountain, I could frequently see whales playing about, spouting long plumes of water in the air. Now, years later, I can still see in my mind the whalers going by, towing a whale fastened by the tail, sometimes one on each side of their boat, often to the accompaniment of orchestra music on my radio. It made it seem almost like a movie.

Between our house and the mountains on Sitkalidak Island were Barling Bay and Three Saints Bay. It was there in 1784 that the Russians landed and established their first colony. The beautiful and excellent harbor told why. The water was deep enough for large ships to get right to the water's edge. One could easily imagine their ships being hauled out of the water for repairs and for fortification purposes. History records show that this early settlement had gardens and herds of cows and goats. Storehouses and dwellings were fortified against attacks by the Natives.

The Natives still tell stories of huge bonfires being built on the near mountaintops. These were beacons to warn and to call together various tribes in defense of the Russians. Rites for the first marriage ceremony in Alaska were performed there when a Russian priest presided over a ceremony for a Russian colonist and a Native woman. A Kodiak priest told us that 5,000 Natives were baptized on one day by the early Russian priests. Foster had made a trip to this historic spot, intending to stay overnight in a cabin that belonged to a fisherman friend. He wanted to do a little investigating of the ruins. After he had walked around for several hours, there seemed to be no point in staying because there was nothing to explore. Nothing remained of that early settlement except mounds of vegetation, wild celery and carrots, berry bushes, a few alders and some Queen Anne's lace. There was not a log or upright or anything that suggested previous habitation.

Clam-digging time was every month at low tide. It took no effort at all to walk to a rocky point a few roads down the beach for clams. In half an hour, one had a full bucket, more than enough for several meals. We had them baked, fried, stewed, and in chowder. We were very fond of clams, so this was a constant delight for us.

We had many good meals. We could invite you to a dinner of delicious fresh leg of lamb roast brought from a nearby sheep ranch, canned vegetables of all kinds, and perhaps a fresh berry pie or pudding.

The sheep ranch was about fifteen miles away on Sitkalidak Island, nestled in a partly hidden bay. One suddenly came upon it from around a point. A charming old house was surrounded by gnarled trees, and there was an immense barn at the back. It reminded me of

Boat and whale, Old Harbor, Kodiak Island, 1938.

a Michigan or Midwestern farm. High green hills rose from the water. The tiny moving dots on the hills were the sheep. The openings in the hills were broad meadows, wildflowers, and good garden spots. There was always a welcome from the old caretaker and an invitation to dinner. Cats, dogs, and sometimes little lambs were there to play with. There was no shelter for the sheep and cattle. They sought the sunny south slopes in winter. Going home with half a sheep or some beef, perhaps a fresh fish caught in the bay, and taking back a sense of peace and quiet beauty, of something outside the wild rugged spirit of Alaska, something that suggested Old World ruggedness, this was one more example of the paradoxical land of Alaska.

On the same island and within five miles of this place was a whaling station. It was in full operation when we first went there, but it later closed. Once while we were there, the workers were just beginning to cut up an eighty-four-foot whale. The size of these monsters of the sea was almost incredible. We were invited to stay for lunch, but we declined because the smell was more than we could stand. Workers get used to this smell, they told us, and do not mind the food being saturated with it. We found this to be true as our visits continued, until we could stay for lunch and enjoy everything, not minding the smell. After the whaling station closed, we had many pleasant visits with the caretakers. They were fine people.

The old skin bidarka [traditional Aleut kayak] *was not in use when we first went there, but there were two still in the village. One old* man was pointed out as a mighty hunter of whales from the bidarka. In one hunt, he was badly injured by an angry whale, but he managed to escape with his life. He still carried scars of the injury.

Vi and Jack McCord were prime examples of Alaskan hospitality. We usually made the fifteen-mile trip to their place in our outboard motor boat, often with the waves almost covering the stern. When we arrived, hungry and windblown, we were met at the dock with a cheerful welcome. We were then escorted up the long boardwalk to their comfortable cabin. "Take off your things and make yourselves at home. There's a roast in the oven and dinner will be ready soon." Vi was a great radio fan and she had a remarkable memory. She knew all the stations, their announcers and sponsors, the bandmasters, singers and actors, and all of the theme songs and little idiosyncrasies of radio land. She sent in questions and answers and joined contests. She was a really remarkable person.

After a good dinner, and a couple hours of animated chat, we returned home again across the huge ocean swells, although sometimes it was quite calm. On this trip we passed several small islands and an old four-master sailing schooner anchored in a quiet bay. It was left there for years, gathering barnacles. After especially violent storms, we used to wonder if the schooner was still there. It was the general opinion that someday it would be missing. Once we boarded her, and we imagined what had happened on her decks in the old days.

Some of the islands were very tiny, and the gulls and other sea birds laid their eggs there on the cliffs. Every spring the Natives went on egg-gathering expeditions to all these islands. One island consisted of high perpendicular rocks. There was no way to land except by scaling the rocks, and attempts at this were not very successful. Nests there were so thick the birds seemed to almost tread on each other. They seemed to know they were safe.

Old Harbor, Alaska
December 7, 1939

Dear Clarence [Clarence Leeds, a former neighbor of Etta's in Vineland, New Jersey] :

Amateur radio is a blessing, isn't it? We do appreciate

the messages you sent about Mother. Foster doesn't do much "hamming," but he has a schedule twice a week with the operator at the Standard Oil digging at Jute Bay, Kanatak. That isn't very far from here. Roy Wilson is the "ham." I think his amateur call letters are K7HJI. We get him on his commercial frequency under KAYR. Perhaps you could hook up with him sometime. He has a schedule with a relay league "ham" in San Francisco twice a week. It was an easy matter to get messages through, but, unfortunately, we had a long spell of bad radio conditions just when we wanted most to get through.

We have a new receiver. It's a Howard Communication 460. It is fine, but too complicated for me. I am almost afraid to touch it.

I had about made up my mind to take a trip back home next summer, but now that Mother is gone, I won't attempt it alone. [Etta's mother had died six days earlier, on December 1, 1939, in Pleasantville, New Jersey.] Foster is too busy with his mining to think of going, but we may meet again sometime. Who can tell? In the meantime, best wishes to you and Bessie.

Sincerely,

Tetts

Years later, Etta's former students recalled her with great fondness and respect. They related the impact the Joneses made on the Old Harbor community. George Inga said, "They were real nice people. She liked people. Mrs. Jones was a good teacher because she never spanked me." George went on to say that Foster was a hard worker. "[Foster] dug a tunnel under the school," he said, "to put in a light generator, and he let us students help him. He taught us how to work it, and that was very exciting." George was fifteen years old at the time. Before the generator was installed, the village had used gas lamps. George said that Etta and Foster were "kind, wonderful people who never raised their voices at the villagers."

Foster continued to hone his radio skills. He used a transmitter radio to communicate with other villages, and he taught some of the students how to use it. Annie (Inga) Pestrikoff, another former student, wrote in 2004: "After the Joneses left, there was a bad flu in the village. It's a good thing that [Foster] showed Alex Inga how to use the radio because when the flu hit, he used the radio to call Kodiak, and that saved a lot of people." Annie and George both said the Joneses were actively involved in the village, attending dances and Native games. The villagers were very happy to have the Joneses living in Old Harbor, and Etta and Foster were well established and content. Etta's Service Rating Form validates what Annie and George said. It stated, "She is well adapted to life in Alaska. She is loyal and interested in being of service to the people she serves."

Etta's former students Annie Pestrikoff (top) and George Inga (bottom), Old Harbor, 2005. PHOTOS BY GEORGE INGA.

The employees of the Alaska Indian Service were accustomed to frequent transfers to remote Native villages, so it did not come as a surprise to Etta and Foster when they were offered yet another move. They had endured separations, appalling weather conditions, and unfamiliar foods as they had been shuffled around Alaska. Therefore, a move to another village seemed like duty calling from another corner of the land they loved, the Aleutian Islands.

Juneau, Alaska

March 17, 1941

Mr. Charles F. Jones, Special Assistant

Old Harbor, Alaska

Dear Mr. Jones:

     For your information, it may be that we shall open a school at Attu, the extreme end of the Aleutian Islands, this summer. If so, we shall wish to send there a man and wife. The woman

would teach and the man would be appointed by the Weather Bureau as a C.W. [Continuous Wave, Morse Code] operator. It occurred to us that if this plan is carried out, you and Mrs. Jones might be interested.

In this connection, we should like to have the following information about your qualifications: (1) How many words per minute can you send by C.W.? (2) How many can you receive? (3) Can you service and maintain a simple C.W. and radiophone transmitter and receiving unit? (4) Can you service and maintain a lighting plant such as a $1/2$ KVA 110 V AC Kohler or similar type of plant?

Your duties in this position would be to make and report four weather observations per day, every day, including Sundays and holidays. The observations would be made regularly at six-hour intervals. You would also have to do the maintenance work on the plant and other duties as special assistant similar to those you now perform.

The minimum salary offered would be not less than $100 per month for your weather observations and reporting service, and it is quite likely that the combined salaries, where you work as special assistant and weather reporter, would approximate $2,000 per year. Mrs. Jones's salary as teacher would continue at her present rate. There would be the usual deductions for Q [Quarters], F [Fuel] and L [Lights]. The radio equipment and weather instruments would be furnished by the government, as would also the gasoline and other supplies necessary for the operation of the light plant.

You should understand fully in considering this possible vacancy that it is in an extremely isolated area. You would have no access to medical or dental service and you would have mail service not more than three or four times a year when boats call at your station during the summer. Your quarters would be comfortable and reasonably well furnished. You and Mrs. Jones would be the only white people in the community.

We should like to have you think this over and, if you are interested, give us the information requested, sending your reply in duplicate. This letter is an inquiry and not an offer, since the position is not yet definitely considered and will be if and when the school is established.

Very truly yours,

Fred R. Geeslin, Acting General Superintendent,

Alaska Indian Service

Foster responded in a letter to Mr. Geeslin's supervisor, Claude M. Hirst.

Old Harbor, Alaska

April 22, 1941

Mr. Claude M. Hirst, General Superintendent for Alaska Indian Service, Office of Indian Affairs, Juneau, Alaska

My dear Mr. Hirst,

Regarding your letter of March 17th, concerning the possibility of opening a school and weather station at Attu: Mrs. Jones and I have thought carefully of the matter, and consider it favorably.

Answering your questions as to my qualifications, I have held an amateur operator's license for six years. Regarding your questions: (1) I can send fifteen words per minute by C.W. (2) I can receive thirteen words per minute by C.W. (3) I can service and maintain a simple C.W. and radiophone transmitter and receiving unit. In this connection, I have built and successfully operated at least a dozen small transmitters, both phone and C.W. (4) I have had considerable experience with many types of gas engines and light plants, and, therefore, feel confident that I can service and maintain a 1 1/2 KVA 110 V AC Kohler or similar type of plant.

We fully understand the isolation and attending difficulties of life at Attu.

Very truly yours,

C. Foster Jones

Weather stations in the Aleutian Islands were few in number

and hundreds of miles apart. Attu was the birthplace of weather patterns that moved across the chain and onto the mainland. Coast Guard and military stations depended on accurate weather information, which was critical locally and globally. The Office of Indian Affairs in Juneau felt it was so important to have a weather station on Attu that the General Superintendent, Claude M. Hirst, wrote to the Commissioner of Indian Affairs in Washington, D.C., that there would be a personnel change in Old Harbor.

> Juneau, Alaska
> June 11, 1941
> **Commissioner of Indian Affairs**
> **Washington, D.C.**
> **Attention: Danielson**
> **Regarding Old Harbor: We are recommending the transfer of Etta and Charles F. Jones to Attu, one of the new stations allowed in the budget. Attu is a very important weather reporting station, where the special assistant will also be appointed by the Weather Bureau to make weather reports. The person sent to this station must be thoroughly reliable and a good radioman; therefore, we are recommending the transfer of Mr. and Mrs. Jones at government expense to Attu. It will be necessary to find a teacher and a special assistant to replace them at Old Harbor.**
> **Signed,**
> **Claude M. Hirst, General Superintendent,**
> **Alaska Indian Service,**
> **Office of Indian Affairs, Juneau**

Once the decision was made to establish the weather station and the new school, arrangements were made to get Etta and Foster to Attu as quickly as possible, and a telegram was sent to Washington, D.C.:

INDIAN AFFAIRS
JUNEAU, ALASKA
JULY 5, 1941
COMMISSIONER INDIAN AFFAIRS
WASHINGTON, D.C.
ATTENTION: DANIELSON

NECESSARY WE REQUEST YOU EXPEDITE TRANSFERS
ETTA AND CHARLES FOSTER JONES FROM OLD HARBOR
TO ATTU RECOMMENDED OUR LETTER JUNE ELEVEN
ON ACCOUNT ONLY TRANSPORTATION WILL LEAVE
VERY NEAR FUTURE ALSO WEATHER BUREAU DESIRES
EMPLOYEE ARRIVE IN ORDER TO START MAKING
WEATHER REPORTS PROMPTLY

CLAUDE M. HIRST, GENERAL SUPERINTENDENT
ALASKA INDIAN SERVICE
INTERIOR

United States Department of the Interior
Division of Personnel, Supervision and Management
Washington, D.C.
July 8, 1941
Mrs. Etta E. Jones:

You should report to Attu, Alaska, at the earliest practicable date. If you cannot do so, advise the Commissioner of Indian Affairs immediately by letter. This transfer is at government expense, and you will be allowed transportation and subsistence expenses and expenses of packing, crating, unpacking, and uncrating, and shipping household goods in accordance with travel regulations in Alaska. This transfer is not for the convenience of the employee. Use of own conveyance is authorized if desired. You will continue to be subject to provisions of the Retirement Act.

Signed,

J. Atwood Maulding, Director of Personnel

Planning ahead, Etta and Foster had gone to the Seattle area in July to purchase property where they would build their retirement home. They chose some acreage on Whidbey Island, located fifty miles north of Seattle.

Juneau, Alaska,
July 19, 1941
Mrs. Etta E. Jones, Government Teacher
Old Harbor, Alaska
Dear Mrs. Jones:
    We have your letter of July 16 stating that you are returning to Old Harbor in order to pack and proceed on the *Cordova* as soon as possible.
    We are attaching travel orders. As the method of your transportation is rather uncertain, you should have the transportation company bill this office for the transportation of yourself and Mr. Jones from Old Harbor to destination. This letter will be your authority for having this done.
    We are glad to know that you are on your way, and we hope that you will like your new assignment and get along nicely.
    Very truly yours,
    Claude M. Hirst, General Superintendent,
    Alaska Indian Service

Transporting personnel and their possessions in the Alaska Indian Service always depended on the weather and the availability of boats. Not this time. Rather than make their usual, almost leisurely runs, Coast Guard cutters were ordered to sit and wait, even for two weeks if necessary, until the Joneses and all their freight were ready. Within one month of receiving travel orders from Washington, D.C., Etta and Foster were on their way, escorted at government time and expense, to a remote island so far west that it technically fell within the Eastern Hemisphere. En route to Attu, Etta took time to write her sister and brother.

The freighter SS Dellwood, *which Etta and Foster traveled on
from Seattle to Old Harbor after a brief trip to the Lower 48 in 1941.*

FROM LUCILE MCDONALD, "ALASKA STEAM," *ALASKA GEOGRAPHIC*, PAGE 80

Kodiak
August 12, 1941
Dear Nan and Russ:

I'll write to you both together, thus saving time. It seems as
if the days fly by so fast, there is no time for half of what we want
to do. I think I wrote you last from Seattle. I thought I would
surely have time in Old Harbor to write. We landed there at 6:00
one evening, ten days after we left Seattle. We had a good trip
on the freighter *Dellwood*. Weather was ideal, and the passengers
and crew congenial.

The day after we landed in Old Harbor, packing was begun,
and then cleaning up, and then two weeks had gone by and it
was time to be on the go again. Foster's mining partners came
to the rescue with a boat, thirty-nine feet long, and a hold big
enough to take all our trunks and bags and boxes, about two
tons of freight. In Kodiak it was impossible to get a room or
any place to stay. Foster knows the chief of police very well,
and we had him racking his brains. Finally, I asked him to get

someone with a boat to take me over to a nearby island where my friend, Mrs. Magnusen, lives. She had invited us to stay with her, but since it was so late when we landed in Kodiak, I thought we could spend the night in town and go to her place in the morning. Foster spent the night on the boat with the other men, while I landed on Mrs. Magnusen long after she was in bed and asleep.

The next day, Foster came over with the bags, and here we have been six days waiting for the boat that will take us to Unalaska. It should have been here before this, but, for some reason, it has been delayed. We have had wires from the Department [of the Interior] that a Coast Guard cutter is waiting at Unalaska to take us on to Attu. It is over 500 miles from here to Unalaska, and more than 800 miles from Unalaska to Attu, so we still have something of a trip before us. We both wish it were over and we were settled there, but this has been a lovely place to stay.

Love to all, and I'll write again when we reach Attu, if there is time.

Tetts

Attu

1941-1942

In winter, snowdrifts cover the soaring mountains of Attu, America's most isolated parcel of land, which is located at the western tip of the Aleutian chain. Cold, dense, impenetrable fog soaks the island. Howling winds and piercing cold make the island's environment inhospitable, if not forbidding, to most. Severe storms can suddenly usher in violent winds that cause rain and snow to blow horizontally. During stormy weather, williwaws—very strong blasts of wind that sweep down from the hills and lift the water up off the surface of the bay—often occur. Storms can last for days. In winter, the spongy tundra becomes slick, frozen muck. Fifty-foot waves are not uncommon, and reefs offshore make navigation treacherous.

The quiet, dignified Aleuts of Attu had survived their exceedingly rugged environment for thousands of years. Their effective self-government was still in place. The village chief, chosen by the villagers for his trustworthiness and leadership, handled all of the community's affairs as well as those of the church. In the absence of a Russian Orthodox priest, he conducted church services and taught at the village's new school. Although the population had diminished to only forty-five Natives—half of them children—these strong, independent people were living the way their ancestors had for centuries on their secluded island.

For all the autonomy that the island enjoyed, for all the preferred isolation and the agreeable nature everyone on the island shared, there was a certain uneasiness that prevailed. The source of this anxiety was not the weather. They had faced all of its fury and capricious nature. They had a tradition of successfully keeping themselves warm and dry. This apparent utopia was breached every time the subject of the Japanese came up. This uneasiness was attributed to periodic encounters with the Japanese in previous years.

Japan had been at war with China since July 1937. In protest, the United States imposed an embargo on the natural resources intended to go to Japan. Rather than look elsewhere for resources, Japan set out to expand its empire. By 1941, the British and Dutch colonies of Southeast Asia had already been conquered and only the United States stood in Japan's way. Fleet Admiral Isoroku Yamamoto's grand plan was to destroy the entire American fleet in the Pacific. It is possible that Japan wanted to conquer the Aleutians in order to get a foothold on American soil. It is also possible that the American military considered attacking Japan via a northern route, that is, through the Aleutians.

No military decisions had been made when Etta and Foster announced to their friends they were going to Attu. The reaction was still one of alarm. "Don't go to Attu! Why, that is practically in Japan's back yard!" The Joneses disagreed. Etta said, "We laughed at them. What would Japan want with Attu?" Both Etta and Foster were sixty-two years old. They had enthusiastically accepted the position and planned to stay there until they retired.

Their first impressions of Attu were not disappointing. In August 1941, Etta wrote to her brother, Russ.

> **Dear Russ:**
>
> **I am sending you a copy of a general letter I wrote to several of you. Saves time and we have plenty to do getting unpacked and settled. We expect another Coast Guard cutter tomorrow, bringing the rest of our equipment including a light plant. After that I don't suppose we shall have another boat till January.**
>
> **It is lovely here—warm and sunny and balmy. It is hard to realize we are only 450 miles from Siberia. We have a very**

comfortable house, well furnished with all the comforts. We
know we shall like it. Write when you can.

> Love to you and Skeets [Russ's dog],
> Tetts

Attu, Alaska
August 31, 1941
Dear Family and Friends:

It was just a week ago that we landed at Attu, eight in the
morning, and glad to get here.

We had a lovely trip from Kodiak to Unalaska on the
Cordova, a comfortable passenger ship. It was filled almost to
capacity with men and families of defense workers bound for the
navy base at Dutch Harbor, just across a narrow channel from
Unalaska. The *Cordova* stopped first at Unalaska where a Coast
Guard cutter was waiting for us, so we did not get a chance to
see much of it. The hills all around are honeycombed with new
roads, new buildings, etc., and the whole place bristles with
guns. Dutch Harbor commands both the Bering Sea and the
Pacific, and, apparently, they are leaving nothing undone in the
way of defense. We found the Coast Guard cutter *Atlanta* tied to
the dock, and the captain was impatient to be on his way. He had
waited two weeks for us, but orders were to wait until we got
there.

There were about a dozen officers, the finest of the fine.
As Foster says, "All gentlemen." We ate with them, used their
office and bathroom, and tried not to be too much in the way. I
must admit that I skipped most of the meals, although they were
the best, served with formality by waiters. Foster did not miss
a meal. Just the last night I was a little sick, and vomited once.
Most of the rookie sailors were worse than that.

There were no easy stairs going up to the deck, just an
almost perpendicular ladder to climb, clutching both handrails
desperately.

That boat was fast. In less than three days we were here,
800 miles from Unalaska, making one stop at Bogosloff Island.

That is a most interesting place. It is called the floating island because sometimes it is there and sometimes it can't be found. One of the sailors told us the last time he saw it there was only one peak showing, and this time there were three high peaks, one of them looking distinctly like a volcano formation, black lava. There were literally thousands of sea lions basking on the shore, and as soon as the anchor was cast dozens of them swam out to investigate. Two boats were lowered and the men were afraid they might upset the boats. Officers and men went ashore to take pictures and to report on formation, bird life, etc. There was a greater variety of sea birds there than I have ever seen in one place.

We are going to like it here. We may not see another boat until January when the trader comes. Don't worry if you don't hear from us.

With love,

Tetts

Etta wrote to Claude Hirst, General Superintendent of the Alaska Native Service, telling her impressions of the village and its people.

September 8, 1941

There are forty-five people in the village. They are progressive, intelligent, clean, and friendly. They live and work as a community, making their living from blue fox trapping. They operate as the Native Community of Attu, pooling the season's catch of pelts, and selling them in the name of the community to a fur dealer in New York. The proceeds, after ten dollars for each skin is taken out for the trappers, are divided equally among all members of the village, children included. Thus, widows and helpless ones are taken care of. There are no indigents here.

The houses are models for construction, neatness, and furnishings. There are nine houses, having from four to seven rooms each, and they are well lighted and beautifully painted, inside and out. All have excellent stoves, good linoleum on the floors, gas lamps, and all but one have running water piped into the house from a spring. The yards are neat, all refuse being

*Three Aleut children (left) and an unknown adult, Attu, spring 1942.
Two Aleut boys (right) at Attu, spring 1942.*

*A barabara at Attu, 1941. This traditional dwelling of the Aleuts and
Eskimos is built over a pit and made of sod supported by driftwood or whale ribs.*

ALASKA'S DIGITAL ARCHIVES, ASL-P27-038.

Attu village and Chichagof Harbor, August 1941.
ALASKA STATE LIBRARY, DORA M. SWEENEY, ASL-P421-195.

Left: Russian Orthodox church at Attu, 1936. COURTESY OF ALEUTIAN/PRIBILOF ISLANDS
ASSOCIATION. *Right: Interior of Russian Orthodox church at Attu, 1936.*
ALASKA STATE LIBRARY, AMRC, AMRC-B833-7-7.

carefully disposed of. The American flag, flying from the village
flagpole, was one of the first sights that greeted us as we came
into the harbor on the Coast Guard Cutter *Atlanta*. They have
a beautiful Russian Orthodox Church, electrically lighted by
means of a small light plant.

They speak a little English, much to our astonishment,
considering their extreme isolation. People from occasional
boats that stop here are the only ones outside the village they
see.

The villagers have used the schoolroom for dances on
various occasions, but have left everything in good condition.
Written on the blackboard we found the chief's orders to the

School at Attu, 1941. ALASKA'S DIGITAL ARCHIVES, UAF-1992-176-12.

villagers: "Pealse don't spate on the Flower and don't brake loking Gleese" [windows]. They are cooperative and helpful in all work concerning the school.

All want to help without pay when there is building or lifting or special work to be done. They have an abundance of all kinds of fish and the boys are generous with their gifts of fish. At first we paid them, but the chief asked us not to pay. The boys themselves made that request. They have plenty of fish and they wanted their gifts to be free.

They are a proud people—proud of the fact that they differ somewhat from the people of Atka and Unalaska. There has been no intermingling with the Japanese. In fact, they dislike and distrust the Japs. They accuse them of stealing their foxes, and even of killing some of their trappers years ago. But for three years, they haven't seen a Jap or a Japanese boat.

Attu was a self-sufficient village that had survived as a subsistence society for thousands of years. With the establishment of a new school, education guidelines from Washington, D.C., 5,000 miles away, would be introduced to help "civilize" the community.

As outlined in a U.S. Department of the Interior Field Service directive, Etta's tasks at this isolated and remote village were to: conduct regular classes of school children, giving them instruction in oral and written English, number processes, and related subjects; help children to form the right habits of living and learning; adapt the educational program to the major concerns and problems of the community, putting most stress on those things that will tend to make living conditions healthier and more pleasant and will aid the children in making a living; cooperate with the health and reindeer officials and other agencies for the betterment of conditions in the area; visit homes in the community regularly, becoming acquainted with the parents of the children, helping them to understand the purpose of the schools, and securing their cooperation in making them function to the greatest possible extent; promote community gatherings, such as P.T.A., community forums, community singing, play days, pageants, wholesome Native games and dances; encourage interest in community gardens, home improvement, Native crafts and industries, according to the particular conditions encountered; and perform such other duties as may be necessary in connection with the community needs.

Foster's responsibilities were to: assist in the teaching of manual training to the boys and men of the village; do the janitor work in connection with school and quarters; assist in the repair and upkeep of government property; direct the band music and programs of entertainment for the school and village.

Given the island's rich history of subsistence and its economic independence, these directives hardly seemed necessary. With the exception of formal instruction in oral and written English, math, and related subjects, Etta and Foster's role was that of facilitators to an already highly functional community.

Foster's family was well established in the small town of St. Paris, Ohio. Members of the community were always anxious to hear the news of Dr. Jones's adventurous son in faraway Alaska. The *St. Paris Dispatch* reported in October 1941: "From lonely Attu Island, seven degrees east of Greenwich and the most westerly of the Aleutian Islands, Uncle Sam now is receiving regular weather reports for the first time, Howard Thompson, Weather Bureau meteorologist for Alaska has announced. C. Foster Jones, who established the first Office of Indian Affairs on the island, 'worked' the new system recently, his wireless report being relayed by the navy radio station at Dutch Harbor to the Weather Bureau. Jones, a licensed radio operator and classified as a special meteorologist by the Weather Bureau, is equipped with wireless and weather instruments furnished by the bureau and with a power unit from the Office of Indian Affairs."

With the holidays approaching, Etta was anxious to send greetings to her family. If she had enough time before the supply boat arrived, she always wanted to make sure she had letters ready to mail.

Attu, Alaska
November 21, 1941
Dear Nan and Russ:

I am writing to you both at once. Saves time and that may be important just now. There may be a coast guard cutter in here any time. We do not know. Foster talks to one every night so there is one in these parts, and the fact that they want to keep in touch with Attu and know our weather gives us hope they

Aleut adults and children with fishing boat and nets, Attu, September 1941.

may call in here, so I am getting letters ready, just in case. They will take mail out for us even if they do not bring us any, and we hardly hope for that since they have just come up from the south, probably California. They never give a hint as to their position or their plans or intended stops. There are strict regulations, and stricter now with war looming in the near future, so we can just hope.

We like Attu. It grows on one, and the people are fine. There is no drinking, and that means much in a Native village. Consequently, there is no fighting. All is peace and harmony. The people are very industrious, even teaching their children to work. Most Native children escape that.

Today is a big church holiday. We watched them march to their beautiful white church, all dressed up. The girls wore white shoes and stockings, white dresses and sweaters, with white hair ribbons and sashes, and the boys were in neat blue suits and white caps. They will stay dressed up for the rest of the day, and not even think of school, so that gives me time to get caught up on my letters. We can make up the school days later. We are supposed to get in 180 days for the year, and if not at one time, then another, just so it is done before the last of July.

We celebrated Thanksgiving yesterday. It rather goes against the grain to follow Roosevelt's tinkering with our national holidays, but we thought something might prevent us from celebrating next week. To be sure, a celebration merely meant opening a can of chicken, another of mincemeat, and making two pies. One was lemon chiffon, and it was good. So was the gravy. We are getting hungry for meat. When our trader's boat comes in January, we expect him to bring us three pork loins. I am hoping we can get some reindeer meat before long. I surely do like reindeer. We find quite a little reindeer moss on this island, so we may be able to persuade the government to put some reindeer here for the Natives. There is no game here at all, not even rabbits. Incidentally, there aren't even mice. What do you suppose the cats do here with no mice to catch?

Now I have three women visitors, but they are busy playing checkers, so I can still go on with my letters.

I'll wish you all a Merry Christmas, hoping you get this before then.

With love,

Tetts

Attu baskets were considered *among the finest in the world. Men from every ship that stopped tried to get baskets. When it became known that we were going to Attu, from all sides came the plea, "Get me some Attu baskets."*

In the fall, whole families went out on grass-hunting expeditions, sometimes being gone for several days. Some years, there was no grass because of unfavorable weather. After it was cut, it was allowed to lie in the field to cure, then husked, then hung up to dry in the houses until it was ready to use. The manner of basket weaving was a wonder to behold. How the nimble fingers did fly! Various colors of embroidery silk were skillfully woven in to form flowers and birds. The younger women were not too eager for the basketry; it was the older ones who excelled.

The village council set the prices of their famous baskets. They sold for ten, fifteen, and twenty dollars each, according to size and quality, and the men did the selling.

Aleut baskets from Attu were woven for functional as well as aesthetic purposes, and they ranged in size from that of a thimble to large enough to hold food staples. Learning to make these traditional baskets required years of patience and practice. For this reason, young women were not usually taught by their mothers; instead, an aunt, grandmother, or nonfamily member in the village was the teacher. Beach rye grass was collected, and dried and split several times until the strands were as fine as silk threads. The intricate weaving created more than 1,300 stitches per square inch. By the twentieth century, colorful designs were woven into the baskets using silk and cotton thread.

These baskets were highly sought after by museums and

Prep House: Place these 4 photographs together as one photograph with the same black background - it now has a mottled look.

Aleut baskets given to Etta in 1942 by the Natives of Attu,
and now owned by the author.

collectors around the world. They were noted for the fineness and evenness of the weaving. This art has been handed down, but today there are only a few artisans skilled enough to replicate the great work of the past.

January 10, 1942

Well, here we sit, and still no boat. We knew one was just about to start for this place when Japan started her dirty work at Pearl Harbor. Then all coast guard ships were needed elsewhere. We have new hope now since the commanding officer at Dutch Harbor wired us a few days ago to send in a list of "immediate needs and future requirements." Just how much in the future that means, we can only guess. Perhaps next summer means a far distant future to him, while to us it means fairly soon. Anyway, we sent a long list, including the MAIL. That is a most important need, both immediate and future.

I suppose some of the young Schuremans and Joneses may be included in the draft. That is frightening, but I suppose they want it that way. If I were younger, I should want to do something myself.

All [non-Native] women and children have been evacuated from Dutch Harbor and Unalaska. That is understandable because Dutch Harbor is a Naval base, heavily fortified, and Unalaska is a small town just across a narrow strait from Dutch Harbor, perhaps a mile or less. I think women and children have been sent from other places too, in Alaska. We do not hear

Aleut children, and toddler in Attu, May 1942.

those things over the air, but when letters begin to come in, we shall know many things. Our nearest neighbor is at Atka, 500 miles away. They have more boat visitors than we do, and he [Ralph Magee, radio operator at Atka] has developed a code of his own, so he has told us some things, some I am afraid even to write in a letter. The radio operators now are forbidden to communicate in any way except purely business, and that in code, so we don't hear much except a lot of meaningless numbers and words going over the air. Of course, we hear the regular broadcasts, especially on the shortwave. From Tokyo, we hear curious things about our country. For instance, in the first weeks of the war, the United States was very short of gasoline, so much so that rickshaws are soon to be seen on the streets of Washington. It is about the only way, according to Tokyo, that Chiang Kai-shek can repay the immense loans the United States has been making to him. Japan, on the other hand, has plenty of gas. Their domestic consumption allowances have been much increased, etc.

Foster is just now having trouble with his transmitter. It is a very complicated affair, and suddenly it went haywire while he was talking with Dutch Harbor this morning. He has had trouble with it before but always got it fixed. If he does not get

back on the air soon, they will think the Japs have gotten us. He
still has his little battery set of his own making, and will use
that in case he does not get the other fixed. The trouble is it does
not reach very far, except when radio conditions are good. We
are almost 900 miles from Dutch Harbor, and that is a long way,
about as far as you are [New Jersey] from Mexico.

Hope everyone is well. It will seem so good to get letters
again. When our boat comes it will not stay long, so there will
be no chance to answer letters.

With love to all,
Tetts

The Japanese had bombed Pearl Harbor on December 7, and the
United States military was concerned that the Aleutian Islands would
be the next target. Foster was sending and receiving four weather
reports per day, and he had been instructed to notify the U.S. Navy,
in code, if he ever spotted the enemy. The entire Attu community,
including Etta and Foster, felt confident that Attu would not be
bombed because it was not a military base and it was too small to be
of any significance to the Japanese. Etta explained in a letter to her
friend, Ella:

Attu, Alaska
February 6, 1942
Dear Ella:

Your long newsy letter was most welcome. Yes, your Los
Angeles letter came, also the card from Atlantic City. You seem
to be doing quite a lot of gadding around in the late summer of
life. I am glad you can. There were many years when you were
tied down with your growing family, and you and Howard must
plan a long visit with us on Whidbey Island if and when. . . . You
may even be neighbors of ours. Who knows?

Of course, the Japs know there are weather stations all
along this coast. We feel they are listening in all the time,
and Foster's transmitter is so powerful it reaches right into
Japan, which is no farther from here than Dutch Harbor is,

and they have no trouble getting him in Dutch Harbor. What he transmits now will do the Japs no good because everything is in code. No friendly conversations are allowed over the air. Twice our villagers have discovered a Jap boat anchored on the other side of this island. What they were doing there we don't know. Foster reported it to the naval base at Dutch Harbor, and a few weeks ago one of our minesweepers, bringing us supplies and doing a little reconnoitering (or more likely, a thorough reconnoitering), picked up a Jap boat somewhere in this vicinity. We don't know the particulars, but Foster arranged a little code with the officers. They do not use their radio, except to listen, but if Foster has anything to report, he uses certain words in his weather schedules with other weather stations, and the officers, stopping at these weather stations, leave messages to be transmitted to Foster in code. In that way, we know they nabbed a Jap boat. We'll get particulars when they visit us again.

They were a fine bunch of fellows, mostly from Seattle and vicinity. Their boat is based at Puget Sound Naval Shipyard in Bremerton, near Seattle. They were itching to grab some Japs. At first, their sudden appearing outside our little harbor was rather startling. We knew some boat was headed this way, but we rather thought it was a freighter. Just about noon one day, the Natives came running, "Big boat coming," and there it was at the harbor, an ugly looking customer, a dark, dirty looking gray, with big guns bristling on the deck. We could not see a flag, but we ran up the Stars and Stripes. We knew they were anchored, but for two hours there was no sign from them that they were coming ashore. Finally, we saw the motor boat loaded with men coming in. Foster remarked after we had waited half an hour for them, "Well, it can't be a Jap ship or they would have shelled us by this time." The explanation of the long wait was a reasonable one, of course. It was just about lunchtime when they anchored, so they waited for that, and there was some little trouble launching the small boat, and freight had to be unloaded and put into the small boat. The time did not seem long to them. They were here until after dark. They brought us four big mail sacks filled to overflowing. It was the first we had had since we landed last August. You can imagine how we feasted for days. Now we are expecting a small trader's boat in a few days. It will have supplies for the village store and us and more mail. The minesweeper captain gave us orders for a village blackout every night. It seems unreal covering up our windows each night because of the Japs. All boats travel without lights. That is a pretty risky business on these rocky, storm- and fog-ridden coasts.

Foster is writing to Tobe Toback [Etta and Foster's friend from their years in Tanana]. He sent us a hilariously funny letter. One doesn't suspect his keen sense of humor until one gets very well acquainted with him. He had only seven more months to serve before being retired, but I imagine with this war on, he won't be allowed to retire. He envied us our trip and said he would not care what ship he traveled on, just so it was Alaska bound.

Tell Howard when he wants to go on a real fishing or hunting trip to come to Alaska (after the war).

Well, it is near midnight and I must hie me to bed. Foster is transmitting the weather to Dutch Harbor. He enjoyed your letter and says "Hello" to you and Rose.

Don't worry about us. We feel as safe here as anywhere. The teachers at Atka [Ruby and Ralph Magee]—500 miles nearer Dutch Harbor than we are—are leaving.

March 3

The small trading boat arrived yesterday bringing mail and supplies. A lovely woman on board was traveling as co-pilot with her husband, the captain [Ginger and Don Pickard]. We had them for dinner last night. She was the first white woman I have seen since we came last August. We were to have had dinner with them tonight, but the storm is so great, we can't get out to their ship—wind, rain, hail, and snow.

Love to all,

Tetts

Attu, Alaska
February 8, 1942
Dear Nan and Russ:

At last, our long-looked-for mail arrived on January 16th. It was a long time coming, the first we have had since we came here last August, but it was worthwhile when it did get here. Four big mail sacks were stuffed to overflowing. You can imagine how we feasted for days. In fact, we are still enjoying it. There was a letter from Ella McLaughlin telling me of her visit to Atlantic City with Howard. They were there a week and had a grand time. Too bad you were not able to see them, Russ. I am sure you would like Howard.

There was a long letter from an old friend of the family. I am sure you would never guess who. Young Philip Gross, the weatherman, who kept the maps on the Boardwalk, and who used to board with us. He is now in Germantown, and is making some special kind of candy—nonfattening. He sent me a circular on which was his picture. He is pretty bald, and I would never have known him. He got my address from Carrie [Russ's estranged wife].

Thanks for the pictures. You look about the same, but Skeets does look old and too fat. I hope he is better. And there were four letters from you, Nan, the first one written last July, when it was "red hot and a-heatin', " according to Pearl Birch. Also, your package arrived with everything else. Many thanks for it. Yes, I can use everything in it. I love the little saucepans. We have plenty of large ones, but none that size, and there are so many things to use them for. And thanks for all the news of the wedding. I am glad everything went off well, and that Elinor is so well established. I hope this war does not take Erling away. Married men do not seem to stand any better chance than the single ones. I shall be glad to get pictures of the wedding.

A Mrs. Massey of Cardiff also wrote me a letter. She says she was a friend of Mother's and also of yours, Nan, but I do not remember her. Perhaps sometime I shall get around to answering it. She seems like a nice soul, but I have so many letters to write. There are huge stacks of official mail to get ready each month, both Weather Bureau and Indian Service, and I have to do them all. I am on the go all day long—school, housework, and other things. I never get a chance to even sit down till evening. Foster is just as busy. He doesn't finish with his weather broadcasts till after midnight, and then it is get up early and begin all over again. It is not an easy job here, but the pay is good. We get $280 per month and heat and light and living quarters furnished, so we are glad to have it until we are ready to retire.

March 3

Mail arrived yesterday. Thanks for Elinor's picture and the novelty ring. Yes, I can use them. Elinor makes a very stunning bride. Wish I could have attended the wedding, but it was impossible.

Love,

Tetts

Nothing in the following letter, Etta's last from Attu, foreshadows her friends' and family members' greatest fear—the Japanese invasion of Attu.

Attu

April 9, 1942

Dear Nan and Russ:

I suppose it is time to write again although I have no idea when there will be an opportunity to mail letters. Life goes along very peacefully here. The days pass quickly. We like to see these winter days go—the sooner the better. Even now, when it should be showing some signs of spring, winter hangs on. There is a nine-foot snowdrift by our front door, and at least three feet of snow on the level ground. The temperature is below freezing, about twenty-eight, and more snow is coming down. No thawing, but a few weeks ago we did have one hard warm rain.

The people of Attu say they have never known such a winter. We hope next winter will be an improvement.

Thanks for the brooches and pins, Nan. Yes, I can use them. I am always glad of such things. I finally got a letter written to Mrs. Massey. I feel mean for not writing, especially when she is something of a shut-in, but my big stack of unanswered letters weigh enough on my mind without adding to them. This last mail brought a letter from C. L. Andrews, who has written several books on Alaska. I met him in Kodiak a few years ago, traveled with him to Seward, and liked him a lot. He wants to know all sorts of things about Attu. That letter will take me hours to write but I must do it.

Say, if you have any seeds of houseplants or pansies of any kind you don't want, you might send me some. I did not bring a slip of any houseplant or a seed of any kind. There wasn't time. I don't think we can have a garden here, but I might raise something in the house.

Russ, we were glad to get a Christmas card from Leslie [Russ's son] and family. Tell them "hello" for us when you see them.

Will sign off now.
With love to all,
Tetts

12

Invasion

1942

❦

Visitors to the remote island shared Etta's feelings about this pleasant sanctuary. Ales Hrdlicka, a noted anthropologist, wrote about his visit to Attu: "The dreamless restoring nights. Have tasted simple pure values." A visitor in 1937 recalled the generous hospitality afforded her party by Mike Hodikoff, the Attuan chief, and fellow Aleuts on "the shores of their little Eden." Coast guard officers who knew the area claimed that Attu's people "are by far the happiest and best of all the Natives because they live in such a remote situation and bad influences don't come so easily their way. They . . . don't want to be brought into closer touch with the world. They are always the most friendly and helpful . . . lending a hand if required." Alice Petrivelli, an Atkan leader, described Attuans as "dignified, quiet, laid-back, calm."

Even though they were aware of events at Pearl Harbor, these independent people seemed to feel immune to the possibility of war reaching their own isolated shores, with one exception.

MIKE, IN A REMINISCENt *mood one day, told us of their hatred and distrust of the Japs. On one occasion, some thirty years before, a party of Attu fox hunters camped on the far side of the island were surprised by Jap marauders who had a bundle of fox skins stolen from the Attu people. In the battle that followed, some Attu men were killed, Mike's father among them. After that, they never went trapping or hunting*

Top: Aleut boys with pet fox, Attu, spring 1942. COURTESY OF ALEUTIAN/PRIBILOF ISLANDS ASSOCIATION. *Middle: Aleut girls, Attu, spring 1942.* COURTESY OF ALEUTIAN/PRIBILOF ISLANDS ASSOCIATION. *Above: Aleut children at Attu, spring 1942.*

Main Street, village of Attu, spring 1942. ALASKA'S DIGITAL ARCHIVES, AMRC-b83-7-5.

without arms. If an enemy was encountered, there was only one order—
kill him. One time, they came upon a party of Jap marauders who got
away before they could be dealt with, but a storm soon came up which
must have wrecked the Japs' boat because, later, a bundle of furs, which
the Attu people recognized as belonging to them, was washed ashore,
together with wreckage of the Jap boat.

So they were always prepared for the Japs, but for the past three
years, Mike solemnly assured us, no Japs had been seen. That November
[1941], he came excitedly to report that one man had sighted a strange
ship anchored on the opposite side of the island. No one was visible
on the ship, and he saw no one on shore, and our Attu friend, being
alone and scared, made tracks for home. Then, late in December, after
war had been declared, one of them came suddenly upon a ship quietly
waiting in a bay. He said it was too dark to see a flag or anything about
it except the lights. At once, he heard the anchor being raised stealth-
ily and it slipped smoothly away. He seemed quite sure it was not an
American ship. Foster, of course, reported both these incidents to the
commanding officer at Dutch Harbor, as was his duty.

And so the winter passed. We were too busy to be lonesome. There
were ten or twelve children of school age, but students were not limited
as to age. There were three-year-olds and forty-year-olds. Attendance
was necessarily irregular. Nine o'clock meant nothing to them, nor the
ringing of the school bell. Like most Alaska Natives, mothers did not

dream of waking children for school. When I made ten o'clock the time of opening, there were still laggards. On stormy days, when the blizzards were so thick I could not see the houses, and no one turned up, I would declare a holiday.

I have no recollection of our official record of stormy and clear days, but looking back, it seems that I could count on my fingers all the fine days of that winter. The wind velocity instrument sometimes indicated 100 miles an hour, and several times Foster was picked up bodily by the wind and carried several feet, usually toward the ocean, though he never actually landed in the water. Mike said it was a bad winter, that sometimes there were many sunny days and little snow. But our thermometer never reached zero; seven above was the coldest. Neither the harbor nor the shores were ever icebound, although snow covered the ground right to the water's edge.

Radio reception was good. We heard stations from all over the world, our news coming chiefly from England. Oddly enough, the clearest and loudest station was Tokyo. We listened often because their statements amused us. And it was from Tokyo that we first heard that war had been started not by America, but by Japan. 🌿

Etta remained optimistic, as evidenced in her letters. She referred to not getting mail out until "next summer," and, in reference to the weather, "We hope next winter will be an improvement." She continued to tell her family, "Don't worry about us. We feel as safe here as anywhere."

AMERICAN SUBMARINES, minesweepers, and various naval vessels visited us from time to time, cautioning us about lights [blackouts], and giving us news. It was through commanders of these vessels that we learned of a rescue ship coming to take the whole village to a place of safety. It was to come before the first of May, and everyone in the village was to be ready to board her at once since, under the circumstances, they could not wait for us if we were not ready.

As May passed, our friends from these vessels still advised us to be ready, the rescue ship was on the way. We were to be replaced by twelve men—radiomen and weathermen, a cook, and others. 🌿

170

Top: *Attu adults and children, spring 1942. Bottom left: Mike
Hodikoff, Aleut chief, and son, Attu, spring 1942.* Courtesy of Aleutians/Pribilof Islands
Association. *Bottom right: Aleut girl at Attu, spring 1942.*

In her last quarterly report, written to the General Superintendent
of Indian Affairs in May, Etta wrote, "School closed abruptly upon
orders to have the entire village removed to a safe place for duration
of the war."

Where boats were concerned, Etta and Foster had developed
patience. For twenty years, the arrival of boats had been entirely
dependent on the weather. They had grown accustomed to delay, so
the fact that the evacuation boat didn't arrive exactly on time didn't
concern them.

After the first of June, *several of these men who were to replace us
did arrive, but as our ship had not come, they went off again, saying
they would be back the next day.*

Being occupied with getting a few sick ones ready to travel, we were not in the least perturbed when about daybreak on June 7th, the Natives came to tell us that a ship was outside the harbor—a big ship. After an hour or two, a plane flew over. We paid no attention because we were still busy with last things to do. It would be nice to get south again.

Then Alex, one of the assistant chiefs, became much disturbed because he had seen a red spot under the plane's wings. "I think it is a Jap plane," he said. But we assured him he must have been mistaken. How could it be? At eleven o'clock, Martha came running over. "Japs coming!" she cried, and pointed to the hills. They were swarming down like an army of ants! They must have surrounded the island in their landing barges, closing in from all sides at once.

A Japanese invasion force of almost 2,000 men made a clandestine landing by ship in Holtz Bay, three miles over mountain peaks from the village of Attu.

Admiral Isoroku Yamamoto, who was in charge of Japan's Pacific fleet, had assembled a flotilla large enough to destroy any fortifications he thought existed. Two aircraft carriers, the *Junyo* and the *Ryujo*, each had about fifty planes. The main gun armaments of the warships *Maya* and *Takas* were ten eight-inch guns and sixteen twenty-four-inch torpedo guns. Three destroyers were equipped with torpedoes, antisubmarine equipment, and antiaircraft guns. Japan had the largest submarines in the world. They had the fastest underwater speeds, could carry three floatplane bombers, and employed the best torpedoes available. Five of these submarines were in the flotilla and had Attu in their sights.

The ground troops had silently made their way up the snow-covered mountainside until they reached the summit of a mountain pass where they could see the tiny exposed village down below.

Unaware that they were about to witness the beginning of the end of their village, the Attuans leisurely walked the short distance from church to their homes on Sunday morning, June 7, 1942. As they looked at the mountains that normally sheltered their homes, they were horrified to see armed men in unfamiliar uniforms slipping, sliding, and running down the snow-covered side of the mountain, all the while shrieking and shooting their guns. Instead of an organized march into the village, the attack was utter chaos. The Japanese lost their footing in the ice and snow and while yelling unintelligible words, they fed on each other's fear and that intensified the assault. When they slipped and fell on the icy terrain, their guns went off, random bullets sometimes wounding or killing some of their own. They quickly learned that the merciless island landscape was as deadly as a bullet. The screaming intimidated the intended victims and bolstered the invaders' courage. Consumed with sheer terror, Attu adults quickly gathered their frightened families and barricaded themselves in their houses while the gunfire and yelling continued to assault the village.

SUCH A WASTE OF EFFORT *because one rowboat could have come right in through the open harbor and encountered no resistance. Foster's shotgun was the only working weapon on the whole island. They could not realize the island was not heavily fortified.*

Aleuts with bows and arrows, Attu, spring 1942.

173

Bullets began raining through the windows, and stones were dislodged and came crashing down the chimney. At almost the moment of their arrival, Foster had been trying to send the weather through to Dutch Harbor on his regular eleven o'clock schedule. Reception had been bad, and he sent it blind, as he had often done. But now, he added something else. Four words: "The Japs are here!"

Foster and I did two things. As the Japs swarmed down the hillsides, I thrust into the fire all the letters and reports that I could find. Foster smashed the radio. I do not doubt that the Japs had much more information than were contained in those letters and reports, and they brought their own transmitter.

When the hail of bullets lessened, Foster went out to give himself up. A young Jap officer then burst through the door and thrust a bayonet at my stomach, saying over and over, "Do not cry. Do not cry." It exasperated me. I had no intention of crying.

The Jap officer was young, and could speak enough English to make himself understood. He was very nervous, certainly, but he finally made me understand that he wanted me to go outside. "Take nothing," he said. "We must search."

I went outside to find Foster surrounded by four Japs with bayonets. The Natives had been brought from their houses, and they herded all of us to an open tundra area near the school. There, we received mimeographed copies of a proclamation and, when we were all together, I was told to read this to the assembled company. I tried to keep one copy for myself because it was a document worthy of a place in our history, but it was taken from me. It was addressed to the inhabitants of Attu and informed us that the Japanese had come to rescue them from the tyranny and exploitation of the Americans! We had nothing to fear. The Japanese had only our best interests at heart. We would be allowed to pursue our normal way of life, but we must not try to hinder the Japanese and must strictly obey all orders. The Natives must not try to help the Americans. If they did not obey, they would be severely punished. We were introduced to the commander, a squat, typical Jap, and we were instructed as to the niceties and joys of the "salute" to him. He made a speech, too, through an interpreter, but I could not now for the life of me tell what it was about.

Etta Jones and Attu Natives, in a photo taken by Masami Sugiyami,
Japanese photographer who accompanied the Japanese invasion force,
June 7, 1942. FROM MASAMI SUGIYAMA, ICHIMAI NO SHASHIN O OTTE ARYUSHAN O YUKU..

The speech was received in stoic silence. One woman had been
shot in the leg, but they would not let me dress it. Their own first-aid
men looked after it. These men had shoulder kits marked with the
familiar Red Cross. They carried her into the schoolhouse and dressed
her wound. While all the houses were being searched, we were kept in
the schoolroom the remainder of the day.

The Natives, for whom the Proclamation had been designed, were
finally allowed to return to their homes where an armed guard was
standing at the door. Upon entering, they found that while they had
been detained in the school, Japanese troops had destroyed their homes.
The previously neat, clean, organized houses were now in shambles.
Broken furniture, destroyed household goods, food and clothes littered
the floor, shattered dishes spilled out of demolished cupboards, and religious icons were damaged or missing.

Foster and I were kept in the schoolhouse because Jap officers
had taken our home. While waiting in the schoolroom that first day,

Foster and I talked with some of the officers. Most of them spoke a little English, and all carried English-Japanese dictionaries. When an English word that they did not understand cropped up, the dictionaries were brought forth and the word was industriously looked up. They spoke freely about themselves, telling of their families in Japan, and of how long they had served in China. They were seasoned, crack troops. We wondered if the English preparation and the apparently picked men might not signify the Japs' expectation of going on into the States.

Foster and I were told to go to an empty house because the Japs wanted ours for themselves. We were allowed to take whatever we could manage to carry. The Natives were not allowed to help us, and so I had to carry part of a heavy bed. The fog had turned to a drizzle and it had grown dark. The ground was getting treacherously slippery, as it will in the Aleutians. I did not move fast enough to suit the soldier in charge, so he knocked me down with the butt of his rifle. He kicked me then, and ground his heel into my stomach until I thought I would faint. He seemed to enjoy it. During that trip, I saw them knock my husband down three times—for no reason at all. That night my husband and I spent together in this barren house, with no lights or other comforts. Neither of us mentioned to the other about how we had been treated. It was simply a subject we didn't talk about.

Foster Jones (back to camera) and Japanese soldiers, just before Foster was shot, Attu, June 8, 1942. From Masami Sugiyama, Ichimai no shashin o otte Aryushan o yuku..

176

The next morning, the commanding officer sent for my husband to come to headquarters. 🌸

The main purpose of the Aleutians operations by Japanese task forces was threefold: (1) to defend the Japanese homeland from an attack by United States naval carrier task forces through the Northern Pacific Ocean, (2) to protect Japan from an attack by the United States land-based bombers using air bases in the Aleutian Islands, and (3) to create a diversion from the Battle at Midway. The Japanese knew Foster sent daily weather reports to the naval base at Dutch Harbor, and they accused him of including military secrets in the weather reports. Foster was the only male non-Native on the island, and he was the only one who knew how to operate the transmitter radio. Through an interpreter, his captors demanded to know what secrets he had passed on to the U.S. Navy. Foster responded to his captors time and time again that he did not have any knowledge of military maneuvers or secrets. The interrogation dragged on, hour after hour, the Japanese insisting that Foster was withholding information while Foster emphatically denied all accusations. The Japanese demanded that Foster repair his smashed radio and show his captors how to send and receive messages. When he responded that he did not know how to repair it, the Japanese shot him in the head, killing him instantly.

Kept in isolation, Etta was terrified for her sixty-three-year-old husband. Where was he? How long were the Japanese going to hold him? They had heard about Japanese atrocities in China and she was afraid he might be victimized the same way. She was frantic with worry and fear.

Foster was dead, but instead of telling Etta the tragic news, guards frequently came to her while she was alone and told her Foster was well, that he was warm, and he sent her his love. Etta wondered to herself about these assurances, but gratefully accepted them rather than let her hostile captors sense her doubt. In mental and emotional turmoil, the hours dragged on until, finally, some guards ordered her to come with them. She was taken to a room where, lying on the floor in a pool of his blood was the body of her husband. Even though she had known in her heart this was how it would probably end, seeing him lying there dead was too much to comprehend. The Japanese, however, were not yet finished. They forced her to watch as they beheaded him. Barely able to stand, she was roughly ushered back to her isolated quarters.

Gripped with fear, Etta languished in solitary confinement, struggling with the unspeakable horror she had just witnessed and the enormity of her situation. She fixated on the image of her husband's murder. She anticipated her own imminent death. Would she also be shot? Or worse? The brutality of the death of the only man she had ever loved overwhelmed her. They had spent nineteen magical years together. They had shared experiences that others could only dream of or read about. Now he was dead.

On November 28, 1945, Mike Lokanin, one of the Attu Natives, wrote to the *Seattle Post-Intelligencer*, telling what happened to Foster's body after Etta was led away by the guards. "[The Japanese guards] call us in, [Foster] was half sunk in his own blood. They wont let me see his face or body. He was wrapped in blanket. The tol me to bury him without cofin. So I dug a grave by our church. Measure destains from corner of church with my eyes and try to remember wind direction. It was burried in SW corner of church grave depth 7 ft. disent from church to grave 15 ft. After that I bury him that was end of them then and I never try to forget where I berried his body. And Iamai [one of the Japanese guards] was by me all the tiem I work. We don't know what Japs might do to [Etta]. She is sick. . . . Mr. Iamai received 3 stars. He got high after Foster got murdered."

I WAS PUT INTO A SMALLER CABIN, *and the chief was told to appoint some of the villagers to stay with me, but they could not talk with me. A Jap guard stood right outside the door. I heard some of the news in whispers. Mike [Hodikoff] said he was allowed to go to the commander with requests and complaints, and he got results. For instance, the soldiers had stolen all their outboard motors. They were unable to go out for fish. When he complained of this, every motor was ordered back. Then, the soldiers stole the fish! After this complaint, the village was roped off, and the soldiers were forbidden to go inside the ropes.*

A Japanese soldier said one morning the commander was coming to see me and I was to be prepared for questions. When I saw him, I could understand the change in treatment. He was not the same little monkey we had bowed to. This one was tall and grave in manner, intelligent, and gentlemanly in bearing. His uniform was of excellent material, well made, and covered with gold braid. He spoke entirely through an interpreter, wanting to know all about our business in Attu, all about the Natives, about surrounding islands, what I knew of Kamchatka, and what business my husband had with the Russians. He seemed satisfied with my evasive answers, and urged me to send for any of our things that were in the schoolhouse.

Next day, I was told a naval commander was coming to see me. He was a cocky, arrogant little person, and his eyes stabbed hatred. He plainly did not believe what I said, and, through an interpreter, remarked that if I did not tell the truth, I would be "severely punished." He looked quite capable of dealing the punishment. He was sure we had communications with Russia through Kamchatka. He wanted me to tell him all about an island near Dutch Harbor. I think now he meant Adak, but I knew nothing of Adak, or of any other place he asked about. Finally, he said that my husband had warned the Americans of the approach of the Japanese. They had heard him on the ship. That Foster had said, "Japs coming, Japs coming." And I answered just as positively, "No he did not say that. He said, "The Japs are here."

I was not sure what was going to happen to me after that interview, but I did not care. The whole world seemed to whirl and totter, and those bleak Aleutian crags, almost lost in the gray-white fog, seemed as unreal as a nightmare. I had to cling closely to God, to the certainty that He was still on His throne, that what was happening to me on this strange and lonely island was not happening everywhere. Yet, I was soon to know, it was happening almost everywhere, everywhere but down in the States. And I could not be sure that it would not happen there. These Japs were poised and arrogant. Attu, Kiska, Dutch Harbor, Juneau, and then down to Vancouver and Seattle.

That was the whirl of my mind. And then, one morning, I was notified suddenly that I had one hour in which to prepare to sail for Japan as a prisoner of war.

179

With a resilience of the human spirit that few people possess, Etta did her best to obey the order. Into her trunk went winter and summer clothes, family heirlooms and photos, Native-made artifacts, and some colored construction paper, crayons, colored pencils, scissors, and stationery.

> I TRIED TO SAY GOOD-BYE *to the Natives, but I could not see them all. I learned from the chief that Foster had been buried in the hallowed ground by the church.*
>
> *I was put into a launch with my baggage and taken to the big ship outside the harbor. Looking back, I saw Martha, one of the Attu women, waving to me from her doorway. She waved until I could no longer see her.*
>
> *On the floor of the launch was something I tried not to see, but it kept burning itself into my eyes, into the very core of me. It was the American flag, torn to ribbons and soaked in the dirty bilge water of the launch.* 🌿

The Japanese troops had deliberately soiled the flag with the soles of their boots, all the while sneering at Etta. When she averted her eyes, a soldier knocked her to the deck and viciously kicked her. Stunned by the violence, the pain increased her determination. She pulled herself up to her full height of five feet. She was then taken to a cabin on the ship where interrogations began. The Japanese were convinced she and Foster had been communicating with the Russians as well as the Americans, but after endless hours of accusations and denials, the Japanese finally acknowledged that she was not withholding military information. A bruised, grieving, and exhausted Etta was led to a tiny room on the ship where she was pushed inside. The door closed and locked behind her.

Etta was scared, and felt more alone than she had ever been in her life. Everything she had known and loved was gone. Her world had changed. The entire world was changing. War had reached Alaska.

13

The Australians

January–July 1942

❦

The United States' Pacific military leaders General Douglas
MacArthur and Army Chief of Staff General George C. Marshall
overestimated the power of their own forces and underestimated the
strength and ability of the Japanese. Like Sherman's army during
the Civil War, the Japanese Army obliterated everything in its path
while gaining complete control of the South Pacific. By May 1942,
the Japanese had succeeded beyond their wildest expectations. A vast
new empire had fallen into their hands so quickly, and at so little cost,
they were tempted to go farther. If their forces could move into the
Solomon Islands and the southern coast of New Guinea, they could
threaten Australia and cut the American line of communications to
MacArthur's base in the Philippines. If they could occupy Midway
Island, only 1,000 miles from Honolulu, Hawaii, they could force the
American fleet to pull back to the United States' West Coast.

Compulsory evacuation orders were issued in December 1941,
for all Australian women and children at Papua New Guinea who
were dependents of missionaries or men in the military. Due to the
threat of a Japanese invasion, they were to return to their homeland. Feeling a strong sense of duty, civilian, Australian Army, and
Methodist missionary nurses chose to remain behind. Very soon,
however, it became too dangerous for them at their outposts, so they
were evacuated to the safety of the Sacred Heart Catholic Mission at
Vunapope, Papua New Guinea.

This self-sustaining settlement was nestled between the water-front and the mountains. Several hundred people of seventeen nationalities lived in this complex of three convents, boarding schools, a seminary, dormitories, a hospital, a magnificent cathedral, large vegetable gardens, and lush flower gardens. Germans were on staff and Red Crosses were worn and posted throughout the grounds, so the residents felt the Japanese were not a threat. They were wrong.

There was nothing unusual about the morning of January 25, 1942. Then, just as in the invasion at Attu a few months later, this quiet setting was disrupted as thousands of Japanese, shrieking and poking the air with machine guns, bayonets, and swords, ran across the mission grounds and surrounded the hospital, their guns aimed at the nurses. At the same time, screaming armed soldiers drove at breakneck speed up the gravel driveway and came to a halt beside the hospital. The soldiers jumped out of the vehicles, yelling, all the while gesturing with their rifles and machine guns for the nurses to line up. All residents of the mission, even those who were bedridden, were forced at gunpoint and fixed bayonets to form lines, hands raised above their heads. Some of them would stay this way, standing in the hot sun, arms raised, for hours as they were interrogated one by one.

Dora Wilson, one of the Methodist nurses, said she was too numb to be afraid. Many of the soldiers looked very hot, and dirty, and she guessed that they had been shut up in a ship's hold for weeks, waiting to go into battle. Some of them looked so very young, and valiant, charged with the great task of taking all before them for the emperor. Their great moment had come and, weapons in hand, intoxicated with patriotism, fear, and tension, fingers on the triggers, they were facing their enemy. "Their enemy. We are their enemy," she thought, "nurses and [100] sick men, nuns and mission staff. It was ludicrous."

The questioning went on for endless hours while nurses and their patients stood, their shoulders aching and perspiration soaking their entire bodies. If the response to a question was unsatisfactory, the Japanese slapped the startled nurse's face or hit a patient's open wound with his sword. Tootie Keast, one of the army nurses, said, "I got the most fearful whack, and I was knocked down and got a few kicks because I didn't bow deep enough. I did bow my head, very begrudgingly, but, from then on, I did bow deeply." At long last, with the questioning over, the nurses and patients were ordered to bow and bow low. The Japanese told the nurses and their patients, "You will not be shot today," and they were allowed to return to their duties, but not before twenty of the patients were taken away, executed, and buried in a mass grave.

In light of what they had just experienced, it was difficult to resume a routine as simple as returning their patients to their rooms and beds. And when they returned to their own quarters, they discovered that their neat rooms were now in shambles. Broken beds and ripped mosquito nets lay in a tangled mess on the floor, food containers with bayonet holes in them were thrown everywhere, and glass from broken bottles was scattered across the bed sheets. All of their personal possessions were either gone or broken beyond repair.

They did their best to put things back in order, and anticipated getting some rest after what had been a most traumatic day. Rest, however, would not come because the drunken Japanese soldiers had different plans. Away from their officers' watchful eye, the soldiers, staggering around from the effects of alcohol, snuck into the nurses' rooms and tried to fondle and kiss the women. When the women protested, the soldiers wrenched their arms and hit them in the face. In the hope of finding someplace safe, the nurses sometimes slept under the patients' beds.

Tenko meant roll call. When *tenko* was yelled out, the nurses were to line up and they were counted over and over and over. The women wondered if the Japanese could actually count because they did it so many times, never seeming to get the number correct. They thought, "How can it be so difficult? There are only seventeen of us." *Tenko* was yelled or whistled frequently and randomly during the day and night. While the women stood in line for the endless counting, the soldiers would brandish bayonets, slap the women for no reason, and threaten them.

Tootie recalled, "Some of the Japanese were so dreadful, and they thought we were just big jokes. Many is the time they chased us trying to urinate on us while the rest of them just stayed back and screamed with laughter. It was nothing for them to take their trousers off and things like that. We just had to put up with it."

One day, the nurses saw a disheveled woman escorted to the mission by Japanese guards. Kathleen Bignell, a British national in her fifties who was estranged from her husband, had remained at her plantation when all other civilians evacuated the island. She escaped into the jungle hills with several men and hid for a month until she learned that her son, Ted, an Australian soldier, was at the plantation looking for her. Risking her life, she returned, but, instead of finding her son, she was captured by the Japanese and taken to Vunapope. The Japanese put her with the group of nurses and they now numbered eighteen.

The women's daily rations of rice, fish, and milk started to diminish in February. The mission kitchen had provided them with bread but the quantity began to markedly decrease as ordered by the Japanese. No longer allowed to work in the hospital, the women settled into a mundane routine that was dictated by a daily schedule, printed in English and enforced by the guards. All activities, including their scanty meals, cleaning their rooms several times every day, and trips to the bathroom, were signaled to begin and end with an annoying whistle. There were constant searches of their quarters and frequent *tenko* with bayonets poked in their backs, and threats of assault, rape, and violent death. The women had often seen Australian men walking by the mission carrying shovels and ropes. They were flanked by Japanese guards armed with bayoneted rifles. This sight was most often followed by a sound that struck sheer terror in their hearts. They learned that the shovels were used by the men to dig their own graves.

The guards were always present, and the women were repeatedly made to bow low. The women feigned respect with this gesture, but they did respect the fact that the unpredictable Japanese soldiers had the power, and they might use it at any time.

Elsewhere, beyond the compound, Allied prisoners of war were suffering at the hands of the Japanese. In April, the Bataan Death March cost 10,000 American and Filipino lives due to starvation, dehydration, and malaria. Violent deaths at the hands of the Japanese were the result of random beatings, torture, and execution by bullets, bayonets, or beheadings. The Battle of the Coral Sea in May set the stage for the Battle of Midway in June.

Looking toward the waterfront, the women watched helplessly as more and more Japanese ships and thousands more Japanese troops came ashore. They also witnessed daily military flights out of Rabaul, now a Japanese stronghold. Some of the women had been evacuated to Vunapope from their beloved Rabaul. They had been holding out for rescue by the Allies, but the buildup of Japanese forces made that seem less likely every day. They were distraught, hungry, and sick. Due to the lack of nourishment, dysentery set in. They did have rich coconut after their bread supply was cut off, but it didn't stop the dysentery. Soldiers guarded the bathrooms, and every time the women had to use them, which was frequently, they had to bow before entry was allowed.

On June 22, at 4:00 A.M., the soldiers yelled to the nurses to get up, and with bayonets fixed at their backs, the women were forced to line up outside. This time, they noticed the convent nuns were also in line. Soldiers went into the living quarters, got everything that was in the rooms, and threw it all on the lawn—clothes, books, personal possessions, and diaries. The women stood in line for seven hours for seemingly no reason, and were then told to disperse. On that same day, a priest, Padre John May, told the women that all the Australian men in the POW camps in Rabaul, including most of the mission doctors, had been put on the *Montevideo Maru* and were shipped out. They had been given no warning and their destination was unknown. Those not sent were army officers and a dozen or so civilians who were kept to do specialized work. Mary Goss was the only married nurse, and her husband, Tom, was a member of the New Guinea Volunteer Rifles, the coastal defense group that was quickly overpowered when the Japanese had invaded Rabaul in January. The priest couldn't find out anything about Tom, but he

The Montevideo Maru, *the Japanese ship that transported*
captive Australian military and civilian personnel from Rabaul, Papua New
Guinea, to Japan. En route, the ship was torpedoed, and all those on board were
lost, spring 1942. FROM WWW.MONTEVIDEOMARU.INFO/INDEX.HTM.

did have information that Mrs. Bignell's son and son-in-law were on the ship. The prisoners included more than 800 in the Australian Lark Force, the remnants of the New Guinea Volunteer Rifles, and over 200 civilians and plantation owners and managers, senior civil administration officers, missionaries from all denominations, and Norwegian sailors who had survived the sinking of their ship, the *Herstein*. The priest told the women that because one of them, Grace Krueger, was sick in the hospital, she wasn't worth the trouble and because of her, the women were not included in the *Montevideo Maru's* departure.

The ship was not appropriately marked as one carrying human cargo. Had it been, attacking forces would have known that hundreds of POWs were on board. No one knows whether this was an oversight or a cruel joke, but the missing insignia cost the lives of everyone on board when the ship was torpedoed by the American submarine *Sturgeon*. Mrs. Bignell would not learn the news until after the war was over.

On July 5, almost six months after their capture, the women were ordered to pack their belongings and be ready in one hour. They were told they were going to "Paradise," where there was no malaria. They were too afraid to ask about this paradise because experience had taught them that to ask a simple question could provoke beatings or worse. The women hurriedly packed what was left of their meager belongings and were taken to a truck where the mission nuns were waiting for them. The nuns and priests gave them more clothing, old fancy dresses, towels, blankets, soap, and bottles of wine that were used in their religious services. The clergy and the nuns were the only ones allowed to see the women off. Together they sang "Auld Lang Syne" and "Home Sweet Home" before saying a tearful goodbye.

For six months, the nuns had provided a compassionate sanctuary, and words couldn't express the women's gratitude. Weighted down with shoulder bags, cans, bottles, wooden boxes, and a few suitcases, the women struggled to get themselves and their possessions onto a truck. With a final look at what had been their temporary residence, albeit a hostile one except for the kind nuns and priests, the women were taken to the seaside town of Rabaul a few miles away.

What had been a picturesque, tropical waterfront resort was now a visual testament to the ravages of war. Shells were all that remained of formerly elegant buildings. Landmarks were destroyed. Along the waterfront, tiny huts were barely visible because of the debris that threatened to bury them. Uprooted trees were used as posts for barbed wire. Broken trees covered the landscape and parts of sunken vessels protruded above the water. Wharves and landing strips cluttered what used to be an inviting and tranquil swimming lagoon, where the women had spent pleasant times.

When the truck rumbled closer to the wharf, the women could see several ships in the harbor, none of them very big. Under the guards' vigilant eyes but with no offer of assistance, the women were told to get their possessions off the truck and onto a barge anchored at the dock. Then, bouncing over the waves and leaving the ruins of Rabaul behind, they were taken to a freighter whose smudgy white letters gave her name as the *Naruto Maru*. There was no insignia to indicate that prisoners of war were on board.

A rope ladder was suspended alongside the hull of the ship. Bobbing up and down in the ocean swell and hampered with their cumbersome parcels, it was difficult to transport their belongings from the barge to the freighter. Swaying with the motion of the waves and clinging to the ropes with clammy hands, one by one,

The Naruto Maru, *the Japanese ship that transported Australian POWs from Rabaul, Papua New Guinea, to Japan, July 1942.*

the women somehow maneuvered it all and struggled to the top of the hull. Next, they had to grope their way backward down another ladder onto the deck. Once there, they put down their belongings and waited to be told what to do. The guards, however, appeared to be consumed with indecision. After several minutes, one pointed to an opening in the deck and ordered, "Down there!" Once again picking up their luggage, and led by army nurse Kay Parker, they trudged backward down the steep ladder into the ship's hold. They had been captives for more than five months, but this seemed like a literal prison, more like solitary confinement, in terms of light and airflow. It was hot, dark, and empty—slatted wood floors, high walls, some shelves, but no beds or furniture. In an attempt to make light of the situation, Kay announced that in spite of the lack of food, water, light, and a view of the sea, things could be worse. The others wondered how that might be possible.

Several hours later, there was a sudden commotion on the deck above. They heard the stamping of feet and the murmur of voices, and those voices were speaking English. When long brown legs descended the steep ladder, the women were astonished to see men they knew! There were men from the New Guinea Volunteer Rifles, officers of the 2/22nd Battalion including the commanding officer, a handful of men from the 1st Independent Company of Kavieng, and a Royal Australian Air Force Intelligence Officer, sixty men in all. When the last man entered the hold, the hatch was slammed shut.

Seeing these men gave the women hope that their men were still alive. The women couldn't wait to start asking for news about their doctors, government officials, and enlisted men who were captured in Rabaul. Mrs. Bignell was especially anxious to know the whereabouts of her son and son-in-law. Mary Goss was concerned about her husband, but all the officers could tell the women was that they had seen the men marched out of camp with their luggage, but never saw them again.

The anchor was pulled and those in the hold embarked on what would be a most unpleasant journey.

It was comforting to have the men with them, but with the hatch closed, the hold was unbearably hot. Overcrowded conditions and the lack of the most elementary hygiene made life below decks oppressive and intolerable, especially during the long nights. When they were ready to sleep, the guards opened the hatch, but sleep was difficult because the only source of air was the hatch, and they tried to squeeze in so they could benefit from the air that came through the small hole. The group was crammed so tight, sleep was a problem, one they tried to solve by sleeping in shifts. While some tried to doze off on the hard wood floor, others stood and quietly waited their turn. Although seventy-eight bodies were packed in a small twenty-by-thirty-foot space, the Japanese managed to crowd some of their own into the hold to guard the prisoners. This seemed absurd. How could they escape? Where would they go?

As time wore on, the heat in the hold made it almost literally suffocating. The odor of sweating bodies permeated the enclosed space. The Japanese solution to the problem was salt baths. Each person was given the equivalent of two cups of salt water per day to wash their clothes and themselves with soap that did not lather. The water caused those with sensitive skin to break out in a rash. Many of the men had suffered bouts of malaria while being interned in Rabaul, and others had tropical ulcers. The stifling, unsanitary conditions in the hold did nothing to improve their condition.

Privacy was a distant memory, although the men tried to create a semblance of it with the use of a screen. Toilets were cubicles attached to the top deck, hanging over the side of the ship with no doors. There was no privacy from leering eyes, and the POWs were afraid of falling overboard and becoming food for the sharks. They all suffered from diarrhea and dysentery. There were frequent trips to the toilets, but there was never any toilet paper. Added to this, the group felt the ship zigzag at times, and they wondered if they were darting around submarines.

As in the previous months, food continued to be a problem. They ate meals of watery rice while squatting on the floor in the hold. The men had planned ahead, somewhat, by smuggling some fruit on board, but with seventy-eight mouths to feed, portions were ridiculously small. Drinking water was very limited.

Time passed agonizingly slowly. One endless day would finally succumb to nightfall only to be followed by another. There was nothing to do, nowhere to go, and nothing to see. All they could do was talk with each other, and even that could be frustrating. They worried aloud about their families and wondered where they were. Concern for the safety of their men in the Australian Army and Navy was consuming. Less stressful conversation centered on gourmet meals and the wonderful times they would have when they were all free again. The hope was that they would be rescued, but that would mean bombing and death, so, for the first time, they were hoping the Allies or Australians would not bomb the ship and that they could be rescued peacefully.

The group speculated on where they were going and why. The men reasoned that the Japanese wanted the women out of the way so the enemy could continue its deadly maneuvers. It was suggested that because there were so few of the women, the Japanese could not possibly put them in large prison camps filled with men, so perhaps the women would be used in exchange for Japanese prisoners of war. If that were true, wherever they were going, it would not be for very long. Reflecting on their experiences over the previous months, the women were reluctant to place their hopes on exchange, but they could not help but wish for it.

One morning, all of the prisoners were brought on deck to observe the ceremony that honored the ashes of the Japanese war dead. The ship had been entrusted to return the ashes of war soldiers to Japan. It was also rumored that the list of those on board the *Montevideo Maru* was in the officers' possession, but the prisoners were told nothing of this. The question of where the ship was going was answered—it would be somewhere in Japan. It also meant the women could hope they were going to be exchanged for Japanese prisoners of war. The men resigned themselves to the fact that, in all likelihood, they were going to Japanese prison camps.

After nine insufferable days and nights in the ship's hold, the boat docked. The seventy-eight POWs, among the first to arrive in Japan, emerged from the hold, dehydrated and bewildered-looking, carrying suitcases and shoulder bags from which dangled tins, bottles, and bags. When they got their first glimpse of Yokohama in Tokyo Bay, on one side they saw an industrial center enveloped in smoke. On the other side, a steep, green, tree-covered bluff rose above the water's edge. They saw no warships. Instead, fishing fleets and sailboats with striped sails dotted the harbor. The fact that Japan was at war with the Allies was not evident in this deceptively peaceful setting.

A small, black-coated man and six bureaucrats dressed in white uniforms heavily trimmed in gold met the group on the dock. The leader was from the Foreign Office, and after this first encounter, the women called him the Undertaker because they felt his black uniform matched his dark demeanor. Like the indecisive Japanese when the women boarded the ship, the Undertaker seemed undecided as to what to do, then made them line up, and, because of their experience with *tenko* while at Vunapope, they did this quickly and efficiently. He checked names and numbers, and pointed with his index finger several times while yelling to make sure everyone was there and accounted for. As the men were taken away, they tried to reassure the women they were probably going to be exchanged. The women were encouraged not to give up hope. They wondered whether they would ever again see these men who were their only semblance of protection. Anxiety gripped the women as they watched the men depart.

The first stop for the women was the Customs Shed. The lackadaisical attitude of the officers lounging inside the building made them wonder whether the Japanese were drugged. The women were searched lethargically for cigarettes and books, had to sign "no escape" forms, then were loaded onto the back of a truck, which they labeled the Black Maria. They were so used to being forced to bow low, and being screamed at and poked with bayonets, they reeled from this new indolent approach. Confused and anxious, they were hastily transported from Yokohama's wharf area through city traffic.

Everything about the place was strange—the people, the demeanor of those in charge, the architecture, and the signs in Japanese. Because of their work at outpost mission stations, some of the women had not been in a city for three years. The new sights, sounds, and smells were disconcerting. They didn't have long to take in everything that surrounded them because in a very short time, the truck started to slow down.

14

Bund Hotel, Yokohama
July 1942

❦

W hen the lurching motion of the truck finally stopped and the women got out, they were amazed. They did not see a POW camp with barbed wire and armed guards. Instead, they were standing in front of a beige two-story building with the words BUND HOTEL in English above the hotel's entrance. The front of the hotel had garden beds, potted plants, and windows adorned with lace curtains. Fighting hunger, fatigue, and the disgust at the sweaty, makeshift garments clinging to their dirty skin, the women wrestled with

Bund Hotel, Yokohama, the first camp in Japan for Etta and
the Australian women as prisoners of war, July 1942.

193

their cans, boxes, and suitcases as the Japanese guards herded them into the hotel. At one end of the lobby was a sitting room with comfortable chairs, ottomans, sofas, and coffee tables. The furniture and potted plants gave the room a cozy ambiance. At the opposite end of the lobby was a large, well-appointed dining room. An impressive traditional Japanese garden and quality furniture filled the lobby. They were at a hotel that had originally been used for Western guests; in another time, this could have been a charming vacation spot, and as prisoners of the Japanese, their accommodations could have been a lot worse.

The Undertaker led the women upstairs, where they discovered the Bund itself was infinitely more inviting than their host. The bathrooms, with hot running water and all the comforts of an Australian hotel, were a welcome change from their dark captivity and the other perpetual reminders of their status as prisoners of war.

The first thing the women wanted to do was get rid of nine days of filth and pointless salt baths they had taken in the confinement of the ship's hold. After each had luxuriated in a hot tub, albeit with soap that would not lather, the women were led downstairs to the dining room. They were fed a decent meal, their first in six months, and were then introduced to the hotel's short, stout manager, Mrs. Saito. With a scowl on her face and a harsh tone of voice, she told them they were at her hotel out of the goodness of her heart, effectively dispelling any feelings of good will on behalf of the Japanese. She said that no one else would have them, and her portrayal of the reluctant hostess made them wonder why she would.

After their meal, Mrs. Saito's stinging words resonated in their heads as the women enjoyed a leisurely walk on the waterfront with armed guards as their escorts. They were prisoners who had been snatched away from their work, homes, and families. The men they saw as depraved and evil now had control of their lives in this hostile land.

During their walk, they observed that some Japanese mothers were dressed in traditional, elegant garments while others were wearing Western attire. The children were running, playing, and laughing under the watchful eyes of their parents who quietly conversed among themselves. The Japanese civilians were simply going about their everyday lives, as if a war was not going on. The women were struck with the irony of it all. The civilians they saw were just people, and the experience of observing them humanized the Japanese people for the Australians. The women decided then that they would be exchanged for Japanese prisoners. They looked in the harbor and saw the black ships with white crosses, similar to the International Red Cross logo, emblazoned on them. Those were their ships. It wouldn't be long before they were on one of them, heading home where they belonged.

With this conviction, the women returned to the hotel lobby, where they saw someone they hadn't noticed earlier. From behind the potted plants appeared a diminutive white-haired lady, with tears streaming down her cheeks. Whytie, one of the Australian Army nurses, later wrote, "There was this dear little sad lady who told us later she had never been so happy in her life as when she heard us speaking English. She had arrived before, and was so alone on her own and did not speak Japanese. From that moment, she became one of us." She introduced herself as Mrs. Etta Jones. She had been there, by herself, for a month, and had thought she might go crazy. But now that these girls were here, she might be all right. "We were young (twenty-five to thirty-five years old), and she was always Mrs. Jones to us."

All except one of the Australian women had a nursing background. Kay Parker, Eileen (Cal) Callahan, Andy Anderson, Lorna (Whytie) Whyte, Tootie Keast, and Mavis Cullen were Australian Army nurses serving in Malaya and New Britain. Dorothy Beale, Jean Christopher, Dora Wilson, and Mavis Green were nurses from Methodist missionary hospitals at Malabunga and Vunairima, inland from Rabaul. Civilian nurses Joyce Oldroyd-Harris, Joyce McGahan, Grace Krueger, Alice Bowman, Jean McLellan, and Mary Goss worked at Namanula Hospital, the Australian government's Administration Hospital in Rabaul, on the island of New Britain. Dorothy Maye had been stationed at the Government Hospital at Kavieng, on the island of New Ireland. The exception to the nursing profession was former plantation owner Kathleen Bignell.

Over the next few days, Etta gradually told them how she had ended up at the Bund, after the brutal murder of her husband. When recounting her story, Etta could not have known that news of the Attu invasion had spread across the United States. The Army base at Fort Richardson in Anchorage wired the Naval Air Station at Kodiak on June 12, 1942, requesting information about the weather station and personnel at Attu. Captain R. C. Parker, Commander of the Alaskan Sector of the United States Navy, responded, "I regret to inform you that Attu appears to be in the hands of the Japanese and the white residents there are presumably prisoners. What disposition was made of them, whether they have been detained at Attu or are on board some Japanese naval vessel, or have been taken back to Japan for confinement with other U.S. prisoners, I cannot say. I would suggest that you communicate through the official channels of your Department—first, to notify the relatives of the white people who were at Attu. . . . "

Etta's family was not notified through official channels. Instead, they learned of the invasion in newspaper accounts, most of which were riddled with errors. A Seattle newspaper article read, "The only white inhabitants of Attu, Mr. and Mrs. Charles F. Jones, school teachers of Marion, Ohio, attempted suicide rather than be captured by Japanese when they seized the island on June 7, 1942, Army authorities disclosed. Jones succeeded in killing himself, officers said, but Mrs. Jones survived and was taken as prisoner to Zentsuiji, Japan. . . . The Joneses were probably the first Americans in this war to attempt suicide to avoid capture." Another newspaper wrote, "Old time friends of Mr. and Mrs. C. Foster Jones are much concerned over their present whereabouts and [are] wondering if they are being given the right kind of treatment by the Japs, who took them prisoners when they seized the island of Attu where they were teaching and maintaining a weather bureau station for the U.S. government. On July 10, friends in Dutch Harbor and Kodiak are reported to have recognized the voices of the Joneses in a long-distance radio conversation from Attu. Permission was granted by their captors, and they named individually the forty-five persons who were inhabitants of the island and engaged in raising blue foxes, fishing, and making Native crafts noted the world over."

Foster's sister, Anita, who was living in New York City, wrote to the Alaska Indian Service seeking accurate information, and was told on June 29, 1942, "I regret very much that we cannot give you any definite information regarding Mr. and Mrs. Jones; however, we received a radiogram from the General Superintendent of our Alaska [Indian] Service in which he stated they were probably taken as prisoners of war when the Japanese occupied Attu Island. The Office of Indian Affairs regrets exceedingly that it was not possible to evacuate the employees and Natives of Attu prior to the attack by the Japanese."

In response to an inquiry by a friend of the Joneses who was also a former Alaska Indian Service employee, the general superintendent, Claude M. Hirst, wrote her, "I regret to inform you that it now appears that Mr. and Mrs. Jones are prisoners of war. We have heard nothing from them since the morning of June 7, when Mr. Jones sent in the weather report for that station."

Superintendent Hirst wrote to Foster's brother, Dr. Xerxes Jones, in Detroit, Michigan, "As you no doubt read in the papers, Attu Island has been taken by the Japanese, and we must presume that Mr. and Mrs. Jones are prisoners of war. The last message to come from them was on June 7. Mr. and Mrs. Jones have been in our Service for many years, and it is with much regret that we must advise you of their present plight."

In the hotel, the women saw and heard American and European missionaries who had come from China but were forbidden to speak with them. When the missionaries boarded the exchange ships, the nineteen women had renewed hope that they would be next. They were under the impression that the Japanese didn't know what to do with them, because they were given no chores, so the ladies decided they were just there to wait until they were exchanged.

Although they marveled at the blue sky, bright sun, little shrub-like trees, and tiny houses scattered on the hillside surrounding the bay, their own surroundings were permeated by a pervasive stench. With nothing else to do but wander the halls and look out the windows, they soon discovered the source of the putrid smell. Open

sewers in the streets combined with the odor of rotting garbage contributed to the problem, but the primary source was the fertilizer

Bund Hotel brochure, outside (top)
inside (bottom), June 1942.

of human feces used in the vegetable gardens. With their nursing backgrounds, they were appalled at the possibility of diseases being transmitted by this unsanitary practice.

One evening, accompanied by guards, the women were taken for a walk. They noticed people living above small shops and wondered why they engaged in the seemingly pointless practice of hanging laundry on vertical poles that stood perpendicular to the flat roofs. To them, it would never smell clean. Added to these nauseating smells were the unpleasant perfumes both sexes used in excess. The women remarked to each other that it was no wonder the Japanese wore nose and mouth masks.

The presence of mosquitoes and the biggest rats they had ever seen only added to the POWs' already overwrought state. They missed their mosquito nets from the tropics, and were horrified to see that the rats had the run of the hotel, chewing anything and everything they wanted, including small children who would cry in pain. These same young children were puzzling to the women: they couldn't figure out whether the parents were hotel employees, guests at the hotel, or homeless. The children ran around the hotel all day, playing, yelling, and screaming, then would fall asleep whenever and wherever they happened to be at the moment—in the lobby, in the hall, or on the stairs.

Officers from the Foreign Office made daily visits to the women, always lecturing them on their negligible significance to the Empire of Japan. If that were true, the women wondered, then why not just let them go home? The guards pestered them with personal questions that they found offensive and annoying: "Are you married? Why aren't you married? How many children do you have? How old are you?" Since they weren't told why they were in Japan and were being held against their will, why should they answer such invasive questions?

In spite of their distressing circumstances, this group of optimists continued to watch the harbor for the exchange ships—big black beauties with white crosses painted on them. Very little international commerce was going on, but they could always see the exchange ships, at least one every day. Most of their conversations centered on their exchange which they felt was more and more imminent.

These feelings were validated when the women were sent to a doctor for a physical examination. It made sense to have this exam because the Japanese would send the women home in good health, and their enemies could report how well they were treated. Also, the POWs felt this precaution would be a required health clearance for the shipping line. Entering the examination room, however, they were horrified to see that it opened directly onto the street. The doctor told them, in a very stern voice, to take off all their clothes. While doing this, the women could be observed by people passing on the street. Worse, their guards and the police stood nearby in the room, carrying on conversations, occasionally looking at the women, acting as if nothing unusual were happening. Nudity, the women learned, was an accepted part of Japanese culture, but they weren't Japanese. In what would become part of their coping system, they steadfastly refused to allow their captors to see them weak or embarrassed, so they acted nonchalant, but they were mortified and humiliated.

In addition to verbally abusing the women, Mrs. Saito's contempt for her Australian and American detainees was obvious in the food she gave them. The quantity and quality diminished drastically after their first meal. To compensate, the women started stealing carrots, onions, and anything that couldn't be detected by the guards. They were concerned about the fertilizer that was used on the vegetables, but they were hungry, and all they could do was hope they wouldn't get sick.

Occasionally, the POWs would find a discarded copy of the *Nippon Times* in the potted plants. It was a pro-Japanese newspaper, written in English, used primarily to give its readers news of the war. The publication was a source of delight for the POWs because it gave accounts that they were fairly confident were not accurate. It reported splendid Japanese victories, but never recounted Japan's losses, which they would later learn were many.

While at the Bund, the women marveled at a culture that was so different from their own. They compared everyday items—shoes, cars, buses, baths, bicycles, dresses—with what they missed from back home.

The method of watering the indoor and outdoor gardens was a lesson in how to make a simple task more complicated. Every morning, an old Japanese woman came in with a bucket of water and a ladle. She scooped the water into the ladle, slurped the ladled water into her mouth, then spit the water onto the gardens until each plant had moisture. The procedure took a great deal of time. It was obvious to the POWs that, rather than use this prehistoric method, it would be so much quicker and easier if she just used a watering can or hose directly on the plants. It was the women's first experience in how menial tasks were made complex. It was all but comical to them.

The large dining room was sometimes used for social occasions, and the women could observe these gatherings from a distance. One evening, the event was a recital. The audience was all male, and every man present performed. There were several intermissions, during which everyone drank *sake* and shoveled what the women thought was disgusting-looking food into their mouths with chopsticks. The recital went on for hours, and the Oriental music made the women long for Western melodies from home.

While leaning out of their windows one day, the POWs observed a funeral procession. Crowds lined the street, houses were swathed with flags, bands were playing, and men dressed in brilliant traditional dress, complete with high black headdresses, carried the ashes of a fallen soldier. This was the essence of *bushido*, the ancient Samurai code of honor and behavior for a Japanese warrior, which emphasized self-discipline, courage, and loyalty. To the Japanese, the ashes of a dead soldier had great, almost God-like power to do incredible things for the emperor. The warrior should prefer death to laying down his arms. To surrender would be the most disgraceful act. Like almost everything else they had observed in the Japanese culture, this was completely contradictory to what the women believed.

Etta had packed pens, pencils, and paper when she was evacuated from Attu. She could have had no idea at the time how significant those supplies would become. As with any group, latent talents can surface under the most unusual circumstances. People find they are much more skilled in certain areas than they had previously thought—music, art, mechanical ability, sewing, cooking, and so on. In Mrs. Bignell's case, it was poetry. Before the war, she had been so involved with her various businesses, she hadn't had time, perhaps not even the inclination, to devote any effort to writing poetry. Now, however, with plenty of time on her hands, she began to describe, in poetry, her impressions of events as they occurred in their lives. Mrs. Bignell's poetry and the women's journals and diaries were written surreptitiously, some even in code, because if the guards discovered their writings, punishment would be swift and harsh.

While waiting for their exchange, time passed monotonously. There was nothing to do but wander the halls, eat their skimpy meals, and hope. Everything focused on the day they would be set free. They talked about what they would eat, what they would wear, whom they would see, how they could find out what had happened to the men in their families, how they could catch up on family news as well as war news, and how they could help the Australian and American war effort.

As the end of the second week approached, the women were baffled by Mrs. Saito's heightened animosity toward them. She made an ominous declaration: "I do not like policemen in my hotel. You will be moved to a place near the sea, but it is not nice like here." Ever since their capture in Rabaul, seven long months ago, they had been subjected to the unreasonable and erratic behavior of the Japanese. Where were they going, and why? Since they were to be exchanged soon, why were they being relocated temporarily? The women kept vigil on the exchange ships in the harbor. They watched as Americans and Europeans came through the hotel and went directly to the ships, so it was logical to assume they would also be boarding one soon. But one day, they looked out the window, and saw that the exchange ships were gone.

15

Yokohama Yacht Club

1942-1943

On August 3, after one month at the Bund for the Australians and two months for Etta, they were ordered to pack their things. Mrs. Saito had been right. They were leaving the Bund. With their meager belongings in hand, the internees boarded the Black Maria. The guards and driver were well armed. Japanese and German nationals lined the streets and jeered as the bus bounced along the bumpy roads. The women were frightened enough traveling to an unknown destination with their armed captors, but the riot-like atmosphere and blatant hostility coming from the crowd intensified their anxieties. Relief washed over the group when, after several miles, the bus stopped in front of the white, two-story Yokohama Yacht Club, a former waterfront recreational facility for foreigners. In the high cement wall that surrounded the club, there was a metal gate. The irony of the gate was not lost on the women: while it was originally there to keep "a certain element" out of the club, now it was used to keep prisoners locked inside it.

The guards led the women through the gate, and the women saw tennis courts and a swimming pool. Ushered through an elegant lobby, the facility's tacit hospitality reignited their hope that the Japanese meant them no real harm, and talk of an exchange again became their preoccupation. They reasoned they were going to be treated well and fed adequately enough, and their short stay at the "Club" wouldn't be so bad. Once upstairs, through cracks in the high walls, they could see another exchange ship. They kept their eyes peeled on that ship, thinking they would be boarding it very soon.

The man in charge of the kitchen was Fuji-san. Bowie [Alice Bowman] described him as "a spritely old Japanese and the nearest approach to our alleged ancestors that one could ever wish to see. His wrinkled face was like a dried up prune from which two slender beads glittered. From the back he looked pure chimpanzee—elbows stuck straight out from his shoulders. To complete the picture, all he needed as he tottered around in his *geta* was a fur coat. *Geta*, the clumsy, thonged, wooden shoes worn by all Japanese for any occasion, seemed to me to be the cause of this tottering gait, especially when the soles came in varying heights and styles. Fuji—we had no intention of calling him anything else—made no secret of his dislike for us, and in his presence we kept a certain wariness. He spoke with a brand of pidgin English exclusively his own. No other Japanese we encountered used pidgin, though some used very odd English. Fuji had once been a seaman and so this must have been where he picked up this useful jargon. We had no difficulty understanding him, nor he us. Old Fuji was a great thorn in our side, because he understood Europeans better than any other Japanese we had been in contact with. We felt he could read our minds. Fuji had very keen hearing and we were certain he understood what we were saying when we whispered to each other. As time went by, there seemed to be no doubt that Fuji's role was to spy on us. He was invaluable to the guards and others as an interpreter. Any new guard who was reasonably affable toward us would soon change his attitude after morning tea sessions with Fuji. Often, when we were working in the kitchen, Fuji banged his cleaver on the wooden table and made threatening remarks, such as 'More better *Junsa* beat you, more better you die. Japanese soldier like die, no like come back.' During these episodes we were petrified with fright."

The facilities did not provide the privacy they had at the Bund. The women now had sleeping quarters in what had previously been a large dance hall. Their beds were Japanese *tatami*—thin floor mats woven of rice straw, normally used to sit on while eating. They clustered their mats together in three groups: the civilian nurses in the middle, the Australian Army nurses and Etta at one end of the ballroom, and the Methodist mission nurses at the other end. Mrs. Bignell, always independent and now consumed with the unknown whereabouts of her son and son-in-law, chose to be by herself. Also in the room was a Japanese female guard who positioned her *tatami* in the room so she could keep a watchful eye on the women. They had learned that every name ended in "san," so they named her Mama-san but never used the term when addressing her. Very soon, Mama-san's animosity toward the women became evident.

Formerly the housemother at a home for delinquent boys, and not very happy with her duty as a guard for nineteen white women, Mama-san started telling the male guards untrue stories of misdeeds the women had committed, just to get the women in trouble. On the rare occasion when Red Cross supplies arrived, Mama-san's feigned attitude toward the women was very friendly. On her own, she ate her hot, nourishing meals in front of them while they ate their tasteless meals of watery rice soup.

In Japanese culture, guarding prisoners was almost as dishonorable as being a prisoner. Therefore, the Japanese assigned misfits and troublemakers to the task. Basher and Komatz occupied adjoining rooms. The women never learned Basher's real name, so they gave him one they considered appropriate. As a coping mechanism, they labeled people and things to create a shared understanding of the frighteningly unfamiliar. Basher and Komatz had recently been discharged from the army, and they embraced their new assignment. They now had the opportunity to inflict fear and terror in the hearts of the enemy, and they were zealous about it. The women could tell that Komatz was very sick with tuberculosis, and they also felt he was mentally impaired. They thought Basher was manic-depressive because he displayed extreme mood swings. Sometimes he ranted and raved at the terrified women, while at other times he was meek and docile. Whatever the guards' mood, the women learned very quickly to appear as if they understood everything that was incoherently screamed at them, just to avoid getting hit, knocked down, or threatened with a sword.

Komatz and Basher taught the women how to serve the healthy and nutritious meals that were prepared for the guards. They were to bow very low and say in Japanese, "Deign to accept this honorable food," and while still bowing repeatedly, withdraw from the room by taking small steps backward to the door. The guards taught the women to be polite while serving food, but the women made their own observations about the guards' manners. When they ate their hot meals, the guards squatted on the floor, held the bowl of food to their mouths, and literally shoveled large quantities of food into their mouths. Eating was interspersed with many grunts and a lot of belching, then they wiped their mouths on the sleeves of their uniforms. Mac [Joyce McGahan], raised on a farm in Queensland, commented, "Just like the pigs on the farm. Makes me feel homesick."

After a few days, they noticed the exchange ship was back in the harbor. Cautious optimism returned. They resumed their care- ful watch of that ship, hoping against hope they might still be exchanged.

Kay Parker held the highest rank among the army nurses. With her rank, leadership qualities, and her height, the women decided she should be their spokesperson. To the short Japanese, Kay's imposing six-foot stature was a source of intrigue. While she stood up straight, the Japanese walked around her, looking her up and down. One of them got a stool, placed it in front of her, stepped up on it, looked her in the eye, then got down and walked away without saying anything. During *tenko*, Basher used the same stool to reach her face so he could slap her. Outwardly, Kay was impassive to the scrutiny and slaps, but she silently raged at the humiliating spectacle.

At all hours of the night, while the women were trying to rest, Basher and Komatz would charge into the room and scream at the women to stand in line. Satisfied that their order had been obeyed, they would then retreat to their private rooms. Later, the guards would again burst into the women's room just to make sure they hadn't gone to bed—they were to remain standing. These frequent and petty intrusions went on until the guards finally retired for the night, and only then could the women collapse on their thin straw mattresses, cold, exhausted, and hungry. They had only been at the

Yacht Club for a month, but this routine was well established, and the POWs had already learned to do exactly what they were told, no matter how ludicrous. They were holding onto the hope that the exchange ship would eventually liberate them.

One day, when they peeked through the cracks in the wall, expecting to see the familiar and comforting sight of the exchange ship, their hearts sank when they saw that it was gone. The emotional pendulum swinging from high hope to utter despair was taking a toll on their nerves. The women came to the realization that they might be prisoners in Japan until the war ended . . . maybe for years. They even feared they might never get home, but they refused to accept that. They were determined to wage their own war of survival.

Mama-san decided they could do something useful, so she had them knit little silk bags. The bags, two inches by one inch, with fringe on the bottom, were used by Japanese soldiers to hold religious icons. The women also folded and glued envelopes, although they were never allowed to use the envelopes to mail letters to their families. When making the envelopes, the women discovered that, in spite of the putrid smell, there was a slight taste to the glue. Out of sheer hunger, they started eating the glue—whenever the guards weren't watching.

The women were confined to the Yacht Club building, with no trips off the grounds. Several times a day, they were ordered to stop knitting and gluing, and stand in line while Basher and Komatz screamed at them. Basher would frequently brandish his sword and glare at the women menacingly. He would lunge at them and knock them down. During the frequent lineups, they were slapped in the face for no reason. Most of them were taller than Basher, so slapping their faces posed a problem: sometimes, while standing on tiptoe, he was able to reach the victim's face. Other times, he barely came up to the woman's shoulders, so he would get his stool and step up on it so he and the victim were at eye level. After glaring at her for several minutes, he would proceed to viciously slap her while screaming, *"Gosha* [Australian] pig!" The women were also struck with the butt of the guard's rifle. They learned to respond stoically, refusing to let the guards see them defeated or humiliated. But when they were alone, they cried.

The tedious nature of their daily lives soon gave way to overwhelming boredom. All nineteen were used to hard work, and their monotonous daily tasks were so menial in nature. Day after week after month, they sewed the little bags, folded and glued envelopes, and responded to *tenko* for lineups. Someone was always slapped at the conclusion of *tenko*.

Their immediate needs were threefold: more food, better beds, and hope. To break the tedium and boost morale, they worked up the courage to request permission to hold religious services. Surprisingly, permission was granted. The women were of different faiths, so they combined liturgies and sang songs everyone knew. Writing out the words to different hymns helped break the pattern of the endless days. During the services, the guards carried on loud conversations among themselves, ignoring the women's attempt to worship. The services were not attended by all nineteen women. There were those who wondered where God, if He existed, was, and why He would allow them to be victimized. Those who had faith felt reassured by the services.

The eighth day of every month was "degradation day." The women were lined up and forced to watch as the guards threw fresh vegetables into a cesspool. The POWs then had to rake the vegetables out, boil, and eat them. At the conclusion of the meal, they had to kneel and bow in the direction of the emperor's palace. The repugnance of bowing was barely tolerable, but they managed to keep their hostile feelings to themselves.

"Humiliation day" occurred whenever the guards were feeling especially hateful. The women were forced to put their heads in pig buckets and eat a sparse meal while the guards laughed. This was the Japanese way of letting them know they truly were *"Gosha* Pigs."

During the summer months, each woman wore a single dress, but as fall approached, the weather cooled and the dress was not adequate. Some of them didn't even have a sweater because they'd been living in the tropics. Etta's trunk was full of warm clothes, and she offered them to the others, but her short stature of barely five feet made them useless for the tall Australians. In October, Mama-san arrived with a bolt of thick fabric suitable for making new clothing. "For winter," she explained, and cut it into four-yard lengths for each woman. Within days, a sewing machine arrived—"for three weeks only"—and their normal chores of envelope making and bag knitting were set aside while each POW sewed a warm garment for herself. The fabric was coarse and very prickly against the skin, but at least it would offer some protection from the cold weather.

While they were sewing, the ship with the white crosses was seen in the harbor again. It seemed to come and go each month. "Maybe we won't need to wear these horsehair things after all—it's spring in Australia and we could easily be home in time for summer!" they thought hopefully. When all of the garment sewing was completed, the women lined up for their own style show. They had varying sewing skills, and Kay tried to make light of the situation. She had a good laugh and said, "All we need is a new hat each and we'll be really flash for our Melbourne Cup party" [similar to the Kentucky Derby]. "Just look at us! I hope you've all left room to move in these elegant garments so we can bow deep enough to satisfy the chief."

The Japanese guards, *junsa*, came from the Foreign Office once every month. The POWs were forced to bow to any and all visitors who arrived, *junsa* included. At that time, a uniformed Japanese officer, whom the women named "Chiefo," carried out an inspection of the prisoners and handed out toiletries, including sanitary napkins. Because her white hair revealed something about her age, he didn't give any to Etta, but she insisted that she receive the same items as everyone else. After the inspection, she gave hers to the other women.

Fuji had fed them nothing but thin, watery soup, and they suffered from malnutrition. They had stopped menstruating, but they hoarded the sanitary napkins just to feel like they had something of their own. Chiefo always ended the inspection and dispensing with a speech that never varied in content: "Do good works and obey!" At the conclusion of his speech, the women were made to bow in the direction of the Imperial Palace. During the second bow, they were forced to kiss the Japanese flag as it was passed among them. Only then was the flag raised to the top of the flagpole and the women allowed to return to their chores. On the surface, this was a very civil ceremony, but they were quietly seething at this forced display. Later, one of the nurses said to the others, "You know when we were supposed to kiss the flag this morning? I spat on it." Then, with an unemotional tone and a straightforward gaze, she told her fellow captives what she would like the soldiers to do with the emperor they revered.

There were infrequent visits by a doctor. In spite of their emaciated appearance and complaints of diseases they had contracted—they were nurses and knew the symptoms—the doctor declared them fit. He prescribed aspirin for every illness.

The temperature continued to drop. The women were issued no blankets, shoes, or warm clothes. No hot water was available, but they were allowed to take a cold shower once a week. It was too cold to sleep comfortably, so they tried to get warm by lying in pairs on one thin *tatami* and putting the other *tatami* over themselves. They would rub each other's hands and feet in order to keep their blood circulating.

As Christmas approached, they decided to celebrate it. They were determined to uphold tradition with the people who were functioning as their families. They even began to think the Japanese were being tolerant of their efforts when a Christmas parcel arrived from the American Red Cross. The package was given to them, but the contents had been removed, proving the Japanese were anything but supportive of their captives' religious holiday. But Etta had a limited supply of colored construction paper and crayons in her trunk, and the women were given permission to decorate their room. Whytie later wrote, "You have no idea how those crayons were treasured. They were like pieces of gold. We all wanted to borrow them at odd times." They made a construction paper horseshoe and placed it over the door for good luck. That particular decoration was removed by the guards because they thought it was a "V" for victory. After removing the horseshoe, the guards followed up the gesture by again slapping some of the girls in the face.

In spite of their limited supplies of Kleenex and paper, they worked hard to make gifts for each other. This had to be done surreptitiously, when they were supposed to be knitting and gluing. For Etta, the homemade gifts reminded her of those she and Foster had received from the Alaskans. The Natives had used the scant materials available to them, but the gifts were heartfelt and sincere.

Making cards for each other helped raise spirits. Birthdays, Mother's Day, anniversaries, relatives' birthdays—any occasion was a good excuse to fill the paralyzing, mind-numbing days.

The diminishing food supply was turning the women into accomplished thieves. As they walked through the kitchen, they furtively stole anything they could tuck into their armpits or clothes so it wouldn't be detected by the guards. They didn't care if the food was old or moldy. Once in their rooms, they put the pitiful contraband between the wallboards. When they were able to steal a few moments away from the watchful eyes of Mama-san and the guards, they eagerly retrieved it. Because of the small size of the group, theft or any other deviation from Japanese rules could be detected easily. So they had to stay on "high alert," which was wearing on the women.

The freezing weather, scant meals, and cold showers caused most of them to become ill. They were told it was the coldest winter in seventy years, and the guards did nothing to improve conditions for them. For a short time, they had a tiny hibachi stove over which they tried to warm their hands and feet, but like other privileges, it was suddenly taken away for no apparent reason. That day, Basher yelled at them for several hours. Early the next morning, he ordered *tenko* and the women were forced to stand in line all day. That night he lunged at them with his sword, and if the women hadn't dodged out of his way, they would have been killed. During *tenko* on the next day, he hit the girls in the face, head, and chest.

The women felt even more isolated when they became snowbound. The white landscape gave a tranquil appearance to the grounds, but it also made worse how cold, hungry, and sick they were. They were sometimes able to steal half a biscuit from the guards' tray; they didn't care if the guard had coughed over his food.

Last Letters from Attu

Diarrhea, dysentery, beriberi, and tapeworms were persistent problems because of their lack of nutritious meals.

The guards continued to give the women what they thought were lessons in manners during *tenko*. They repeatedly taught the women to bow, walk backward taking tiny steps when serving meals, all the while making polite comments about the delicious food and showing respect for the Japanese flag. The women had also taught themselves a few things about coping with these ridiculous rituals. They learned to remove their glasses and false teeth before *tenko* so they wouldn't be broken when their faces were slapped. But even this action backfired because sometimes these items were confiscated and not returned. One guard took the glass out of one of the women's pair of eyeglasses and wore the frames.

Yokohama Yacht Club

1943-1944

While Etta was struggling to survive in Yokohama, back in the United States the Red Cross, the military, and bureaucrats in Washington, D.C., were aware of how letters of inquiry were circulating, seeking answers to the whereabouts of Etta, Foster, and the Attuans after the Japanese invasion. Sketchy and inaccurate information continued to be all that was available.

Alaska Indian Service, Juneau, Alaska
April 23, 1943
Carol Rivers, Executive Secretary, The American Red Cross
Tanana Valley Chapter, Fairbanks, Alaska
Dear Mrs. Rivers:

In reply to your letter of April 13, 1943, this is to advise you that Attu Island was captured by the Japs last summer at which time Mr. and Mrs. Charles Foster Jones and the Aleuts residing there were presumably taken prisoners of war.

To date, we have not received any information regarding their circumstances or where they may be located. The Juneau Red Cross Chapter has recently written to the American Red Cross in San Francisco, California, for information, in case they have been able to ascertain definitely what treatment they may be receiving.

Yours very truly,
Fred R. Geeslin, Acting General Superintendent,
Alaska Indian Service

Alaska Indian Service, Juneau, Alaska
June 9, 1943
Mr. F. A. Latimer, American Red Cross
1115 Fourth Avenue
Seattle, Washington
Dear Mr. Latimer:

This is in response to your letter of May 26, regarding Mr. and Mrs. Charles Foster Jones. We have not had any information on Mr. and Mrs. Jones since June 7, 1942, when the Japs landed on Attu Island. We have wondered whether the Red Cross could obtain some information. On April 23, we wrote to Mrs. Carol Rivers, at Fairbanks, Alaska. If the Red Cross can secure any information, we would appreciate receiving same as we are very anxious to have any news concerning them, and in case we hear of anything we shall notify you immediately.

Yours very truly,
Claude M. Hirst, General Superintendent,
Alaska Indian Service

Also in June, Frank Lundin, Foster's prospecting partner and best man at Etta and Foster's wedding, wrote the Bureau of Indian Affairs, seeking information about the fate of his friends.

U.S. Bureau of Indian Affairs
Juneau, Alaska
June 25, 1943
Gentlemen:

I am somewhat hopeful that your office may have some knowledge regarding Mr. and Mrs. C. Foster Jones, whom I believe were on Attu Island [at] the time of the Jap invasion. The writer and Mr. Jones were prospecting and mining partners in Ruby, Alaska, for a number of years and I also knew Mrs. Jones at Tanana, Alaska, so you can readily see my interest in them and my hopes that nothing serious has happened to them. [If you have] any information about them at this time and if your department is at liberty to report such information, I would appreciate hearing from you.

Yours truly,

Frank Lundin

American military forces recaptured Attu in May 1943. The battle was a bloody one, second only to Iwo Jima in the number of casualties. After the American victory, Claude Hirst, General Superintendent of the Alaska Indian Service, wrote to the Acting Director of Information of the Alaska Indian Service in Chicago, Illinois.

June 16, 1943

Dear Miss Williams:

Since my letter to you of June 12, I have a report from one who has just come from Attu that the Jap prisoners who were taken there stated that the Natives and Mr. and Mrs. Charles Foster Jones were taken to the island of Sakhalin as prisoners of war.

I was given this information with the understanding, however, that no publicity would be given this matter. All the buildings in Attu village were completely destroyed.

Yours very truly,

Claude M. Hirst, General Superintendent,

Alaska Indian Service

In July 1943, the Office of the Assistant Chief of Staff for Military Intelligence wrote to the Acting General Superintendent of the Alaska Indian Service in Juneau, Mr. Fred R. Geeslin.

Dear Mr. Geeslin:

It is a matter of regret that we can tell you nothing verified or quotable about Mr. and Mrs. Charles Foster Jones.

I have been on the ground you mention, and am deeply interested in the fate of the fine people you name. I have information from a man who was with the Joneses shortly before the enemy occupation, indicating that they were alive, well, and were doing a splendid job for you, for the other agencies they served, and of living generally. The picture was one of people who enjoyed their work, loved life and people, and could not be expected to take the way out that is suggested by the story you quote.

For your information and not for publication, unverified reports stated that Mr. Jones shot and killed himself when the enemy landed, that Mrs. Jones attempted to cut her wrists in a suicide attempt that failed, that Mrs. Jones is a prisoner in a Japanese camp, and that forty Aleuts from Attu are safe in a Japanese camp. I cannot vouch for the source of these reports; it is even possible that they came from Radio Tokyo.

We shall keep your inquiry on file. If and when any positive information becomes available, we shall rush it to you. Meantime, it is requested that you do not quote any part of this letter. Facts that in themselves may be of no consequence can, here and now, provide a valuable index to the enemy with respect to sources of information we are or are not using. American lives might pay if channels were closed or erroneous information planted.

Sincerely,

Luther Meyer

City of Atlantic City, New Jersey

On July 23, the Executive Department in the City of Atlantic City, New Jersey, however, felt they had official confirmation of the fate of Etta and Foster. The mayor wrote to Etta's brother, Russ.

Mr. R. T. Schureman

9305 Winchester Ave.

Atlantic City, New Jersey

Dear Mr. Schureman:

The people of Atlantic City deeply regret the untimely demise of your brother-in-law, Charles Foster Jones, and the imprisonment of your sister, Mrs. Jones, in a concentration camp at Zentzuji, Japan.

The City Commission, recognizing the various expressions of sympathy and appreciation of all our citizens for the outstanding courage, bravery, and gallantry of your sister and her husband, have forever with indelible ink, impressed upon our records his passing, a copy of which I am forwarding to you herewith.

With heartfelt sympathy in the sad bereavement over the loss of your brother-in-law and with every good wish that your sister will soon return to you in good health, I am

Sincerely,

Thomas D. Taggart Jr., Mayor

Claude M. Hirst responded to another inquiry in August 1943.

Dear Mrs. Call:

I have your letter of July 12 inquiring as to the fate of Mr. and Mrs. C. Foster Jones who were at Attu. There have been rumors and some reports given out over the radio recently to the effect that Mr. Jones committed suicide and that Mrs. Jones was taken prisoner with a number of the Natives. However, none of these reports have been confirmed by official sources. I regret, therefore, that we can not state definitely what did happen to Mr. and Mrs. Jones.

Very truly yours,

Claude M. Hirst, General Superintendent,

Alaska Indian Service

In Yokohama, conversation among this unlikely band of internees centered on their families. It seemed impossible that their relatives would be doing anything but searching for them, yet, they wondered if the folks back home had given up on finding them alive. The women hadn't received any letters, so the tangible proof of thoughts and prayers from home was absent. Etta's family members were doing all they could to find out what had happened to her. With no word from any source as to Etta and Foster's whereabouts, they contacted the International Red Cross, but the Japanese Red Cross refused to respond to inquiries. Foster's sister had written to the Alaska Indian Service in 1942, then again in 1943, always hoping for a definitive answer to what had happened to her brother and sister-in-law. The Service replied as follows,

Miss Anita Jones, Assistant Director, Maternity Center Association
654 Madison Avenue
New York, New York
October 26, 1943
My dear Miss Jones:

The Secretary of the Interior received a letter from the War Department, Bureau of Public Relations, dated September 11, transmitting a copy of a letter to Miss Ruth Gruber, Field Representative for the Department of the Interior, from Russell Annabel, United Press correspondent, which was forwarded by the Alaska Defense Command. The letter is stamped "confidential" because the information is based upon Army Intelligence information gained from the diary of a Japanese correspondent. The letter and the circumstances surrounding the acquisition of this information as to Mr. and Mrs. Charles F. Jones, your brother and his wife, are not for publication. The following is an excerpt from the letter. "Information on Mr. and Mrs. Charles Foster Jones came from 'A Journal of the Aleutian Campaign' by Domnei correspondent Mikizo Jukujawa, who spent some months with Jap forces on both Kiska and Attu. According to him, all prisoners were removed to Sakhalin Island. No mention was made of the disposition of prisoners taken on Kiska. Mr. Jones, according to Mikizo Jukujawa, slashed his wrists and died. Mrs. Jones slashed her wrists, and Japanese doctors saved her and took her to Karafuto, where she is healthy and happy as a prisoner of war." We have no way of verifying this report at this point, but thought that you would like to have the information, even though the original source may or may not reflect a true report. We shall advise you if further information is obtained.

　　Sincerely yours,

　　Paul Fickinger

The news was devastating. The families knew that in all probability the information was incorrect, but they still didn't have answers as to the location or fate of Etta and Foster. The incident at Attu had occurred sixteen months before, and after all this time, there was no accurate information about what had really happened. Etta had not tried to commit suicide, nor was she being held at Karafuto, Sakhalin, or Zentzuji, as reported by U.S. government agencies. But the drudgery of her and her eighteen companions' life was excruciating. *Tenko* continued, along with the customary bowing in the direction of the Imperial Palace. The meals were always the same—moldy bread, watery soup, and tea—and the serving portions continued to diminish. The women wondered every day why the Japanese were keeping them barely alive. Was it possible that exchange might still happen? They could only hope, and that hope was what kept them going.

Boredom, apathy, and illness were their constant companions, and the sameness threatened to be just as damaging as their hunger or illness. There was no radio, mail, or newspaper except for the occasional copy of the *Nippon Times*. At first, the women had enjoyed access to a bookcase full of bad novels written in English and outdated technical manuals. But soon, even those items were taken away. It was as if the Japanese wanted to take away any little thing that they believed might break the insufferable monotony. The women had made tens of thousands of the little sewn bags and folded, glued envelopes.

Fuji, the cook, had given them seeds to plant in a garden. The garden work was a welcome relief, and they hoped this chore would mean they might get more to eat. They looked forward to lovingly tending the garden and harvesting the vegetables, even though they weren't familiar with the strange seeds and plant names.

One day, the guards told the women to pack their belongings. This was finally it! At long last, they were going on the exchange ship. They each retrieved one good dress that they had saved for just such an event, and with hopes held higher than they had been in a year and a half, they dressed and quietly lined up for what they thought might be the last time. With their meager belongings in hand, they boarded the familiar Black Maria. Instead of going to the ship, however, they were taken to the police station.

They were shown to the room where they would be staying, and they were appalled at the "amenities." Contrary to their first impressions of the Bund Hotel and the Yacht Club, this place did not look promising at all. The toilets were slits in the floor, and the toilet area was not partitioned off. The police officers, or anyone who was in the building, could watch the women while they relieved themselves, so they decided to use the toilets in pairs, one guarding the other's privacy. There were no showers or baths, so personal hygiene was nonexistent. Fuji rode his bike to deliver their meals. Rice was virtually the only food they got, but the women were thrilled that the size of the portions increased while they were at the police station. They reasoned Fuji didn't want to get caught serving the inadequate amounts that he had gotten away with at the Club.

The women soon discovered that they were moved to the police station to clean it. But they took on this task almost lightheartedly because the knitting, gluing, and *tenko* had stopped. The cleaning took two weeks, after which they were returned to the Club, only to discover that their garden, which they had so carefully tended, had been demolished.

Their disappointment made life at the Club infinitely worse. They continued to sew the little bags, glue envelopes, and stand in line for hours while Basher and Komatz screamed their tirades. They were given a small amount of money in return for the sewing and gluing, but this, too, was akin to the empty box at Christmas, because a certain percentage of the money was taken back by the Japanese and spent on sweets that were given to the children of Japanese sailors. The women used their paltry wages to buy extra food, but the guards who purchased it for them usually consumed it.

Large rats and cockroaches lived in the building, and the women were ordered to get rid of them, Japanese-style—chase them with a broom. This method made as much sense to them as the woman who spat water on the plants at the Bund. They had to wash the hotel bar area, the large main rooms, and the wooden kitchen floor. In summer, the floor would dry, but in winter, with no heat, the floor was transformed into a sheet of ice.

In December, Claude M. Hirst responded to yet another inquiry, this one to a former employee of the Alaska Indian Service:

December 4, 1943
Dear Mrs. Hurst;

I have your letter of November 22, 1943, and the only information we have had regarding Mr. and Mrs. Charles Foster Jones is what appeared in the newspapers soon after Attu was taken by the American troops. This was to the effect that Mr. Jones committed suicide by slitting his wrists and Mrs. Jones was removed to a concentration camp at Zentsuju, Japan, as a prisoner of war. It was also stated from the same source that Mr. Jones was killed by the Japs, which we think is probably more nearly true.

Mr. and Mrs. Jones were very dear personal friends of mine and I have been most anxious to get information that she at least is alive. If you should by any means obtain information from the Red Cross, I will appreciate receiving same. So far, we have not heard through that organization.

Yours very truly,
Claude M. Hirst, General Superintendent,
Alaska Indian Service

As winter wore on, the women were losing weight at an alarming rate. When they complained to Chiefo, he laughed at them. Whenever someone from his office came to check on conditions, the women were served good food, so in spite of their emaciated appearance, the visitors were under the impression that the internees were not being starved. When Chiefo was not present, hearty meals intended for the women were given to the family and friends of Fuji, as well as the *junsa*. The guards and Mama-san continued to eat their hearty meals in front of the women.

The only excursion outside the confines of the building was when the POWs took out the garbage. They looked forward to the task because then they could sneak some bits of food. Another chore was to get coal for the cook's stove. This required heavy buckets, and because of their decreasing weight and their ill health, this was a difficult task. Fuji would throw the used ashes outside, and it was the women's job to move the ashes to another spot. They had no shovels or tools to scoop them up, so they used broken drainpipes. After completing the task, bathing was even more a necessity, but their efforts to get rid of the ashes and soot were ineffective with the cold showers, soap that refused to lather, and no towels.

Basher and Komatz were bored with their duty, so they resorted to petty, mean behavior. During the winter months, they used tenko to mock the women. They made the women repeat the phrase, "Spring is warm in Japan!" while they stood outdoors, barefoot, in the snow. The POWs did get a small measure of revenge for their cruel treatment when the opportunity arose for language lessons. When Basher and Komatz seemed to be in a decent mood, the women asked if they'd like to learn more English. They taught their guards how to say "God save the King!" Basher and Komatz were proud of their new language skills, and they repeated the phrase over and over. There was an element of danger in tricking the guards like this, but the women somehow managed to avoid retaliation for it.

Spring finally did arrive, and the women were allowed to plant another tiny vegetable garden. They took great care with the plants and looked forward to the harvest.

With the arrival of spring and warmer weather, the rule against leaving the Yacht Club grounds was lifted and the women were allowed to walk along the sea wall. Japanese fishermen used this sea wall, and they wrapped their bait in newspapers, so sometimes the prisoners got the opportunity to look at copies of the *Nippon Times*, and could follow the progress of the war by looking at the maps.

They also used this time to get some food. They found that by using sticks with pieces of wire tied to the end, they could fish for seaweed. They never acquired a taste for it, but they ate it anyway.

Throughout the summer and fall, the monotonous routine continued. Once again, they were let down when the guards took all their garden vegetables. Their second Christmas in captivity, 1943, was approaching, and the women wondered: Did their families know they were alive? Was their location known to anyone? Did the American or Australian governments care about their plight? Did they even have a home anymore? Had the Japanese captured their homelands? Their morale was extremely low, and having hope was increasingly difficult. Still, Christmas was coming, and they forced themselves to make plans. They created little cards for each other, then at the appointed time, exchanged the cards, sang songs, and remembered Christmases back home.

Etta reflected on the special times she had shared with Foster. They hadn't had access to stores to do holiday shopping, but they'd had each other. They didn't have an elaborate feast—in fact, their dinner was usually wild game and something out of a can, but they were delighted in their unique circumstances and enjoyed each other's company. The gifts they received from the Natives, sometimes rare and special, sometimes used and "boughten," were sincere expressions of the Natives' respect for Etta and Foster. Now, Etta had eighteen female companions and she was sequestered in a country with which her beloved homeland was at war. Food was scarce and their heartfelt but sad rituals were not enough to help her forget Foster's murder for more than a few seconds at a time.

After that second Christmas went by, one plain winter day led to another.

Due to the lack of accurate information and in light of Etta and Foster's employment in the Alaska Indian Service, William Zimmerman, Assistant Commissioner for Indian Affairs in Chicago, wrote a summary of their careers in June 1944 and had it put in their personnel files. Similar to the reports of their fate, the summary included errors.

The Japs occupied Attu on June 7, 1942, and, since then, nothing has been heard of the former inhabitants, the Natives and C. Foster Jones and his wife, Etta, who went to Attu in August 1941, Jones to operate the radio station and Mrs. Jones to teach. The elderly couple had known when they accepted the post that their work would be arduous, that there would be almost no contact with the outside world except by radio, that the mail boat came through three or four times a year at most, that there was no doctor within hundreds of miles, but they accepted with enthusiasm. The pioneering spirit was in their blood.

Jones had gone to Alaska before the turn of the twentieth century, and before he was twenty-one. Born in St. Paris, Ohio, in 1879, he left there at eighteen to go to Puget Sound University in Tacoma, Washington, where he studied pharmacy for a few months. But the Yukon called, and the next thirty years found him prospecting and hunting in the Far North. Occasionally, he worked for the government on temporary construction jobs and at Tanana, on such a job, he met Etta Schureman, whose desire to serve others matched Jones's spirit of adventure. Etta Schureman had left her farm home in Connecticut to attend normal school at New Britain, and upon receipt of a teaching certificate, she taught grade school for five years. Not content with teaching alone, she studied nursing [for] three years in Philadelphia, and after twelve years of nursing and social service in Philadelphia and Pittsburgh, she accepted a teaching position in Alaska.

That was in 1923. She was a good teacher, and when she married C. Foster Jones, they became one of the best husband and wife teams in the Alaska Indian Service. Before going to Attu they had served at Kipnuk and Old Harbor, coastal towns, remarkable mainly for their remoteness from civilization. It was a background of excellent performance under conditions of hardship that led to their appointment as teacher and special assistant when the Indian Service established a school at Attu, the very last of the Aleutian Islands stretching far into the Bering Sea.

According to Don Pickard and his wife who, before the Japanese Army occupied Attu, operated a boat between Attu and Dutch Harbor, Jones had plans for any Japs who might land at their little island. He had a rifle and a shotgun and an army—which consisted of possibly a dozen able-bodied men—and was ready to fight it out if the Japs came. The Japs did come. No one knows what happened—whether the Attu islanders resisted and died trying to defend their homes, whether they tried to escape to one of the other islands, or whether they were taken prisoner by the Japs.

Until the facts are known, we can only pray that the people of Attu are still alive and perhaps will one day return to resume their rigorous way of life. And the Joneses—perhaps they, too, will return to bleak Attu—to finish a job they had just begun.

One day the women noticed that Komatz and Basher, the guards who had caused such turmoil and terror in their lives, had disappeared. They were told Komatz had died and Basher had returned to the Japanese Army. That was a good excuse for them to hold an impromptu "victory" celebration.

On July 9, 1944, the women were celebrating Bowie's birthday with handcrafted cards, and making light conversation. Suddenly, new guards burst into the room, announced that they had one hour to pack their things, that they were going to be moved again. The women had witnessed an increase in air raids, and were told they were going to the country where they would be safe. There would be more food, and they would have big gardens, but no water. That made no sense. How could there be big gardens with no water? But patience and tolerance were virtues they had mastered. The guards said they could take anything they could carry, and they did. They gathered everything they had accumulated, be it handmade or scavenged, including books, playing cards, secret diaries, tiny cards and gifts they had made for one another, handmade bamboo knitting needles, leftover silk from the endless knitting, and empty cans. They had learned to hoard anything and everything they could lay their hands on and were reluctant to part with even the smallest, most useless item. The internees boarded the Black Maria and were driven west, out of the city, leaving the Yokohama Yacht Club after two years.

17

Totsuka

1944-1945

As the Black Maria rolled through the city, it traced the route it had traveled on the way to the Yokohama police station a year earlier. Now, the city was strikingly desolate. Motorized vehicles were nonexistent—no doubt because gasoline was being used in the war effort. Pavement had been replaced by vegetable gardens and air raid shelters, and there was visible bomb damage. As they rode west beyond the city limits, however, the women saw a refreshing, pastoral countryside. Little cultivated fields and thatch-roofed cottages were surrounded by rice paddies. Tall pine trees dotted the landscape. Peasant farmers in their cone-shaped straw hats were bent over, tools in hand, tending their rice crops. Majestic Mount Fuji, the highest mountain in Japan, rose against the summer sky. The landscape helped the women relax, and they began to think that the accommodations at their next site might be almost adequate.

The bus stopped in the village of Totsuka, a small rural slum with dilapidated buildings. The area consisted of scrawny untended plants. Tree branches littered the ground. The bus emptied its occupants, and they stood in the hot sun while the truck driver and the *junsa* went into one of the shacks that lined the dirt road. Although they were temporarily unguarded, thoughts of escape never entered their minds. The women were too weak to travel any distance on foot, and there was nowhere to hide in this enemy territory. They stood and waited. After about an hour, the *junsa* returned, ordered

Left: Some children of Totsuka, Japan, 1945. Photo taken by a friend
of Etta's after the war. *Right: Exterior of the Totsuka camp, 1945.*
Photo taken by a friend of Etta's after the war.

them to pick up their belongings, and they were led single file on a
narrow path that wound up a hill through a grove of trees.

At the top of the hill sat several long, low, decrepit buildings.
In the main building, the rooms opened onto a verandah, and the
verandah surrounded a courtyard. The facility had once been a hospital for victims of tuberculosis, and the nurses were well aware of
how hazardous exposure to the disease could be. Dirty spittoons
had been discarded all around and under the buildings. Cal had been
showing signs of contracting tuberculosis—she had night sweats and
a sore throat—and this environment would do nothing to improve
her health.

The rooms allowed the women to once again live in small
groups, something they hadn't been able to do since they were at the
Bund Hotel two years earlier. Regrouping was their way of establish-
ing a small sense of order in their lives. The beds were thin quilts on
the floor. The *junsa* and the cook were housed at the end of the building, so they were out of sight and earshot, which was a relief. The
women were unhappy to learn that Fuji, the disagreeable lout who
had methodically cut their rations at the Yacht Club, would again
be in charge of their meals. In addition to cutting their rations, he
always referred to the women as "men." If anything positive could be

gleaned from this, their third location in as many years, there were no high walls as at the Yacht Club, the years of knitting little silk bags and gluing envelopes were over, and they had an unobstructed view of Mount Fuji.

The women who were physically able washed and cleaned the building. They hauled water in heavy wooden buckets to and from a hand pump located 300 yards from the building. Once the building was clean, their work really started. They carried up to 100 buckets per day to the building for cooking. Quite a distance away from the building was another hand pump, but this one had a large vat next to it. They had to fill the vat so the villagers could take their communal baths. Trucks dumped wood and coal on the roadside. The women had to carry it up the hill, stack the coal, and chop the wood. The wood and coal were used to heat water in the kitchen and the water vat. The women were manual laborers for the benefit of the *junsa* with their hot, hearty meals and the Totsuka villagers' baths. Kay Parker was a born leader—articulate, courageous when faced with the *junsa* and their irrational behavior, a tireless worker, fair in negotiations, and never visibly intimidated. She drew up rosters so the women could share the workload, except those who were too sick to help.

By August 1944, the women had been at Totsuka for one month. In the United States, the Department of the Interior had decided that Etta and Foster should be rewarded for their efforts and fate, both of which were still unknown. The department wrote to Mr. Don C. Foster, who had replaced Claude M. Hirst as General Superintendent of the Alaska Indian Service: "When deliberating on the award to Mr. and Mrs. Jones, the Board took into consideration all available information concerning their whereabouts and/or possible fate. Lacking conclusive evidence that they are no longer alive, it was agreed the award should be made. The Board understands that Mr. Jones's sister, Miss Anita M. Jones, is living in New York City and it believes she would appreciate being informed of the recognition given them."

With hope that at some point she would be repatriated, correspondence was addressed to Etta in care of the Bureau of Indian Affairs.

The Secretary of the Interior, Washington, D.C.

August 14, 1944

My dear Mrs. Jones:

Enclosed is a formal notice of salary increase which I have been glad to approve upon the recommendation of the Board of Awards of the Interior Department's Suggestions System in recognition of your outstanding and meritorious service in remaining with the Natives of the island of Attu in the face of Japanese invasion of the island.

In making the recommendation, the board did so with the full knowledge that your present condition and whereabouts are unknown but with the hope that at some future date you can enjoy the accompanying promotion.

The notice carries its own story of material reward for your loyalty and courage, but I wish to add a personal word to express my own appreciation of and thanks for the splendid service that you have rendered. On behalf of the department and the public that it serves, I gratefully acknowledge your outstanding devotion to duty.

Sincerely yours,

Harold L. Ickes, Secretary of the Interior

Her "meritorious service" was rewarded with a pay increase of seventy-five dollars per year.

The Alaska Indian Service sent the following message to Foster's sister, Anita:

September 2, 1944

Dear Miss Jones:

We thought you would be interested in knowing that the Board of Awards, United States Department of the Interior, has given Mr. and Mrs. Jones each a pay increase for meritorious service. In making the recommendation, the Board did so with full knowledge that their present condition and whereabouts are unknown but with the hope that at some future date they can enjoy their promotion.

Very truly yours,
Olive Trower, Administrative Assistant

In all likelihood, Foster's sister was pleased to have this information. But it had been more than two years since the invasion of Attu, and Anita and her family were very anxious to know the whereabouts of Etta and Foster.

Shortly after they arrived at Totsuka, the internees were told to dig air raid shelters. The women took this as a sign that the Allies were approaching. For those who were able, the trench digging started every day at 5:00 A.M. By the time the trenches were four feet deep, the women were too weak to crawl out, so they had to be pulled out. The shelters were an encouraging sign, but air raids didn't happen and, once more, as with their vegetable gardens, the women felt they had been used for unnecessary manual labor. They requested more food in order to bolster their strength, but Fuji's response was to add more water to their already thin soup.

The female guard, Oba-san, lived in a one-room shack next to the lavatories. She was a small, energetic, bowlegged woman in her early forties. She wore her hair in a knot at the top of her head, and her darting black eyes missed nothing. Oba-san would soon become the central figure in a battle of wits—hers for personal gain versus the women for their survival. At first, the women treated her like they had all of the Japanese—with caution. Eventually, they hoped to use what little bargaining power they had with her in order to acquire more food.

Except for a ferocious determination to survive, the women had little in common. They came from different backgrounds and orientations—military, civilian, religious. Since Etta had lived in remote villages in Alaska for nineteen years, she was used to isolation, but her companions at those sites were her husband and caring Natives, not a hostile enemy. Mrs. Bignell had run several business establishments. At the time of their capture, one of the nineteen was married, one was estranged from her husband, and one had witnessed the brutal murder of her husband. There was an age gap of thirty-seven years from youngest to oldest. Their interests were as varied as their backgrounds. The emotional needs of the nineteen almost mandated that cliques would be created within the group.

Although compelled to band together for food and warmth, they got on each other's nerves. They lived in the past, telling things they did when they were younger. They'd talk and talk and talk, telling the same stories over and over. Finally, out of sheer boredom, one would say in exasperation, "Oh, shut up! You already told that six times!" In spite of the hardships Etta had experienced at the hands of the Japanese, she managed to console others. As Whytie told the author, "She was always there like a mother if any of us younger ones wanted a listening ear." But living together was difficult. Oba-san fed into this by pitting one group against another. She would sneak tiny bits of food to one group, defying them to tell the others. Eventually, the women discovered Oba-san's deception, and after that they shared with each other what contraband they could get from her.

When the Japanese sweet potato crop was harvested, the women observed the Totsuka peasants nibbling on the fresh potatoes. They had never placed much importance on sweet potatoes before captivity, but now that food might be the one thing that could keep them alive. Oba-san wanted the women to knit garments for the

Dining room of the Totsuka camp, 1945. Photo taken by a friend of Etta's after the war.

peasants, so in exchange for sweet potatoes, the women agreed. The wool Oba-san gave them had to be washed, sorted, cut, and twined. This done, the women happily began knitting and their work was rewarded with the promised potatoes. Their hunger pangs subsided and sleep came easier. But without warning, the peasants took back the potatoes and the wool. They even stoned the women when they were at the well. Puzzled by this antagonistic behavior, they soon discovered that the peasants had seen Oba-san wearing the garments. She had kept all the garments for herself and had given the villagers nothing.

Oba-san told Dora that if she hand-sewed a suit for a man in the neighborhood, Oba-san would pay her twelve eggs. Dora, skeptical but hungry, accepted the offer. She worked for several days and when the suit was finished, Dora held out her hands for the agreed upon compensation. Instead of receiving a dozen eggs, Oba-san gave Dora only three. Deceit was a way of life for the internees.

The toilets—*benjo*—were the same as those at the police station—slits in the floor with large concrete containers underneath. These were emptied by a man the women called "Dan, the *benjo* man." He opened the door to the containers and scraped out the contents with a long shovel. The contents went into a wooden tub that was placed on the side of the road. The odor was fetid. Situated close to the building was a cemetery. The Japanese did not use coffins, and cadavers were buried close to the surface. The stench was repulsive. The combined odors of the *benjo* and cadavers permeated the air and wafted into the building. The women wore rags over their noses, but it didn't help. On top of the smelly gravesites, the women noticed containers of food that were left for the spirits of the deceased. The food was moldy, hard, and reeked, but at night, when they could avoid the *junsa*'s watchful eyes, they snuck out to the cemetery, stole the food, and stored it in cracks in the walls to eat later.

Rats the size of small cats were everywhere. They scampered around the rooms, scurried in the ceiling, and, at night, they ran over the womens' bodies. One night, Etta woke up with a start. One of the creatures had gotten tangled in her hair. Years later, she said she could still feel its little feet beating against her ear. The women slept with one eye open, always on the lookout for the large rodents. That's when haircuts and sticks started. The women gave each other haircuts to minimize rat bites and they kept sticks by their beds to ward off the rats. All of this nocturnal activity prevented them from getting deep, restful sleep.

The meals of watered-down soup continued. Occasionally, the women saw barely visible pieces of what they thought was dog or cat meat in the thin soup, but they disregarded the possibility and ate it because they were so hungry. They usually saved their paltry breakfast and lunch and combined it all with dinner for one "good" meal per day. Etta told the women how she and Foster had eaten one meal each day while in Alaska, but, of course, they had had ample food for the meal—meat, fresh vegetables, and dessert.

They all had symptoms of malnutrition—distended stomachs, exposed backbones and rib bones, and lumpy hip and thigh tissue. Some of the women had lost teeth. In their weakened condition, they suffered through colds, flu, pneumonia, rheumatism, beriberi, and chilblains [painful swelling or sores caused by exposure to cold, especially on the fingers, toes, or ears]. While the cause of their physical condition was obvious, they continued to serve the *junsa* hot, hearty, nutritious meals. On the rare occasions when they received packages from the International Red Cross, cigarettes were usually in the boxes. Oba-san was a chain smoker, so the women used the cigarettes to barter for extra food. This enterprise was short-lived because, as had happened in the past, they gave Oba-san the cigarettes, but usually received nothing in return.

While the women were struggling to survive, concern about Etta's whereabouts continued in the United States. Her employer, the Bureau of Indian Affairs, received a letter from the New York Life Insurance Company.

August 25, 1944
Re: Charles F. Jones, Etta E. S. Jones
Gentlemen:
     We are told that the above named annuitants were
inhabitants of Attu Island at the time of the Japanese occupation

of that island. We desire to learn whether the fate of Mr. and Mrs. Jones is known to you. If so, will you advise us whether either or both are known to be alive or dead? This information is requested solely for insurance purposes, and any information you can give us will be treated in strictest confidence.

Very truly yours,

W. N. Hutchison, War Service Bureau

The Bureau of Indian Affairs responded as it had in the past.

September 7, 1944

Dear Mr. Hutchison:

This will acknowledge receipt of your letter dated August 25 inquiring of the fate of Mr. and Mrs. Charles F. Jones, annuitants of your company who were inhabitants of Attu Island at the time of the Japanese occupation of that island.

We have no definite information regarding the whereabouts of the Joneses. We received one confidential report that Mrs. Jones was taken prisoner of war and that Mr. Jones died resisting capture. This report has not been confirmed. We have followed up all possible clues but have been unsuccessful in obtaining definite information.

Sincerely yours,

Paul L. Fickinger, for the Commissioner

Their third fall in Japan quickly turned into winter with the early arrival of snow. Bitterly cold wind blew off Mount Fuji and wrapped its icy fingers around the women. They were issued no additional blankets, clothes, or shoes. Their bare feet left footprints in the snow. They still wore their one woolen garment they had made during their first winter at the Yacht Club, and it was threadbare. The women stuffed newspaper inside the wool for insulation. The Foreign Office always promised warm quilts and clothes, but they were never delivered. The women spent as much time as they could huddled together on their flimsy quilts in an attempt to keep warm. The *junsa* and Oba-san had new, warm uniforms and quilts, and heat in their rooms. Later, the weather was so cold the well froze, so there was no water for cooking or baths. The hand pump also froze, but sometimes the women were allowed a bucket of hot water from the kitchen to melt the ice. When they could, they stole hot water from the communal bath and kitchen and used it to wash. When the wood on the roadside was gone, the *junsa* made them look for and dig up tree stumps for the kitchen fire. They wrapped rags around their feet and hands but it didn't help. As hungry as they were, the freezing temperatures affected the women more than it had in the past. Years later, some of the women stated they feared the cold more than hunger. The POWs had two hot baths that year.

November 1, 1944, was the day of the first air raid sirens. This was proof that the Allies were getting closer and the war was turning, so the internees' spirits were lifted. On November 24, the women heard bombs in Tokyo and Yokohama, and they became even more optimistic. Fuji responded by chasing Joyce with a knife. Fearing similar reactions from all their captors, the women stayed as far away from them as they could in the close quarters.

With the threat of Allied bombs increasing, wealthier Yokohama residents used part of the Totsuka building for storage. They would drive to Totsuka on the weekends and drop boxes of their possessions on the roadside. It was the POWs' job to pick up the boxes and put them in storage rooms. But on December 21, the guards said there were boxes from the Foreign Office on the road, and the women were to gather them up and bring them into the building. Bowie recalled: "A few minutes later a lorry pulled up and started off-loading strong cardboard boxes. We all came alive at the same time. 'They've got Red Crosses on them!' No one waited for an order now, as with renewed strength we surged forward and loaded ourselves up like coolies going to market. It was 21st December, so near to Christmas, and we were overjoyed.

. . . from near starvation to what seemed like mountains of food in just a few hours was mind-boggling. Everyone was talking at once and the din almost reached hysteria level as we opened the boxes containing tins of jam, milk, coffee, sugar, raisins, prunes, chocolates, butter, and meat. And last but not least for the trading potential they offered, cigarettes and soap. When the excitement died down a little, each room group decided, more or less according to willpower, to spread this bonanza over as long a period as possible. The nonperishable goods, said the more strong-minded, should be kept. With a good cigarette supply we might be able to get *sashies* [sweet potatoes] and so struggle through the winter without too much privation.

As Christmas Day drew near, it was certain to be another white one, for which there was little enthusiasm. Next year it would be sun, sea, and sanity, and on this subject we were in complete agreement. Privately we all knew, that whichever way the war went, under another winter of these extreme conditions we would find it impossible to survive.

On 24th December 1944, Christmas Eve, the sun shone brightly. The snow-covered peaks of Mount Fuji glistened in the distance, inspiring hope and banishing unpleasant thoughts of gloom. Everywhere could be heard happy forecasts of how we will celebrate this time next year—not of now but tomorrow. Without a doubt the present euphoria was related to the state of our stomachs.

'An appropriate background for Christmas carols,' Chris said as she hung the now rather tatty decorations of other years.

On Christmas Day we wrapped small parcels of sugar, raisins, chocolates, and tea in the only paper available, toilet paper; the fact that we were each giving and receiving almost the same gift made no difference to the pleasure involved. The only one singled out for anything special was Cal. [Early in 1943, Cal had symptoms of tuberculosis. Repeated requests for treatment were denied. By the time the women were relocated to Totsuka, she was bedridden.] We all gave to her what we knew she would be capable of using and eating. A much-appreciated gift of sweet potatoes from the Oba-san added to our tinned Bully beef and made a real Christmas feast. From the kitchen came a gift of bread, which had been off the menu for a long time. Later in the afternoon the Oba-san lent us her kettle, and we rounded off an almost happy day with bread and jam and real tea. This, after all, was a most promising Christmas.

The festivities were short lived however and we faced the realities of the cold winter anew; we had never experienced such low temperatures. Our rags and tatters, when put outside to dry, froze almost as soon as they were hung on the line; they looked like the bizarre shapes of a string of scarecrows. Ragged as our clothes were, they were never thrown away, and any material left over from patching them was used to repair the futons, which were not only falling to pieces, but had taken on that unhealthy damp mustiness when cloth is permeated with grime. By now though, we could almost ignore smells of any kind, and except for the girls with malaria, we had a good idea, too, that we must be immune to most infections, which was one blessing."

Occasionally, Oba-san gave them rice with cooked sweet potatoes, but the food was covered with ice. The women had stolen small pumpkins from Oba-san's garden and had hidden them in the ceiling above the rooms. When they were out of food, they secretly ate the raw pumpkin. Food was their obsession: they dreamed about it, talked about it, and wrote recipes from memory. Over and over, they planned what they would eat for their first "freedom meal." But some were beginning to wonder if they were going to lose their own war of survival.

In February, the air raids increased. The trenches the women had dug months before were now filled with garbage. With threats from the *junsa*, it was their job now to clean out the trenches that housed vermin as well as trash. They continued to shovel snow and dig up tree stumps for wood. When it wasn't snowing, the wind, rain, and sleet blew all around them.

Dora had bouts of illness because she didn't even have a sweater to ward off the cold. The women decided they would knit her one as a surprise, but they were at a loss as to what to use for yarn. Then they remembered watching the Natives in the South Pacific roll fibers together to make thread. They carefully pulled cotton strands from the sanitary napkins they had hoarded, and wrapped the cotton around the leftover silk thread from the bags they had knit for two years. Using the palms of their hands, they rubbed the two strands up and down on their legs, creating a kind of knitting yarn. They set to work to make their friend a very special cardigan. Mavis knit a pattern into it and Chris made buttons out of bamboo.

On March 9, 1945, Tokyo, just fifteen miles away, was bombed relentlessly. Refugees poured out of the city, and they exemplified the antithesis of what the women had experienced when they were on the Black Maria. Instead of a jeering, taunting crowd, this was a slow, dismal parade of bedraggled evacuees who could scarcely realize the enormity of what had happened to them. While plodding along the Totsuka road, there was a heavy silence, which was only occasionally broken by the wail of a small child. The air around them reeked of defeat.

The women finished knitting Dora's sweater, and they gave it to her just before Easter 1945. That special religious day, they created a church service based on the Stations of the Cross, which is the story of Jesus's last days on earth. Some of the internees felt somewhat uplifted after the service, while others still wondered how a loving God could allow them to still be captives in such a malevolent place. Cal's health continued to deteriorate, and she told the women she did not want to die in Japan.

Food. Mail. Those were the two things the women continued to want most. Mail had sustained Etta and Foster in Alaska. Etta and the internees hadn't received a single letter in almost four years.

Day and night, the women watched the drama of war being played out in their own backyard. The women watched planes overhead, heard the screams of the bombs descending, and saw the black smoke of destruction. They counted the number of Allied planes and cheered the pilots when they saw the fires of accurate strikes. Watching the sky and cheering as if they were at a sporting event gave the women hope. With an Allied victory, they might survive their internment—unless the bombs struck Totsuka.

Although they were encouraged by the mounting activities of the Allied forces, concern for their own safety escalated. The women learned that most of Tokyo and Yokohama were destroyed and thousands of people had been killed. The homes of the *junsa* and Fuji were demolished. The Junsa reacted to the devastation by fighting frequently and viciously with each other, and they treated the women even more harshly than before. Now, all at the facility—Australian, American, Japanese—were feeling the effects of the war.

In June, the women saw U.S. planes drop leaflets over the countryside. The printed leaflets told Japan to either surrender or expect to be invaded. The women were horrified. They knew the Japanese would never surrender. Rather, they would opt for suicide and in all probability, they'd kill the prisoners first. The women noticed that kitchen knives had been sharpened and the *junsa* had been given new swords.

July 1, 1945, was a remarkable day for the women. A representative of the Red Cross visited them at Totsuka. The visit was their first from the Red Cross since Christmas Eve, 1942. The representative told them two very important things: No one outside of the camp knew where the nineteen women had been for almost four years, and that, in their case, the Geneva Convention accords had been ignored. Those accords specifically state that prisoners of war must at all times be humanely treated, and be protected, particularly against acts of violence or intimidation, insults, and public curiosity. Basic daily food rations were required to be sufficient in quantity, quality, and variety to keep the prisoners of war in good health and to prevent loss of weight or the development of nutritional deficiencies. Prisoners of war were to be involved with the preparation of their meals. Clothing, underwear, and footwear were to be supplied in sufficient quantities, and allowances made for the climate of the region where the prisoners were detained. Prisoners of war should be allowed to receive and send, by post or any other means, individual parcels containing, in particular, foodstuffs, clothing, medical supplies, and articles of a religious or educational nature, including books and devotional articles.

The women were stunned. All this time, they should not have had to endure the hardships. They could not comprehend what they were being told.

Japan had not ratified the Geneva Convention (of 1929), so it had no legal (or moral, it would seem) obligation to treat its POWs and internees in a humane way. Japan's Prime Minister Tojo had declared all POW food rations cut in order to provide more for the Japanese armed forces. Starving their prisoners was the greatest atrocity committed by the Japanese. It had led to the fatal diseases that afflicted thousands of POWs and internees, those at Totsuka included. The women also learned that the exchange ships, on which they had pinned so much hope, were used only for American and European missionaries who were in Japan before war was declared.

The Red Cross representative gave them world news. The war in Europe had been over for two months. Hitler, Mussolini, Roosevelt, and Australia's Prime Minister, John Curtin, were all dead. The representative also promised the women he would tell the Allied officials about them and their location. After he left, the women had mixed reactions to all the news. The optimists felt the war was over and that they would be free very soon. The pessimists worried that the Japanese culture wouldn't allow them to just walk away.

The women deduced that since Germany had been conquered, the Allies were concentrating on Japan, and that explained the relentless raids. Their present location was a precarious one. Throughout July and into August, the air raids continued. They counted as many as 400 planes in one day. Emotions went from extreme joy at the prospect of finally being free to the depths of despair because the Japanese had been schooled to never give up. They feared for their lives, should the Japanese be forced to surrender. The Japanese had told them no mercy would be shown—all prisoners would be killed.

August was hot and humid. It had been one month since the visit by the Red Cross representative, but no one had come to rescue them. Air activity continued, day and night, and it kept the women on edge. Daisy Keast [Tootie] related what happened next: "Then one night when we had gone to bed, there was a terrible scream for Parker, and poor Kay went out to see what it was. They told her that the Americans had dropped this one bomb on Hiroshima and all the damage it had done. She said, 'Oh, *takusan takusan*, we've got plenty more of those.' She came around, told us, and we all shrieked with laughter. We said, poor silly fools, fancy them thinking one bomb can do that. Then they told us that we had three days to live. All prisoners of war in Japan were going to be killed within three days. Well, a couple of nights later, Kay was called again, and they told her that another bomb had been dropped on Nagasaki."

The women had learned not to believe anything the *junsa* said because the Japanese involved in the war effort appeared to be allergic to the truth. The women were skeptical about this news about the two bombs. However, if the information was correct, they knew they had every reason to be afraid. They had just been ordered to dig the air raid shelters deeper, and were told all POWs and internees would be killed. They figured they had dug their own graves, just like the soldiers in Rabaul.

On August 15, the women saw a lot of the villagers huddled around the radio in Oba-san's house. They didn't know who was speaking in the broadcast and they couldn't understand what was being said, but after several minutes they saw that the listeners—police, farmhands, schoolchildren, adults—were bowing their heads and crying. As the people shuffled back to their homes, they noticed Fuji walking across the field, away from Totsuka. They never saw him again. That night, with a very sad face and barely able to make eye contact with the women, one of the *junsa* told them the war was over, Japan had surrendered. The former captives could hardly contain their excitement. After almost four long years, they were finally free!

But where could they go? When would they be taken away from this horrible place? They needed food and Cal was desperately ill. The *junsa* cautioned the women not to leave the building grounds because the peasants might take their hatred out on them.

The Red Cross representative had done as he promised and had told Allied officials the women's location. Word was received in the United States that Etta was alive. In Washington, D.C., intraoffice memos were sent and received, dispensing information that was not quite accurate.

August 27, 1945, 2 P.M., Zimmerman to McCaskill:
In Commissioner's Annual Report, may we refer to finding of Mrs. C. Foster Jones of Attu? Please advise.

August 28, 1945, 11 A.M. McCaskill to Zimmerman:
War Dept. says no objection referring in Annual Report to the finding of Mrs. C. Foster Jones only American citizen

interned Totsuka Camp, Tokyo-Yokohama area. 18 Australians
also detained there. News reached our State Dept. thru channels
from Swiss Legation, Tokyo. Next of kin Mrs. Erling Meyers,
Muskegon, Mich., notified. The mother of Mrs. Erling Meyers
who is sister of Mrs. Jones, lives in Muskegon. [Etta's sister,
Nan, lived in Montague, Michigan.]

An Allied officer arrived in Totsuka, and told the women that
for the first time in almost four years, they could write to their families, but the letters could not exceed 100 words. They wondered how
they could explain the lost years in 100 words, but, somehow, they
managed. Food soon arrived by the truckload. The amount was
excessive and the women literally ate themselves sick. They knew
the food should be properly cooked and now, for the first time,
they had access to the kitchen stove, but they were so hungry, they
gorged themselves. They had beef, salmon, vegetables, butter, sugar,
biscuits, tea, and beer. Tootie wrote: "I don't remember all the food,
but I do know that 90 pounds of meat—now we hadn't seen meat
for over two years—came, a big tin that had possibly two pounds
of butter in it, a lot of very coarse sugar, 20 tins of salmon, and I
have forgotten the rest. But I got a spoon and I ate the butter and the
sugar, and I was desperately ill, but I didn't care. We fixed a roaster.
As soon as the meat was cooked, the bell rang, and whether it was
day or night, we ate. And our tummies just got fatter and fatter, and
all of a sudden it went flomp. Just vomited! And then we were ready
to start again."

A few days later, more food descended from the sky dangling
from colorful parachutes. One parachute broke the power line to
their building, so the women used a piece of rag in a saucer of butter for light. They didn't care about wasting the butter—they had
an unlimited supply. As barrels of food continued to float down, the
women watched as they landed, then ran into the field to retrieve
and haul them to the building, gleefully emptying the contents and
distributing them.

Japan had surrendered, the women finally had food, but they
were still at Totsuka. When were they going to be liberated? Why

The field behind the Totsuka camp building, 1945.
PHOTO TAKEN BY A FRIEND OF ETTA'S AFTER THE WAR.

didn't someone come to get them? They found sheets, wrote POW on them in big letters, and strategically placed them in the open fields near the hospital grounds, hoping the Allied planes flying overhead would see the sheets and rescue them. Their rescue, the one they had dreamed about for almost four years, happened in a way no one could have imagined.

18

Rescue

August 31, 1945

Allied victory meant the women were free to roam beyond the confines of the building. Despite the *junsa*'s warnings about their safety, the women ventured down the hill to the Totsuka Road, on the lookout for someone coming to rescue them. On August 31, still with the ever-present armed guard nearby, Kay, Liklik, and Whytie were standing behind some bushes that lined the road. Whytie wrote, "Then, to our amazement, along the road to the Atsugi Airport came this huge transport of trucks and little cars (jeeps we had never seen before), and these soldiers with funny helmets on. Now you must remember we were taken POW before the Americans came down the Pacific so they were very new to us. Also, we were a little puzzled because at first glance they looked like German soldiers. But this was General MacArthur's entry into Japan. In his convoy was a jeep with Major Meanley aboard—plus an interpreter who told him we were English women who had been wandering in the fields during the war. He was not happy with that answer, so returned an hour later to see if we were still there—which we were. Well, you can't imagine in your wildest dreams what happened next. Here was this wonderful tall American asking us who we were."

Major Meanley told his brother, Eddie Meanley, the sequence of events. "[Major Meanley] was being driven down a dirt road and was reading a map when his driver said, 'Major, there is a white woman in the bushes.' He told the driver to stop. He also told the driver to

Left: Totsuka Road, circa 1946. Photo taken by a friend of Etta's after the war.
Right: Major William Meanley, member of General Douglas MacArthur's
convoy to Atsugi Air Base near Totsuka, Japan, saw POWs alongside the road
and rescued them, August 30, 1945. Courtesy of Ann and George Meanley.

keep his gun pointed at the Japanese guard, and if the guard made a move toward my brother to shoot him. My brother said that as he walked by the guard, they each eyed the other, but no move was made."

The women could not contain themselves. Whytie wrote, "That poor man. How he stayed on his feet I shall never know. We hugged and kissed him, and the poor guy was wanting to know who we were. Finally, we took him up to the camp."

The women inside the building heard shrieks, squeals, laughter, and the thumping of army boots, but they instinctively knew that these particular boots would not be used for kicking. The major's brother wrote: "When my brother reached the building where the nurses were being held, they were deliriously happy to see him. The two men smiled and laughed as the women crowded around them, touching, hugging, kissing the men and laughing, all at the same time. The major smiled and said, 'Boy, I could take a lot more of this!' " The women's bodies were barely covered with rags, and they weren't exactly beautiful and sweet-smelling, but that didn't seem to matter to anyone.

The building where the women had been living was in complete disarray when they ushered Major Meanley into their makeshift dorm. Food boxes cluttered the hallways and were piled in random stacks, raggedy clothes were hanging on clotheslines, everything they had stockpiled for almost four years was littered everywhere. Eventually, everyone calmed down, somewhat. The women introduced the major to Cal, and told him she was too ill to travel. He made arrangements for her to be transported immediately to a hospital ship in Tokyo Bay, a short distance away. The major's brother wrote: "They told him that all of the women in the group were nurses except one who was an American schoolteacher. They also told him that the Japanese made the American teacher watch as they executed her husband. He told me that the women were wearing paper dresses."

Major Meanley told the former prisoners he would have to make arrangements to transport all of them out of Totsuka but it couldn't happen until the next day. He asked them if they would be all right for one more night. After almost four years in captivity and planeloads of food at their disposal, they agreed, what was one more night? They accompanied the major and his driver back to the jeep, and they noticed the Japanese armed guard had disappeared. Once more joy and exuberance took over, and they hugged and kissed the major, his driver, even the jeep.

A military ambulance soon arrived to take Cal to the hospital ship. Word had spread, and a mob of photographers and journalists arrived. The women were in shock—after total isolation from the rest of the world, they were suddenly surrounded by hoards of English-speaking men. One photographer prompted, "How about a wave, girls?"

When the Americans left, the women hugged each other, to make sure they weren't dreaming. They needed to pack, although except for the handmade gifts, there wasn't a single thing that was worth taking with them. But after hoarding and hiding everything they could get their hands on, it was difficult to part with anything. Thus, into their boxes went empty bottles and tin cans, rags that used to be clothes, scraps of paper, handmade playing cards, souvenir

FREE AGAIN.—Australian nurses and an American woman captured at Rabaul and held prisoners at Totsuka, near Yokohama, photographed upon release. Front row: Misses Mavis Green, Raymond Terrace; Dorothy Mary Maye, Sydney; Mrs. Etta E. Jones, U.S.A.; Misses Lorna Margaret Whyte, Hay; Jean Christopher, Kadina, South Australia; Jean McLellan, Queensland; Grace Dorothy Kruger, Townsville. Centre row: Miss Dorothy L. Beall, Gladstone, Queensland; Mrs. Mary E. Goss, Binalong; Misses Dora E. Wilson, Newcastle; Daisy E. Keast, Junee; Joyce C. McLahan, Warwick, Queensland. Back row: Misses Alice Bowman, Grafton; J. Allroyd Harris, Bowenfels; Jean Anderson, Grafton; Mavis Cullen, Yass; Kay Parker, Croydon, and Mrs. K. D. Bignall, Isabel Island, Solomons. The Australian girls are on their way to Sydney by air.   —"Sun" Special Photo.

The former internees, August 31, 1945. Etta is in the front, third from left.

silk bags, and secret diaries. Dora packed the cardigan that had been so lovingly made for her, and those who still had them took their Bibles. Etta had managed to save Japanese money as well as cards and gifts the others had made for her.

They cooked their last meal in Japan on the same hibachi that had been the source of so much frustration. Then they tried to sleep, but couldn't. Everyone talked at once, wondering aloud about their families and the men who had traveled with them on the *Naruto Maru*. The women had been completely isolated for so long, and they needed to know everything. They hoped to get good news, but realistically feared they might not.

Their first official day of freedom arrived with a vengeance. Typhoon rains and wind came, reminiscent of those on Attu, scattering everything that wasn't nailed down. The Red Cross had arrived

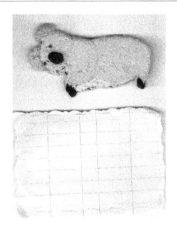

Hand-sewn koala bear and its paper container, given to Etta by one of the Australian internees in 1944.

Above: A note from internee Kathleen Bignell to Etta, 1942 Below: Japanese money Etta brought back to the United States, 1945.

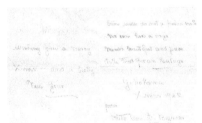

Handmade cards created by the internees for Etta in 1943 and 1944.

with a dress and pair of shoes for each of the women, and in these new outfits, they waited for the promised transportation. A bus, not the Black Maria this time, arrived to take them to Atsugi Airbase. As he watched them leave, one of the guards standing by, now unarmed, had the audacity to tell the women to take good care of themselves. By the time they walked from the building to the truck, they were soaked to the skin, but they didn't care. As the bus pulled away, the women looked back at their former prison and saw Oba-san standing in the road calling, *"Sayonara!"* When she raised her arm to wave good-bye, they noticed she had cartons of cigarettes tucked in her kimono. The women smiled, knowing that Oba-san had obviously schemed with one of the visitors to obtain cigarettes.

The ride to Atsugi was not very long, but halfway there, the truck got mired in the mud. Those who were physically able happily worked in the wind and rain to get the truck out. Laughing as if they didn't have a care in the world, soaked and mud spattered, they got back on the bus and rode the rest of the way to the base. When they discovered how close the air base was to Totsuka, they realized why they had seen so much air activity over the previous weeks. It was a miracle they hadn't become casualties instead of survivors. Later, they were told Atsugi was where the Allies planned to land, so they had deliberately not bombed the base, but had destroyed everything around it.

At the base, they were treated to a breakfast that surpassed their wildest dreams while in captivity—eggs, as many as they wanted, crisp bacon, pancakes smothered in syrup, muffins dripping with honey, hot toast swimming in butter and jam, plenty of fruit, orange juice, tea, and coffee. They feasted until they were full, but were careful not to make the same mistake as in their first feeding frenzy. Even though they were free, old habits were hard to break. As they were eating the sumptuous meal, several secretly put muffins and toast in their pockets. One of the servers observed this and quietly told them, "You don't have to do that anymore. There's plenty more where that came from, ladies!"

Following the meal, the women were given a tour of the brand new, state-of-the-art base. It was built by the Japanese and the Allies planned to utilize it, so they didn't want to destroy it when they invaded. It was so new, in fact, that water hadn't been plumbed into the barracks, so there were no showers. This was almost insignificant to the women because they were free and full of food. A lavish dinner was served that evening followed by more conversations with those stationed on the base. Finally, around 1:00 A.M., each woman literally fell into her own luxurious bed—a real mattress, pillows, and clean sheets and pillowcases!

The next morning, as General Douglas MacArthur participated in the formal Japanese surrender on the USS *Missouri* in Tokyo Bay, eighteen overwhelmed, skinny, but very happy women boarded a C-54 Skymaster, a new luxury plane, headed for Okinawa. They were the first group of former prisoners to leave Japan.

At the end of the six-hour flight, Andy collapsed. She was malnourished, as they all were, but she had complications with exhaustion, beriberi, and malaria. She was hospitalized in Okinawa. The next day the remaining seventeen were put on a plane to Manila, an eight-hour flight. This time, the aircraft was a noisy troop carrier with long wooden benches along the sides. Long tables, groaning under the weight of more food, were set up in the middle of the aircraft. There was a big supply of magazines and newspapers, and the hours passed quickly as they ate, read, and got caught up on what had been happening in the world while they were confined. They remarked about how hair and clothing styles had changed while they were in captivity. Trousers! Women were wearing them. That was unheard of in 1942.

When they arrived in Manila, they were told that Etta was the first American woman rescued, and the Australians shared the same distinction. Families of the former internees were notified immediately.

For the next ten days, the women were thrust into a whirlwind of activities—bureaucratic forms to fill out, interviews, physical and dental exams, immunizations, hair appointments, the distribution of clothes, shoes, cosmetics, and toiletries. On her "Affidavit of Recovered Civilian Form," dated August 31, 1945, Etta wrote that during her captivity, she had performed "menial tasks—made paper

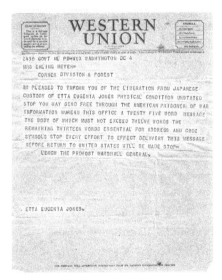

Cable from Elinor Smith Meyers, Etta's niece, written in response to notification from a Swiss Red Cross representative who visited the POWs at Totsuka in July 1945.

Etta's family was officially notified of her free status with this cable from the U.S. government on September 4, 1945.

envelopes, knit silk bags." In reference to Foster, she said: "Husband, C. Foster Jones, killed at time of Japanese invasion, Attu, May 7, 1942. Buried in Attu, Alaska. Told by Natives of Attu." Ettta gave her permanent legal home address as St. Paris, Ohio, and her proposed new address as Seattle, Washington. When looking at her barely legible handwriting, the discrepancy of the invasion date and considering her age and the circumstances, past and present, her confusion is easily understood. As for listing her permanent address as Seattle, perhaps during captivity she had dreamed of building the retirement home on Whidbey Island, north of Seattle, that she and Foster had planned before disastrous events intervened.

For Etta, a joyful activity was receiving and sending messages.

Dear Elinor:

Space is necessarily limited. Your cable through Geneva was delivered to me September 4th, the first and only communication I have received so far. I could send only one cable through the Red Cross and that a collective one with the eighteen Australians. Later we were allowed another collective one, and after the U.S. Army took us, we could send a short individual one. Naturally, I wanted to include you and Russ and family and the Joneses, but I thought if anything had happened to your mother you would be there to carry on; therefore, she seemed the logical one to receive them. Was greatly relieved to know you are all there and well. After almost four blank years, one feels rather doubtful.

> **See you soon.**
> **Love,**
> **E.E.J.**

Etta also wrote to Foster's brother in St. Paris, Ohio.

Dear Cecil:

This is a continuation of a letter I have just finished to Mother Jones, both letters for all, of course. I suppose you received notice from my sister that I left Foster's body on Attu.

Was allowed only one cable and sending it to her seemed the best way. Since talking to Army officers here I learned I am apparently the only survivor of Attu. Having no legal residence now I have given St. Paris, Ohio, as my permanent address, all messages in your care. Hope it will not burden you but I will keep you informed of my whereabouts. We have been overwhelmed with kindness since leaving internment, especially by the Red Cross. Our gratitude is too deep for words.

I happen to be the first [American] woman prisoner released from Japan and for that reason I am receiving special attention—interviews, etc. They had me down for a broadcast from Atsugi Aerodrome just before leaving Japan but it did not come off. It is terribly hot here. All I want is to get back to the States. Almost four years is a long time.

E.E.J.

The remainder of the womens' time in Manila was spent resting, watching movies, and being pampered by attentive personnel. Those assisting the former internees were hopeful they were witnessing the beginning of recovery. The women had suffered as much as any soldier: they had had their lives transformed, and they, too, were survivors.

As the date of departure came, the former prisoners were full of emotions. They were all anxious to go home, but it was difficult to leave the oldest member of their group, who had been so helpful to all of them. They hugged Etta and promised to keep in touch. When she boarded her plane bound for the United States, one commented, "After a few days' rest in Manila, Mrs. Jones said good-bye to us. Along with Bernie and Sam [American POW soldiers], she was flown home to America. Mrs. Jones was an unassuming and uncomplaining woman, who had suffered a great loss and stood up to the years of hardship well. She survived the ordeal in mind and body, as well as, and in some cases better than, those half her age." Etta was one month shy of her sixty-sixth birthday.

19

Return to the United States
September 1945

❦

W hen the Australians reached their final destinations, they leaped into the arms of loved ones. The happy Australians finally reached "home," the place they had dreamed about, talked about constantly over the past four years. As wonderful as it was to finally be home, some reunions were bittersweet because family members and friends had died during their internment. Mrs. Bignell learned that her son and son-in-law had perished on the *Montevideo Maru*. Mary Goss's husband, Tom, had escaped into the jungle, but had eventually been found and executed. For those who had boyfriends and fiances, only one, Mac's Bill, had survived. Attempting to reclaim their own lives and accepting the news, the women continued on their journeys home. Once there, they devoured even the plainest of homemade meals. Every day was a feast and an exercise in readjusting. Warm, familiar bedrooms were ready, most just as they were years before when the women left. It was a quiet and welcoming homecoming.

That was not the case for Etta when she arrived in San Francisco. Her elderly brother and sister could not make the transcontinental trip to meet her—their reunion would have to wait. She was the first Caucasian female taken prisoner by a foreign enemy on the North American continent since the War of 1812, and she was the first female American released from Japan. Instead of tears of joy and hugs and kisses from family members, she was met by blinding

First Woman Prisoner of Japs Is Home

MRS. ETTA E. JONES

Weighing 80 pounds, 65-year-old Etta Jones arrives in San Francisco, September 12, 1945. COURTESY SAN FRANCISCO NEWS, SEPTEMBER 12, 1945.

flashbulbs from photographers, a steady stream of reporters wanting interviews, and the beginning of a bureaucratic process that would go on for years.

Back in America, Etta felt as displaced as she ever had. Without Foster or the Alaska Territory that had been her real home for twenty years, she had much uncertainty. She would travel alone more than 3,000 miles over the next two months before finally reaching home in Margate, New Jersey.

As soon as she arrived in the United States, she wrote to her family from San Francisco.

September 12, 1945
Dear Folks:

Have just arrived. Thirty-eight hours of almost continuous travel in a plane, and I am tired but I must keep going.

I have too much baggage and have had one trunk expressed back to St. Paris, charges collect. That seemed the easiest way. I'll pay you when I see you.

Have been met at all points by correspondents and photographers. I am weary of the sight of them. My reservations to Seattle are now being made through the Air Transport Command. They want me to fly but I have had enough flying. I'll go by train, leaving tomorrow sometime. Will go to the Roosevelt Hotel, where I hope to collect some long overdue letters. If you have written, I have not received any.

Don't suppose I'll be in Seattle more than a week, then I'll visit my niece in Muskegon [Michigan] and then you in St. Paris [Ohio].

Till then, cheerio and love,
Etta E.

Etta received welcome-home letters from her employer, although one was sent to an incorrect address.

Alaska Native Service
Juneau, Alaska
September 11, 1945
Mrs. Etta Jones
c/o Russell T. Schureman
Atlanta, Ga.
Dear Mrs. Jones:

It is with a great deal of pleasure that we learn from the press of your release from Japanese prison camp and your return to the States. The suffering which you and Mr. Jones endured, the leadership which you gave your people in a crisis, have been an inspiration to all of us and a source of pride to our Service.

We can only convey our humble thanks on behalf of the entire Service and with it the congratulations of all of us and the recognition which you have earned from the department and public as conveyed to you in the secretary's letter of July 11.

We are indeed happy to forward the enclosed materials to you and look forward to hearing from you direct. We would indeed welcome you should you wish to return to our Service.

Sincerely yours,

Don C. Foster, General Superintendent,

Alaska Indian Service

September 12, 1945

Mrs. Etta E. Jones

c/o Russell T. Schureman

Margate, New Jersey

My dear Mrs. Jones:

The good news of your release and repatriation has brought great satisfaction to the Indian Office. We want you to know that many efforts were made to obtain information concerning you, your husband, and the Aleuts of Attu, but no word was received from the Japanese government at any time. Please accept our sympathy for your sorrow in the loss of your husband and for the many hardships you have suffered. We hope that rest and good care will restore you to complete health.

When you feel able, will you let us have your story of what happened when the enemy invaded Attu and the subsequent events of your internment? Do you know what became of the Natives of the island?

Sincerely yours,

William Zimmerman Jr., Assistant Commissioner

Etta rode the train to Seattle, where she had friends who were anxious to assist in her recovery. As with most returning internees, Etta just needed rest and wholesome food. Her friends, however, wanted to fill what they perceived as a void in the last thirty-nine months, and they included her in numerous social gatherings. Lulu Fairbanks wrote: "Many old friends gave her a whirl of entertainment and she often felt bewildered because her social vacuum needs much filling. As soon as she can get time, she is going to [go to] the library, get out the complete files of *Life* and *Time* for the past three years, and find out what has happened during this period, for it is a complete blank in her life, so far as news is concerned.

Last Friday evening, I drove Mrs. Jones to the University District to attend the concert given by Alaska's famous musical artist, Simeon Oliver. She had known him in the North, and their joy at meeting was another genuinely happy thrill added to her homecoming. The evening's entertainment was sponsored by another friend, Mrs. A. C. Goss from Unalaska."

While in Seattle, Etta needed to deal with a myriad of personal business affairs. As stated in one of her letters before the war, she and Foster had purchased property on Whidbey Island, where they were going to build their retirement home. With Foster gone, she decided to sell the property. Most of their financial accounts were in Seattle, and she had to settle what had been their joint accounts.

One of the women in Seattle with whom Etta worked in these matters asked if she would mind telling her story to a very small group of people. Etta had been through so much, she was tired, and was trying to regain her strength, so she politely declined. The woman persisted, and finally Etta agreed, having been told the audience would be perhaps as few as twenty people. The time came for Etta to speak, and when she was introduced, Etta stood in front of an audience of 200. Despite her shock, she composed herself and told her story yet again.

The Bureau of Indian Affairs sent their representative to talk with her, a meeting that resulted in the following report to Juneau:

Juneau, Alaska
September 19, 1945
Dear Mr. Foster:

Today, in response to Mrs. Trower's telegram of the 14th,
I contacted Mrs. Etta Jones at her room at the Roosevelt Hotel.
The letter Mrs. Trower referred to arrived in this morning's mail
and I delivered the same to her. She was most pleased to receive
the letters from Mr. Foster and Dr. Dale as well as the one from
Secretary [of the Interior, Harold] Ickes. She requested that I
extend to you her thanks and appreciation, and to advise you
that after she has rested she will write. She is in good health but
very tired both physically and mentally. Of course she has aged,
is very thin, and I believe I would be correct in saying that she is
suffering from shock. Her memory seems to fail her at times, all
of which she freely admits, but she is of the opinion that rest and
proper food is all she needs.

I was able to be of some service to her in taking care of
some personal affairs. Please be on the lookout for a box being
forwarded by freight to your office in care of the Arts & Crafts.
This box, which has been in storage for five years, contains
curios that Mr. Jones collected years ago at Kipnuk. Mrs. Jones
has requested that the contents be invoiced, evaluated, and sold
by the Arts & Crafts Division and proceeds sent to her in care
of Cecil V. Jones, St. Paris, Ohio. I delivered this box to the Bell
Street Dock and the same will be sent on the next boat to Juneau.

Mrs. Jones reports that the Jap invasion took place on June
7th, 1942. Mr. Jones was taken from her on June 8th. The Natives
told her they had buried him in the churchyard at Chichagof
Harbor. The Japs had refused to give them lumber for a casket
but the Natives knew him to be a good man so they placed him
in a place of honor by burying him in this churchyard. She has
no idea just where the grave is located in the yard since they
were not allowed to put up a marker. She reports that on June
14 she was taken aboard a transport ship and taken directly to
Yokohama. At the time of her departure, the Japs' treatment of

the Natives was very satisfactory. She does not think they were taken from the island at a later date.

She plans on remaining in Seattle until the middle of next week, after which she will go to her husband's people at St. Paris, Ohio. Mr. Swanson of the First National Bank is taking care of her property, Mr. Jones's insurance, etc. She plans on stopping over in Chicago and calling at the Chicago office in response to Mr. Lamson's wire of the 17th. She desires to retire and will discuss this while in Chicago.

I am enclosing various items of correspondence and newspaper clippings, which you might want to place in her personnel file.

I will make it a point to be of service to her in every possible way I can during her stay in Seattle.

Sincerely yours,

V. R. Farrell, Acting Director of Resources

Abe Fortas, who would eventually have a seat on the United States Supreme Court, wrote the following letter.

Mrs. Etta E. Jones, c/o Russell T. Schureman

Margate, New Jersey

September 19, 1945

My dear Mrs. Jones:

It was exceedingly gratifying to have the news of your release from Japanese imprisonment and safe return to the United States. On behalf of the Department [of the Interior] and the Office of Indian Affairs, I wish to express heartfelt sympathy in the loss of your husband and the suffering that you have met so bravely during your internment. Secretary Ickes had previously written you in recognition of your outstanding devotion to duty at the time Attu fell.

All of our efforts to secure information about you, your husband, and the Aleuts of Attu were futile. We have continued to hope for the safety of all.

I extend my personal greeting to you and trust that in due time your good health may be restored.

Sincerely yours,

Abe Fortas, Acting Secretary of the Interior

While in Seattle, Etta wrote to Foster's brother and sister-in-law in St. Paris, Ohio.

September 23, 1945

Dear Cecil and Mary:

Thanks for your letters. I can begin to see my way clear to leaving here September 27. Have reservations for then. Suppose I'll get to Chicago about the 30th on Northern Pacific [Railroad]. Will be there a few days (official business) and then go to you. I'll wire you from there when and how I shall leave.

I am feeling a lot more rested and am getting fat. Now weigh 101. I have whirled through a terrific amount of business but still have much to do. May have to go to Washington and New York, so my stay with you at first will be short, but I'll return. This is all about me but we'll talk about you when I come.

Love to all,

Tetts

Etta arrived in Chicago on September 30, 1945, her sixty-sixth birthday. One month and several thousand miles after her liberation, she was finally with family members for the first time. Her sister, Nan, and niece, Elinor, met her at the train depot. "Happy birthday and welcome home!" they exclaimed as they hugged Etta. She eventually told them that the Japanese had killed Foster. The three of them shared a hotel room, and when Etta wasn't meeting with Alaska Indian Service officials, she, Nan, and Elinor tried to catch up on what had happened in the family over the past thirty-nine months. They ate at restaurants, and Etta did some shopping. At Marshall Field's, she purchased a hat for twelve dollars. Nan and

Elinor thought that was an outrageous price, but when they considered the fact that Etta hadn't had an opportunity to spend any money on anything for several years, they decided Etta deserved to spend her money however she wished.

After four wonderful days together, Nan and Elinor returned to Michigan, and Etta boarded a train for St. Paris, Ohio, where she had a bittersweet reunion with Foster's family. She undoubtedly comforted them with her belief that the brutality of Foster's death did not overshadow the light, joy, energy, and love that was his life. Etta's stoic nature prevented her from revealing details of this painful reunion to other friends and family members.

Etta learned that while she was interned, there had been a great deal of intra- and interagency correspondence, about whether, in light of their unknown fate, Etta and Foster should be kept on the payroll, should be given annual pay increases, and just exactly how all this should be handled. Then, less than one month after Etta's repatriation, the Honorable E. L. Bartlett, the Alaska delegate to the U.S. House of Representatives, strongly voiced his opinion. He wrote to William Brophy, the Commissioner of Indian Affairs, Department of the Interior in Washington, D.C.

William A. Brophy, Commissioner of Indian Affairs
Department of the Interior, Washington, D.C.
October 5, 1945
Dear Mr. Brophy:

In connection with the return to this country of Mrs. Etta Jones, who was a teacher for the Indian Service at Attu, I am wondering if she will receive pay for the period she spent in a Japanese prison camp.

I have been told informally that those government employees who were captured were kept right on the pay roll. If it should be necessary to introduce a bill in Congress for Mrs. Jones, I should be happy to cooperate.

Sincerely yours,

E. L. Bartlett, Delegate

Fortunately, it did not literally require an Act of Congress for Etta to receive salary compensation for her period of internment, but there was more to the story. The U.S. Employees' Compensation Commission had some requirements. On November 9, 1945, the Bureau of Indian Affairs wrote the following.

> **United States Employees' Compensation Commission**
> **285 Madison AvenueNew York 17, New York**
> **October 8, 1945**
> **Gentlemen:**
> This is to request information as to whether or not Mrs. Etta E. Jones is entitled to widow's compensation because of the death of her husband, Charles Foster Jones. The circumstances in the case are as follows:
> When the war broke out in 1942, Mr. and Mrs. Jones were employed by the government in Alaska on the Island of Attu. Mr. Jones was employed as radio operator and Mrs. Jones as teacher. When the Japanese invaded Attu, Mrs. Jones was taken prisoner and Mr. Jones was killed. A copy of the affidavit explaining the circumstances of his death, as supplied by Mrs. Jones, is attached for your information.
> Mrs. Jones has now been released, and because of having served the required number of years with the government, is planning to retire. I am not sure that the commission will rule that Mr. Jones was killed in the line of duty, and I do not know whether the time limit for reporting the death claim to the commission would be considered as having passed.
> Will you please advise me as to whether or not you believe Mrs. Jones is entitled to widow's compensation, and, if so, what procedure should be followed in making proper application.
> **Sincerely yours,**
> **Roy Gourd, Employee Relations and Training Section**

This Board wanted to know why Etta hadn't filed for Foster's death benefits within one year of his death. Her release from the Japanese had resulted in a flood of newspaper stories from Fairbanks to Washington, D.C., yet she was required to conjure up the horrible events again to satisfy her own government. Her response exemplifies her patience and fortitude:

> This is to certify that I, Etta E. Jones, am the widow of Charles Foster Jones, whose death occurred at Attu, Alaska, on June 8, 1942, as the result of invasion by the Japanese Army.
>
> The reason I did not file a claim within one year from the date of death of my husband is that I was taken prisoner by the Japanese on June 7, 1942, and held as such in Yokohama until released by the American Army on August 31, 1945.
>
> Etta E. Jones
>
> St. Paris, Ohio
>
> Subscribed and sworn to before me this fourth day
>   of December, 1945.
>
> C. C. Davison (Notary Public)

Etta began traveling the long road back to a normal life. Except for brief reunions with family and friends, her days were filled completing bureaucratic paperwork. The flood of forms, affidavits, and statements eventually ebbed to a trickle, and Etta was able to finally do what she enjoyed—attend her church services, read, visit with friends, but, most of all, write letters.

Home

1945-1965

Eventually, Etta found out what had happened to the Natives of Attu after she was taken to Japan. After the invasion on June 7, 1942, the Attuans were prisoners of the Japanese. Their houses were cordoned off and guarded, day and night. Etta and Foster's house became headquarters for the Japanese. The primary food in the Natives' diet was fish. Now, as captives, when they needed to replenish their supply, the Natives were required to ask permission to use their own dories. Guards accompanied them, always insisting that the Japanese flag be flown on the boat. They were forced to feign respect for this symbol of their captors' country, but they secretly referred to its central design as a "meatball." At the end of the fishing trip, the Japanese took the lion's share of the catch. Systematic starvation had begun. The Natives weren't even allowed to scavenge driftwood for their stoves, so they used boards from their houses when they cooked what little food they had.

In September, the Natives were told that they were going to be shipped to Japan, and that they should take as much food and clothing as they could because necessities would be even more scarce where they were going. The forty Natives had one cook stove. They were forced to board what had been a coal carrier, and were ordered down into the dark and dirty hold. The trip took two weeks, during which time the stench from all of those bodies in such a tight space was overwhelming. They weren't allowed a single breath of fresh air on deck for the entire fourteen-day voyage.

Once in Japan, the Attuans were taken to Otaru on the western coast of Hokkaido Island, the northernmost of Japan's four major islands. Their five-room house was filthy, and it had no running water, heat, or electricity. Men and women were immediately forced to work, most of them in clay mines. At first, with their food supplies from home, meals were adequate. When those were gone, however, they were rationed eight cups of rice per day for the entire group. Some of the Natives foraged for food in the area surrounding the house. When they found a discarded orange peel, they boiled it and ate it. Doctors visited, but they never dispensed medicine. Instead, they performed crude experiments, such as drawing blood from one Native and injecting it into another, just to see what, if anything, would happen. Death threats, brutal whippings, and food deprivation were common punishments for such offenses as balking at learning to speak Japanese.

Early on, tuberculosis, food poisoning, malnutrition, and starvation tore through the fragile population. As family members died, the Japanese would not allow burial services. Instead, the deceased

The house that the Aleuts from Attu were confined in, in Otaru, Hokkaido, Japan, 1943. COURTESY OF ALEUTIANS/PRIBILOF ISLANDS ASSOCIATION.

were cremated, and the ashes were returned to the grieving family. Twenty-one of the forty Attuans died in Japan, most of them children.

With Japan's defeat in World War II, the nineteen remaining Attuans thought they would be returning to their ancestral home. When they arrived in Seattle on November 10, 1945, by way of Okinawa and San Francisco, they were informed by the government that there were too few of them to rebuild their village on Attu. Instead, they would be living in Atka, on Atka Island in the Aleutians, the land of their traditional rivals who spoke a different dialect. Hearing this devastating news, some chose to stay in Seattle, others elected to attend the boarding school at Mount Edgecombe in Sitka. The rest reluctantly settled in Atka.

In 1985, Attu's battlefield and airfields were designated as National History Landmarks and in 2008 the battlefield was one of three Alaskan sites included in the newly designated World War II Valor in the Pacific National Monument. Yet, today, there remains no physical evidence that a thriving community of Aleuts existed on the remote island of Attu. The U.S. Coast Guard operates a Long Range Aids to Navigation (LORAN) Station, manned by twenty-four crewmembers who stay for twelve months, with no dependents on site. The weather—fog, rain, violent storms—and the isolation are considered so extreme that those who endure their tour are given thirty extra leave days and their choice for the next assignment.

In 1946, exhumation orders were issued by the U.S. Army to recover Foster's body. Living at Atka, the Attuans who had buried him, Mike Lokanin and Alfred Prokopioff, accompanied Lt. Col. T. C. Frank of the Army Graves Registration, to Attu. Although the grave was unmarked and the area had been ravaged by the battle to reclaim Attu, the two Natives went directly to the burial site. A small bottle was found, buried at the head of the grave and identified as part of a symbolic ceremony that was performed by the Natives at the time of the burial. Foster's body was clothed in trousers and a heavy blue coat, and he had been wrapped in a Japanese blanket because the Attuans weren't allowed to provide a wooden casket. In the right front temple of his skull, there was a small hole with slightly chipped edges, indicating the entry force of a bullet. The deadly bullet had penetrated at an angle that indicated that Foster was seated when the shot was fired. Found at the grave was a Masonic ring, which was inscribed on the inside "Chas. Foster Jones 8–13–23."

The American soldiers who were killed in the Battle of Attu were buried in Little Falls Cemetery on Attu Island. At the time of his exhumation, it was decided that Foster would also be buried there, this time with a proper marker.

After the new burial, Etta wrote to Foster's friend, Frank Lundin:

9305 Winchester Ave.
Margate, New Jersey
June 7, 1946
Dear Frank:

I am really ashamed that I have let so much time pass without answering.

Yes, I left Foster's body on Attu. The Natives buried him. We were waiting to be taken off the island; had some property on Whidbey Island, near Seattle. He had intended to build a house there and retire, but I don't think he would have ever been content in the States. He was too much a Sourdough. He was very fond of Old Harbor on Kodiak Island and, just toward the last, spoke of returning there. He had located some copper in which he was interested. Once a prospector, always a prospector.

In getting a widow's pension, I had to submit a certified copy of my marriage certificate. I sent to Tanana, and Warren Thompson, who is Commissioner now, sent it to me. There were your name and Marie's, bringing back vividly that wonderful April Fool's Day in 1923. It proved to be anything but an April Fool for me. Foster and I often used to laugh at our temerity at getting married on that day.

With every good wish,
Sincerely yours,
Etta

The headstone for Charles Foster Jones at his final burial site,
Post Cemetery, Fort Richardson, Anchorage, Alaska, 1949.

COURTESY OF TOM PUTNAM, ALTADENA, CALIFORNIA.

A few years later, in 1949, those interred at Little Falls Cemetery were exhumed and buried either in their hometowns, at the Post Cemetery at Fort Richardson in Anchorage, or at Arlington National Cemetery in Washington, D.C. When Etta was contacted regarding these choices, she opted for Anchorage because of Foster's love for Alaska, and she received the following notification.

Department of the Army
Office of the Quartermaster General
Washington 25, D.C.
27 April 1949

Re: Charles F. Jones
Plot A, Row 1, Grave 2
Headstone: Cross
Fort Richardson Post Cemetery
Anchorage, Alaska

270

Mrs. Etta E. Jones
Post Office Box 297
Longport, New Jersey
Dear Mrs. Jones:

The remains of your loved one have been permanently interred as recorded above among comrades who also gave their lives for their country. Customary military services were conducted over the grave at the time of burial.

The cemetery is under the control of the Department of the Army and responsibility for permanent construction, beautification, and perpetual maintenance, including appropriate marking of the grave, will rest with the Army. During these operations, which will extend over a period of several months, visits to the cemetery are not encouraged.

You have received, or will receive, a communication from the cemetery superintendent indicating the type of permanent grave marker to be installed as well as the name and other pertinent date to be inscribed thereon.

You may rest assured that this final interment was conducted with fitting dignity and solemnity and that the gravesite will be carefully and conscientiously maintained in perpetuity by the United States Government.

Sincerely yours,
H. Feldman, Major General
The Quartermaster General

The *Kodiak Daily Mirror*, dated February 23, 1946, reported, "Old Harbor News: In memory of C. Foster Jones, a highly respected former teacher here, who was taken prisoner by the Japs and who gave his life at Attu, his name has been added to our school Honor Roll."

While Etta was recuperating from her ordeal, she read and heard the rumors surrounding events as they supposedly occurred on Attu, and she took issue with them. In an article she wrote for *Pacific Motor Boat* (September 1946) she set some facts straight: "Foster did not broadcast long messages after the landing of the Japs. He could not. Nor had he trained the Natives as a fighting unit. There were no weapons. Neither did we hide in caves, or do any of the other spectacular things such as I have been reading since my return to the United States. Foster and I did two things. As the Japs swarmed down the hillsides, I thrust into the fire all the letters and reports that I could find. And Foster smashed the radio."

While visiting her sister, Nan Smith, in Michigan in December 1945, Etta read an article in the local newspaper that announced that Father Bernard Hubbard (1888–1962), the "Glacier Priest," had a speaking engagement in the area. Father Hubbard, a Jesuit priest from California, led annual expeditions to Alaska's glaciers and used his findings on these scientific expeditions in lecture tours in which he presented his photos, films, and stories. Father Hubbard, Etta, and Nan were photographed together for publication in the local newspaper. In the accompanying article, he told the readers "how he learned from a captured Jap that she [Etta] was a Japanese captive, and relayed the information to Mrs. George H. Smith [Nan], of Montague, sister of Mrs. Jones. Until Mrs. Smith heard from

*(Left to right) Father Hubbard, Etta Jones, and
Etta's sister Nan Smith, in Muskegon, Michigan, December 18, 1945.*

Father Hubbard, she believed her sister dead." Father Hubbard had not contacted Etta's family. In fact, there is no evidence that Father Hubbard ever contacted anyone in Etta's family. They only learned what happened to Etta when she told them herself at the end of the war.

When Etta arrived in Margate, New Jersey, in October 1945, she purchased a home near her brother, Russ. Russ died suddenly, in 1947 at age sixty-six, two short years after Etta's repatriation. Etta then sold her house and moved to Bradenton, Florida, because she had friends there, among them Bess and Gus Martin.

Etta Jones in front of her house in Margate, New Jersey, 1947.

The Martins had been the Moravian missionaries in Kwigillingok, Alaska, who had introduced Foster to the transmitter radio in 1931.

Etta divided her time between Florida in the winters and Michigan in the summers. Her sole surviving sibling, Nan, and Nan's husband, Dr. George Smith, lived in Montague, Michigan, where Etta rented an apartment during the summer months. Just fifteen miles south of Montague, Etta's niece, Elinor, lived in Muskegon. Frequent trips were made from Michigan to Bellefontaine and St. Paris, Ohio, to visit with Foster's family. Once back in the States, Etta spent a considerable amount of time with his family. They also frequently corresponded through the mail.

During their imprisonment, the former POWs had become a close-knit group, helping each other to survive. Those who were capable, counseled the others. When they returned home, their families understandably tried to coax their loved ones back to a state of "normalcy," but amidst all the hovering, the former prisoners felt isolated and alone. When responding to questions about what it was like in the camps, the reaction of listeners was disbelief or tales of how the listening audience had also suffered through the war years.

Added to the pain of their own experiences, there was the devastating loss of family members who had been war casualties or had died while they were interned, so they didn't have the opportunity to say proper good-byes. In some cases, the homes they remembered had been sold, and family members had different residences. This went against the grain of the old homestead they had repeatedly described to their companions. All the women needed was peace, quiet, and time to recover physically and emotionally. It seemed that the only ones who understood all of these feelings of frustration were their fellow internees.

They all kept in close contact through the mail. For years following their ordeal, none of Etta's POW companions enjoyed good health. In letters to her, they spoke of lingering bouts of depression, lethargy, malaria, ulcers, dysentery, rheumatism, anxiety, and eating binges. They marveled at her recovery, asking just where she got her elixir of life. One wrote to Etta that she was "delighted to learn you are feeling so well and have regained some of your lost weight."

Etta was accustomed to cold weather, but the Australian captives had arrived in Japan from the tropics, some without even a light sweater for warmth. When they returned home, they vowed never to

Etta Jones and her car, an English Rover, at Daytona Beach, Florida, circa 1950s.

be cold again. Hunger, they knew, they could handle, but they hoped never again to experience freezing temperatures. One wrote to Etta, "I do hope you can avoid the snowy winters. The thought of snow fills me with horror." Wrote another, "It's getting on four months since we came home. I can't look back to this time last year and think correctly just what we were doing—except freezing." Responding to Etta's letter, one wrote, "Yes, thank goodness and old Uncle Sam

Etta Jones, 1953

that we were spared another winter in that country." The thought of experiencing cold weather made them shudder, although one did write, "It is different looking out at [snow] when one is adequately fed and clothed and a heater is burning in the room."

Talking in their letters about their experience was a kind of therapy for the women: "I've come to the conclusion I'm not the same as I used to be. At times, I still wonder if it is true, and wonder if I won't suddenly wake to hear '*tenko.*' " "It seems almost impossible that we have been away from that dreadful place twelve months. I often look back on those mornings in Japan and wonder just how we did it." "I have just allowed my mind to wander back to Totsuka and our last Christmas there. I think we did do our best to make a miserable life less miserable. I have almost trained the sordid to escape my mind altogether."

The women held Etta very dear to their hearts: "I was thrilled when I received your letter because it brought back so many memories of our happy little chats, and I realized that you are so far away with not much hope of having that privilege again." "I'm sure none of us forget to sing the praises of the wonderful American lady we had with us. How could I help but think of our Sunday mornings and those singsongs which helped us so much?" "We never cease to be thankful for the help you were to us all during those years together. You have a horrible 3 1/2 years to make up." "I find the horrid facts of it fading from my memory. Wishing you all the best, hoping you have many happy and pleasant days and that the days of imprisonment will fade away. Such were those days. Now they are only memories." "Are you still motoring and enjoying yourself as you always do?" One wrote in 1953, "Remember that quilt you gave me? I still have it. You deserve all the happiness you're getting, and I'll never forget you and the way you so often stopped a little more unpleasantness."

In 1957, at age seventy-eight, Etta fulfilled a promise made twelve years earlier to someday reunite with the former internees. Her five-month odyssey took her to New Zealand and Australia, where she was a welcomed guest in the homes of Whytie, Kay, Andy, Tootie, Mavis Cullen, Chris, Mavis Green, and Dora Wilson. Cal had died in 1954, never recovering from the effects of tuberculosis. Between 1945 and 1957, most of the women had married and some had children. She wrote to her niece, Elinor, about her visit.

We had a hilarious time, for there was no gloominess connected with this reunion. There were many funny things to remember. And what one had forgotten, another remembered. Dora had given me a set of snapshots taken by a friend who returned to Japan after the war, gone out to Totsuka where we spent our last year as POWs, and took pictures of the very building where we stayed. We had much fun with those pictures. They recalled so many things, mostly funny. One guard had been a traffic cop in Tokyo, and he entertained us many times showing us how he directed traffic. He asked Kay to teach him English, and she said, "Yes, I'll teach you English," and she taught him to say, "God save the King." Everyday he went about the place repeating his English lesson, and when he neglected it, she prodded him. We were hoping he would not try to show off when some of the English-speaking officials came to visit. When

he asked her what it meant, she said, "It means all same number one emperor."

And then came our TV appearance. It was on a program called "Find the Link," similar to our "What's My Line?" Two people appear together having something in common. In our case the panel was told we had had a common experience, Kay and I. They asked questions which we could answer only "yes" or "no." We thought that one being Australian and the other American, it might be some time before they guessed it, but that panel was smart. In no time at all, they had guessed. We were paid three pounds for that show—about $6.75.

In Australia, word spread that an American was in their midst, and there were requests for guest radio spots and newspaper interviews. Still reluctant to retell her story, Etta was delighted to find that the focus of the interviews was her life in Alaska. This was far different from the interviews in 1945, and she was more than happy to talk about her Alaska.

After her trip to Australia, Etta continued to pursue her passions—immersing herself in cultural events and social gatherings, attending Christian Science services, and corresponding with family members and friends who by now were scattered around the globe. She missed Alaska, but had no desire to return to the place that had brought her so much joy and such unimaginable despair.

When Etta was interviewed or asked to talk to audiences, she continued her unofficial policy of speaking only of her prewar life in Alaska. Her family and friends—and eventually the tea-party givers, politicos, and journalists—respected her silence. But thankfully, for the sake of history and literature, we have her letters.

With her niece, Elinor, at her side, at the age of eighty-six, Etta died on December 12, 1965, in Bradenton, Florida.

Afterword
Ray Hudson

‍‍‍

This remarkable book restores an American hero to her rightful place. Until now, Etta Jones has been little more than a photographic footnote in the history of World War II in the Pacific. She was the American schoolteacher captured on Attu Island during the Japanese invasion of Alaska in June 1942. Photographs of her and her husband appeared regularly in publications about the war, with brief captions, and then, as John Cloe wrote in his excellent history *The Aleutian Warriors,* "Nothing was heard from her again."

Now, through her own words and a careful narrative reconstruction by her greatniece Mary Breu, we learn how an almost accidental invitation led to Etta's years of adventure and service in remote Alaskan villages in the 1920s and 1930s. Government schoolteachers were not always suited to the rigors of the Alaskan "bush," or emotionally equipped to deal with long-established and complex cultures of diverse Native peoples. For twenty years, Etta Jones worked among Athabaskan, Aleut, Alutiiq, and Yup'ik peoples. Her letters abound with details about the lives of trappers, miners, and village residents. Her generous heart and practical goodness are everywhere evident. From Old Harbor on Kodiak Island she wrote, "I loved to go to special services in their church, be it Easter or Christmas. They have good singing voices and good ears for music. In the beautiful chants of the Orthodox Church, without instrumental accompaniment, they sing four parts in perfect harmony." And from isolated Kipnuk, outside of Bethel, where "the tundra was as flat as the ocean," she noted, "No more honest people exist than these people." As the first teacher in the village, she invited everyone to attend school and ended up with sixty-four students and only thirty-three seats. She appreciated the balanced lives Native people led and how they "were never overwhelmed or awed by my material possessions."

If Etta's story consisted of only these years, it would be memorable. The letters she wrote are remarkable. But war, death, and imprisonment followed in harrowing succession. Arriving on Attu in 1941, she and her husband, Charles Foster Jones, were immediately impressed by the Aleut people whom she found "progressive, intelligent, clever, and friendly." A few months later she wrote, "We like Attu. It grows on one, and the people are fine." Then came June 1942. Nothing testifies to the horror of her experiences like her subsequent silence. Mary Breu has done a superb job in piecing together the years Etta Jones spent as a prisoner of war in Japan. These chapters are difficult to read. We witness the prolonged emotional and physical suffering inflicted on prisoners of war by ordinary people.

To all of this, Mary Breu concludes with a coda of reconciliation as she describes her great-aunt's return and reunion with her family. This book, while adding to our understanding of World War II in Alaska, is much more. It is the story of an important American, a woman of courage and resolve, an inextinguishable spirit.

Acknowledgments

I am most grateful to Sara Juday and Tim Frew at Alaska Northwest Books for recognizing the significance of Etta's story. I would also like to thank Kathy Howard and my editor, Ellen Wheat.

The Alaska Humanities Forum/National Endowment for the Arts awarded me a grant to do on-site research of documents in Alaska. Bruce Parham and Diana Kodiak's assistance at the National Archives in Anchorage was invaluable. John Cloe, former command historian at Elmendorf Air Base in Anchorage, took my mother, my son, and me to Foster's gravesite at Post Cemetery, Fort Richardson, Anchorage. We are the only family members who have been able to pay our last respects to the man who gave Etta so much joy, and we want to thank John. After diligent research, John found and gave me copies of Foster's military records. Thank you, Loren Nishimura, Anchorage, for translating Japanese text for me. Lorna Johnston, one of the Australian nurses who was in captivity with Etta, gave me first-hand accounts of what the POWs experienced at the prison sites; I wish to thank her for recalling for me some very unpleasant circumstances. Major William Meanley's sister-in-law and brother, Ann and Eddie Meanley, shared information and pictures to accurately tell the story of Etta's liberation. Elinor Christianson, my mother and Etta's only niece, has provided me with primary source material, background information, and anecdotes. Etta's story could not be told without that information; thank you very much, Mom. Ray Hudson, Jackie Pels, and Verbeck Smith offered advice and encouragement. I am grateful for support from Barbara Sweetland Smith,

Acknowledgments

Bruce Merrell, Marilyn Knapp, Dena Drum, and Alice Petrivelli.

Jim Ducker, editor of *Alaska History*, published my first article in 2003. Meg McKinney Larson, of Valdez, and Jessica Cochran, Anchorage—both associated with Alaska Public Radio—conducted interviews with me in 2004 to raise public awareness of Etta's remarkable story.

I wish to acknowledge the patience and support of my husband, Jerry, my son, Jeff, my daughter, Heather, and my son-in-law, Tony.

Notes

Chapter One, To Alaska

1. Excerpts are taken from Etta Jones' unpublished manuscript. This sixty-four page typed and handwritten manuscript was written in the late 1940s. Hereafter, it will be referred to as Jones manuscript.

Chapter Two, Tanana: 1922-1923

1. Jones manuscript.
2. Frank Lundin, Foster Jones' friend and mining partner, wrote an unpublished manuscript in the late 1960s. Excerpts are taken from this manuscript, and, hereafter, will be referred to as Lundin manuscript.
3. Elinor Christianson is Etta's only niece and the author's mother. Elinor shared anecdotes and answered probative questions during the writing of this book.

Chapter Three, Tanana: 1923-1930

1. Jones manuscript.
2. Lundin manuscript.
3. Elinor Christianson interview with the author.
4. Dena Drum lives in St. Paris, Ohio, Foster's hometown. Intending to write his biography, she researched public records, archival documents, and interviewed Foster's descendants. For now, Dena has set aside her project and has given all her material to the author.

5. George, Dr. Otto. *Eskimo Medicine Man*. Portland: Oregon
   Historical Society, 1979. Written by the last "traveling physician," this book depicts life in remote areas of Alaska in the
   1930s, including the Kuskokwim Delta. Dr. George stayed with
   Etta and Foster for several weeks when they were living in
   Kipnuk.
6. The Alaska Department of Vital Statistics has no record of the
   marriage of Etta and Foster, but the author has the original
   marriage certificate, which was among Etta's documents.
7. Membership records of the Tanana Masonic Lodge and Tanana
   Order of the Eastern Star are in the author's possession.

Chapter Four, Tanana, Tatitlek and Old Harbor: 1928-1932

1. Jones manuscript.
2. Official Personnel Folders/Merged Records Personnel Folders
   and Employee Medical Folders for Federal employment.
   National Personnel Records Center, 111 Winnebago Street, St.
   Louis, Missouri 63118, hereafter referred to as Personnel file.
3. Etta was a prolific letter-writer. To save time and paper, she sent
   multiple copies of her descriptive letters to family and friends.
   The texts of her letters are woven into the manuscript and will
   be hereafter referred to as Jones correspondence.
4. An itemized food list can be found in Eva Alvey Richards' book
   Arctic Mood. Caldwell, Idaho: The Caxton Printers, Ltd., 1949.

Chapter Five, From Kodiak to Kipnuk: 1932

1. Jones correspondence.
2. Jones manuscript.

Chapter Six, Kipnuk Culture: 1932

1. Jones manuscript.

Chapter Seven, Letters from Kipnuk: 1932-1933

1. Jones correspondence.
2. Jones manuscript.

Chapter Eight, Kipnuk School: 1932-1934

1. Jones manuscript.

Chapter Nine, Letters from Kipnuk: 1934-1937

1. Jones correspondence.
2. Jones manuscript.
3. Personnel file.

Chapter Ten, Old Harbor: 1937-1941

1. Jones correspondence.
2. Jones manuscript.
3. Personnel file.
4. Annie Pestrikoff and George Inga were Etta and Foster's students in Old Harbor. Annie and George wrote to the author, sharing their experiences with Etta and Foster.

Chapter Eleven, Attu: 1941-1942

1. Jones correspondence.
2. Jones manuscript.
3. Personnel file.
4. Dena Drum.
5. Recipient of the National Education Association's Leo Reano Award for his work with First Americans and the Alaska State Council Governor's Award for the Arts, Ray Hudson learned how to intricately weave Aleutian baskets when he taught in Unalaska from 1964 to 1992. Master basket weavers Sophie Pletnikoff and Anfesia Shapsnikoff were his teachers. This Native art is described in detail in his book *Moments Rightly Placed: An Aleutian Memoir.* Kenmore, Washington: Epicenter Press, 1998.
6. In the September, 1946 issue of *Pacific Motor Boat,* Etta graphically describes her first impressions of Attu in her article "I Am the Woman the Japs Captured in the Aleutians."
7. Etta stated there was no intermingling with the Japanese because the Natives disliked and distrusted them. The Natives had accused the Japanese of stealing their foxes and killing some of the trappers years before, but for three years, they

hadn't "seen a Jap or Japanese boat." Foster's role, as written in the Weather Bureau directive and in Etta's letters, was to report the weather every six hours and, should he see a Japanese boat, he should report that. Etta and Foster felt comfortable and safe in their location, making long-range plans for the future, suggesting the possibility of starting a herd of reindeer on Attu as a source of food and clothing for the Natives. Foster's reference to the possibility of danger was casual. On December 27, 1941, he wrote to the General Superintendent of the Alaska Native Service in Juneau, "So far, all has gone well at Attu. No Japs have as yet put in an appearance."

Chapter Twelve Invasion: 1942

1. It was reported that Foster had armed and trained "a small army" in case the Japanese invaded the island. In fact, the village was undefended and there was no resistance. There were rumors that when seeing the Japanese running, screaming and shooting while descending a mountain adjacent to the village, Etta and Foster ran in the opposite direction and hid from the invaders, that, while in isolation, they both attempted suicide by slitting their wrists. In fact, when the Japanese approached their house, guns and bayonets pointed at him, Foster stepped outside, arms raised, only to be knocked to the ground and kicked. Another armed soldier entered the house, and, while yelling at her, gestured that Etta should step outside. Etta and Foster were taken into the school where all the Attu Natives, half of them babies and children, were being held at gunpoint.

2. Morgan, Lael, editor. *The Aleutians*. Anchorage: Alaska Geographic Society, 1980. "According to Mrs. Jones' account, her husband '...walked outside and gave himself up. A day later the Japanese reported Jones had taken his own life. Subsequent examination of the body, recovered after the war, conclusively ruled out suicide...' For three months they [Attu Natives] were allowed to remain in their own homes, then evacuated first to Kiska and then to Japan."

3. It was suggested that Etta, Foster, and the Native Attuans were all taken to Japan and imprisoned together. In fact, Etta was transported one week after the invasion. Foster was dead and the Attuans were taken in September.
4. Cloe, John Haile. *The Aleutian Warriors: A History of the 11th Air Force & Fleet Air Wing 4.* Missoula, Montana: Pictorial Histories Publishing Company, Inc., 1991. Using military records and information that were available at the time, the author describes the strategy, planning, and subsequent events at Attu.
5. Cohen, Stan. *The Forgotten War, Volume One.* Missoula, Montana: Pictorial Histories Publishing Company, Inc., 1981. This is a pictorial account of the Aleutian Campaign. The facts, as they pertain to Etta and Foster, are inaccurate in Volume One, but Mr. Cohen corrects the errors in subsequent volumes.
6. Garfield, Brian. *The Thousand-Mile War: World War II in Alaska and the Aleutians.* Garden City, New York: Doubleday and Company, Inc., 1969. This book is heralded as a must read for anyone interested in the Aleutian Campaign. The author found Garfield's information in sharp contrast with her facts. Garfield asserts that, should the Japanese land on Attu, Foster had no intention of being taken alive, that he would head for the hills, a knapsack full of survival supplies already packed and ready for just such an emergency. In Etta's own words, "Foster and I did two things. As the Japs swarmed down the hillsides, I thrust into the fire all the letters and reports that I could find. And Foster smashed his radio."
7. Hrdlicka, Ales. Founder and curator of the Smithsonian Institution National Museum of Natural History, he organized and conducted anthropological expeditions to the Aleutian Islands. His findings are published in *The Aleutian and Commander Islands and Their Inhabitants.* Philadelphia: The Wister Institute of Anatomy and Biology, 1945.
8. Hutchison, Isobel Wylie. *Stepping Stones from Alaska to Asia.* London: Blackie and Son, 1937. Hutchison was a Scottish botanist and filmmaker. Between 1927 and 1936, she travelled the

Arctic regions, stopped at Attu, and wrote her findings in this book.

9. Department of the Interior, Office of the Secretary, "For Release to the AM's of Friday, December 7, 1945." In her story to the secretary and to other associates of the Department of the Interior, she [Etta] emphatically corrected an earlier hearsay account to the effect that her husband had trained a small band of Attu Natives to resist the Japanese landing. "Of my own personal knowledge," she said, "there was never any resistance of any kind. There was nothing to resist with. My husband and one Native had a shotgun apiece for game shooting, but I know that neither of them ever fired a shot at the Japs."

10. While Mrs. Jones' memory as to dates during her long and complete isolation from the outside world is frequently some-what hazy, the details of the capture of Attu are indelibly stamped in her mind.

> WHEN A JAP SHIP WAS SIGHTED *in the outer harbor on that Sunday morning, June 7, 1942, we were not in the least disturbed. We had been warned some weeks previously by the Navy at Dutch Harbor that Attu was a danger spot and were told to be ready for an American naval vessel to pick us up for evacuation. Naturally, everybody thought that what we saw was the long-awaited American ship.*
>
> *Pretty soon, however, some Native fishermen came in and said they had seen a lot of little ships surrounding the big ship. These, we learned later, were landing barges and had not been visible at first. Also, about the same time, some Natives spotted a reconnaissance plane with red circles under its wings. Then we began to suspect that something was amiss, but still we had nothing definite that invasion was near.*
>
> *About 11:00, we suddenly saw Jap soldiers swarming down the mountainside coming from all directions, shooting wildly as they ran. In a twinkling, they were upon us. Some shots rang through the windows of our little house, but there was absolutely no resistance.*
>
> *My husband at the time was at the radio sending the weather report to Dutch Harbor, as was his daily habit as operator of the radio weather station. I rushed to him and cried, 'The Japs are*

here!' He repeated that cryptic remark on the radio, but we never knew whether it was received, since weather conditions were bad for sending radio messages and he was broadcasting the weather report 'blind.'

A moment later, a young Jap officer entered our house, just as I was going to give myself up. He shouted to both my husband and me, 'Come outside, and bring nothing with you.' I did manage to pick up my glasses on the way out.

After a complete search of our house, as well as those of the Natives, we were all herded into the school house for a talk by the commanding officer. The officer gave quite a suave talk about their having 'come to release the Aleuts from American tyranny' and that they would be allowed to carry on their normal life, provided, and this was repeatedly emphasized, that they obeyed orders. The Japs started right in teaching us how to bow low three times each time we met an officer.

Late that first day, the Aleut Natives were allowed to return to their homes, which they found stripped of everything valuable. But my husband and I were not permitted to return to our house. We were told to go to an empty house because, ours being the best house on the island, the Jap officers wanted it for themselves.

I was permitted to have my own bed, but was forced to carry it myself. My husband was cuffed to one side when he tried to carry it for me. As I was lugging it along in the dark, a Jap guard constantly prodded me in the back with the butt of his rifle. Once I fell down in the slippery mud (It had been raining.), and then the guard kicked me in the stomach until I thought I would faint. During that trip, I saw them knock my husband down three times, for no reason at all.

That night, my husband and I spent together in this barren house, with no lights or other comforts.

Next morning, the commanding officer sent for my husband to come to headquarters. I never saw him alive again. From then on, my temporary abode was strictly guarded every minute, and the Natives had been instructed not to talk to me.

A day or two later, however, some of them managed to get near enough to me to whisper, 'We buried Mr. Jones near the church.' I whispered, *'Did you have a box* [coffin]*?' 'No,'* they whispered, *'we were not allowed to have a box.'*

Each day thereafter, as was his daily custom, my Jap guard would say, 'Your husband is well. He sends his love. We've got him where it's warmer.'

One week later, on June 14, Mrs. Jones was taken away to Japan on a Jap ship, which evidently had been converted to war service from a tourist vessel.

11. Kohlhoff, Dean. *When the Wind Was a River*. Seattle and London: University of Washington Press, 1995. Professor Kohlhoff, Valparaiso University, Valparaiso, Indiana, spent six summers in Alaska, researching the treatment of Aleuts at the hands of the United States Army, Navy, Department of the Interior, and Territory of Alaska agencies. Using personal accounts, videotapes of Aleuts telling their wartime experiences, and civilian and government archives, Kohlhoff tells the dark story of Native Alaskans and their relocation, including those at Attu. This scholarly book includes bibliographical references and an index.

12. Oliver, Ethel Ross. *Journal of an Aleutian Year*. Seattle and London: University of Washington Press, 1988. When the former Attu Natives were released from Japan, instead of returning to their ancestral home, the United States government sent them to Atka, the land of their traditional rivals. The appendices in this book include first-hand accounts of the Attu invasion told by Mike Lokanin and Alex Prossoff.

13. Sugiyama, Masami. *Ichimai no shashin o otte Aryushan o yuku.* This is the Japanese account with photographs of events and people at Attu and Hokkaido, Japan, where the Attu Natives were interned. The Japanese text was translated for the author by a Japanese-American who lives in Anchorage.

14. Report of the Commission on Wartime Relocation. *Personal Justice Denied*. Washington, D.C., December 1982. The purpose of the Commission was threefold: 1. to review the facts and circumstances, as directed in Executive Order 9066, issued

February 19, 1942, that resulted in the relocation of Japanese-Americans and Alaska Aleuts during World War II; 2. review directives of United States military forces requiring the relocation and, in some cases, detention in internment camps of American citizens, including Aleut civilians, and permanent resident aliens of the Aleutian and Pribilof Islands; and 3. recommend appropriate remedies. In fulfilling this mandate, the Commission held twenty days of hearings in cities across the country, particularly on the West Coast, recording testimony from more than 750 witnesses: evacuees, former government officials, public figures, interested citizens, and historians and other professionals who have studied the subjects of the Commission inquiry. An extensive effort was made to locate and review the records of government action and to analyze other sources of information including contemporary writings, personal accounts, and historical analyses.

15. Aleutian/Pribilof Islands Association is an Aleut non-profit organization that has an extensive library and archival collection. Photos and records document the history and culture of Attu, including events as they happened before, during, and after the Japanese occupation in 1942.

16. Innokenty Golodoff, as told to Karl W. Kenyon, "The Last Days of Attu Village," *Alaska Sportsman*, December 1966. In reference to Etta and Foster, Innokenty states, "Later on they found the body of her husband. I saw them bring him. They wrapped him up in a blanket. They took Mrs. Foster away from Attu first--she didn't go with us. I never saw her again but after the war we heard she got back to the States. We lived on Attu three months after the Japs came. They guarded our houses all the time. We could go outside for fresh air but not away from the houses except that they let us go out and fish once in awhile. The Japs were ready to leave in September."

17. *Seattle-Post Intelligencer.* Mike Lokanin's story, Nov. 28, 1945.

18. *Pacific Motor Boat*, September 1946.

19. When Native Atkan Alice Petrivelli was twelve years old, she met Etta and Foster when they were on their way to Attu. They

stopped at Atka to visit their friends and fellow Alaska Indian Service teachers, Ruby and Ralph McGee. The McGees introduced Etta and Foster to their students, Alice among them. In interviews in 2003 and 2004, Alice shared her considerable knowledge of the Attu people and their culture with the author.

20. "Aleut Evacuation: The Untold War Story," produced by Michael and Mary Jo Thill, 1992. This video depicts the Aleutian subsistence culture that was disrupted when the Japanese attacked Dutch Harbor, Attu and Kiska. Native Aleuts describe the bombing, dire circumstances during their relocation and life after the war.

21. "The Aleutians: Cradle of the Storms, Part Two," produced by Natural History New Zealand and Oregon Public Broadcasting, 2001. Native Aleuts share their horror stories about life at the hands of their Japanese captors.

22. The following excerpts are examples of propaganda published and distributed in Japan.

In 1943, "Attsu To" (Attu Island) was written by Tomoya Tsuruia.

THE VILLAGE WAS SIGHTED *from a distance of 1000 meters. After the attack on the village had commenced, a large 'American' appeared from the communication post. He took 5 or 6 steps toward the beach, then turned toward us. It was then that he first realized that the village was being attacked from the mountains, not the beach. He quickly ran back into the building. The troop commander noticed that he was an old man. The troops opened fire with light and heavy machine guns, but only to intimidate the occupants of the village, not to wound or kill. The order to advance reverberated across the tundra, and a group of soldiers hurried to the building containing the communication equipment. Another corps, which had already surrounded the village, began to close in.*

The 'American' came out of the communication station, holding his hands above his head. The soldiers realized that he was not on combat duty. The corps commander ran up to the old man, and held his military sword to the old man's chest as he handed the man an ultimatum printed in English. The old man ran his eyes over the ultimatum. *After having read it, he mumbled something unintelligible, lowered his hands and then saluted.*

The Natives began to come out of their houses, hands held high in the air.

'There is a woman inside,' said the man, Foster Jones, who we later learned was a weather observer and communications technician. We opened the door to one of the rooms of the communication station, and inside a plump old lady rose to her feet. She was trembling, her hands flying about her bosom. Both 'Americans' were unarmed.

The troop commander ordered the couple to put on overcoats and go outside. They were given permission to smoke.

All the Natives were also made to gather in front of the communication post.

'The Japanese Army does not kill prisoners, you have nothing to worry about,' said the commander, in imperfect English.

We talked with the islanders and gave cigarettes and candy to them. It was then that we learned that Foster Jones was considered a grumpy old man, and that the Aleuts felt that in his heart, Jones held them in contempt. They also said that Foster had as little to do with them as possible. Mrs. Jones was friendly and vivacious, but wanted badly to return to the mainland. This conversation took place on the same day as that of the Jones' attempted suicide. The Natives, as devout Christians, felt that the old couple were guilty of a sin, and prayed that they should be forgiven. That evening, Foster Jones died from excessive bleeding. His wife was saved, and repeatedly thanked the Army doctor for all his ministrations.

Foster Jones was buried in the graveyard beside the church. A clump of flowers was planted on his grave.

Kirtland, John C. and David F. Coffin, Jr. "The Relocation and Internment of the Aleuts During World War II." Anchorage: Aleutian/Pribilof Islands Association, Inc., 1981. Contained in this report is "Arushan Shugeki Senki" (Attack on the Aleutians) by Mikizo Fukuzawa, Tokyo, 1943. When describing the Attu Natives' homes and buildings, Fukuzawa wrote:

THE SCHOOL WAS, IN ACTUALITY, a U.S. Navy communication post. It seems that America was planning to evacuate all residents of the Aleutians to Alaska, to station troops throughout the islands and to use the islands for military purposes. This was in view of the rapidly changing course of worldwide events, particularly since the Japanese-American problem had come so prominently to the attention of the general public. There was already an order for all of the residents of Attu to evacuate the island by the end of August. Because of this order, the yearly supply ship sent from the mainland—for which the islanders had to pay—had not yet come this year. This in itself was out of the ordinary. The ship had been cancelled to impress upon the Attuans that, if they did not follow the above instructions, there would be no further replenishment of supplies.

For the two 'Americans' on the island, a large house with many rooms, double-pane windows and an oil heater was provided. The attitude of the 'Americans' toward the Attuans is shown clearly by the presence of an electrical generator and running water in the Jones' house. When we occupied the island, the Natives feared that it was an attack by the Germans. The islanders had been told by the 'Americans' that America and Germany were at war, but had not been told that Japan and America were also at war. The islanders were relieved when they saw that we were of the Imperial Army, for they knew of the Japanese from a ship that had put into the bay five years ago. They also felt a kind of kinship because of the similarity of facial features.

The islanders were at first frightened by the presence of the Imperial Army, but were soon impressed by the strict discipline of the troops. As soon as the village was occupied, a rope barrier was placed around the cluster of Native houses, and the soldiers were not allowed to approach the barrier. The Natives first felt, because of the rope barrier, that their freedom had been curtailed, but later became appreciative when they realized that the rope was not to contain them, but to forestall any untoward approaches by the soldiers. The islanders became completely at ease and trusting of the Army when they saw how the soldiers treated the children with affection. They were awed by the bicycles and automobiles, the first they had ever seen. Soon, the young people started to accompany us into the mountains and out onto the bay. The adults also gave us salmon in return for sundries. Soon life settled into a gayer and more peaceful manner than before the invasion and all 42 of the Aleuts lived in complete peace and freedom from anxiety, under the complete protection of the Imperial Army.

The Jones had tried to commit double suicide early this morning by cutting the blood vessels in their wrists. They were discovered by the Natives who had heard their moans of pain. The Natives immediately informed the medical officer, who went to the aid of the old couple. 'They have bled profusely, but maybe they can be saved,' said the doctor. I thought of the plump old couple, who had taken the initiative in helping the Natives adjust to the new situation, and had promised, through our interpreter, to obey all orders of the Imperial Army. Obeying the orders of the troop commander, we did everything within our powers to nurse the old couple back to health, but that evening, the husband died at the age of 65 on a little island at the tip of the Aleutian chain. His wife was saved, and thanked the medical officer profusely. 'Thank you for your kindness. When you first came to help us, my husband said that he was beyond help, and asked that I put him out of his misery.' The medical officer explained all of these events to me. Afterward, the body of Jones was buried with proper ceremony in the graveyard of the church at the foot of the hill. He was buried by the troops.

Chapter Thirteen, The Australians: January-July 1942

1. Bowman, Alice. *Not Now Tomorrow*. Bangalow, NSW Australia: Daisy Press, 1996. While in captivity, Alice, an Australian civilian nurse and POW with Etta Jones, secretly wrote this personal diary.

2. Clarence, Margaret. *Yield not to the Wind*. Sydney: Management Development Publishers PTY Limit, 1982. Margaret Clarence's mother, Kathleen Bignell, was an Australian civilian held in Japanese POW camps with Etta Jones. Mrs. Bignell's experiences are described in her diaries and poems written while in captivity. Biographical photos are included.

3. Nelson, Hank. *POW Prisoners of War: Australians Under Nippon*. Sydney: ABC Enterprises, 1985. The author uses first-hand accounts as told by military men and women who barely survived the horrors of Japanese prison camps.

4. Reeson, Margaret. *Whereabouts Unknown*. Claremont, California: Albatross Books, 1993. Using original documents and first-hand accounts, the author very effectively weaves the stories of Australian families affected by separation and the men and women who disappeared behind enemy lines during World War II.

5. Lorna Whyte Johnston was in captivity in Japan with Etta Jones. Lorna and the author have corresponded for several years and, in her letters, Lorna graphically described prison conditions. Hereafter, Lorna's letters will be referred to as Johnston correspondence.

6. *The Montevideo Maru* was a Japanese ship that transported captive Australian military and civilian personnel from Rabaul, Papua New Guinea, to Japan in spring, 1942. En route, the ship was torpedoed, and all those on board were lost. Website: www.montevideomaru.info.

7. Civilian and military men and seventeen nurses and one female civilian, all Australians captured at Rabaul and the Sacred Heart Catholic Mission, Vunapope, Papua New Guinea, were transported to Japan on the Naruto Maru. www.west-point.org/family/Japanese-pow/PhotoFile.

Chapter Fourteen, Bund Hotel, Yokohama: July 1942

1. Bowman.
2. Clarence.
3. Reeson.
4. Johnston correspondence.
5. Personnel file.

Chapter Fifteen, Yokohama Yacht Club: 1942-1943

1. Bowman.
2. Clarence.

3. Reeson.

4. Elinor Christianson interview with author.

5. On June 29, 1942, Claude Hirst, General Superintendent of the Alaska Indian Service, Juneau, wrote to John Collier, Commissioner of Indian Affairs, Washington, D.C., "There is much concern about our teachers at Attu, Alaska, Mr. and Mrs. Charles Foster Jones. The last time they were heard from was a weather report sent out by Mr. Jones on the morning of June 7th. In their last quarterly report, made up [in] the early part of May, Mrs. Jones stated: 'School closed abruptly upon orders to have the entire village removed to a safe place for the duration of the war.' If you can obtain any information about Mr. and Mrs. Jones, we shall appreciate your notifying us."

6. Claude Hirst wrote to Foster's brother, Dr. Z.K. Jones, on July 1, 1942, "As you no doubt read in the papers, Attu Island has been taken by the Japanese, and we must presume that Mr. and Mrs. Jones are prisoners of war. The last message to come from them was on June 7. Mr. and Mrs. Jones have been in our service for many years, and it is with much regret that we must advise you of their present plight."

7. July 20, 1943, Claude Hirst wrote to Eleanor Williams, Acting Director of Information, Office of Indian Affairs in Chicago, "The information that I sent you in previous correspondence was obtained while I was in Anchorage. Miss Olive Trower, Junior Administrative Assistant in our office, wrote a letter to the Alaska Defense Command which Mr. Fred R. Geeslin signed and the enclosed is the reply. We are all inclined to doubt the statement that Mr. Jones committed suicide because he never seemed to be that type of person. His poise in all situations was excellent and it is difficult for us to believe that he did commit suicide. You will note the statement that he 'shot himself,' while the statement I obtained was that he 'slashed his wrists.' The information that I received was supposed to have been from an account of the invasion of Attu by the Japs written by a Domei correspondent and the substance of this was published in the *Anchorage Daily Times*, June 25, 1943."

8. William Zimmerman, Acting Commissioner of Indian Affairs,
Washington, D.C., wrote to the Bureau of Public Relations,
Navy Department, Washington, D.C. on July 23, 1943, having
sent an identical letter to the War Department on July 10:

> WE ARE ANXIOUS TO OBTAIN *information as to the whereabouts or fate
> of our two employees, Mr. and Mrs. Charles Foster Jones, and the
> forty-five Aleuts who were presumably on Attu at the time of the
> Japanese occupation in June 1942.*
>
> *I realize that military operations in that area have necessitated
> secrecy, but in view of several recent conflicting reports, I am won-
> dering if we might be a little more fully informed about the Joneses at
> this time or as soon as military operations permit.*
>
> *If the Joneses and the Aleut Natives are held as prisoners of war
> on the island of Sakhalin, as has been reported confidentially to me,
> can steps be taken soon to insure their safe removal to American soil?*
>
> *A United Press story datelined May 31, Massacre Bay, Attu,
> states Jones succeeded in killing himself in a suicide attempt. Mrs.
> Jones also attempted suicide, according to the news story, but sur-
> vived and was taken as prisoner to Zentsuji, Japan.*
>
> *The Red Cross in Seattle has directed inquiries concerning the
> fate of the Joneses to our Juneau headquarters where, of course, we
> are unable to give any information.*
>
> *I shall appreciate anything you care to write me, either confi-
> dentially, or a statement for public use.*

Chapter Sixteen, Yokohama Yacht Club: 1943-1944

1. Bowman.
2. Clarence.
3. Reeson.
4. On June 22, 1943, Fred R. Geeslin, Administrative Assistant
in the Alaska Indian Service, Juneau, wrote to Paul Fickinger,
Office of Indian Affairs in Chicago, "In Attu village in the
Aleutians, American GI's have solved two mysteries. One
mystery was the disappearance of the only two white persons
on Attu, at the time of the Japanese invasion. American soldiers
found the body of Charles Foster Jones, who had committed

suicide by slashing his wrists. Mrs. Jones also attempted suicide but she recovered and now is in a concentration camp at Zentsuji, Japan. The other puzzle of Attu village was the discovery of a lot of lipstick and rouge in Japanese dugouts. It was learned, however, that the Japanese used it in place of wax to imprint their names on letters for the folks back in Tokyo. The manager of the station informed us that he had received this information from Washington and it is seemed that it is official."

5. Johnston correspondence.

6. Personnel file.

Chapter Seventeen, Totsuka: 1944-1945

1. Bowman.

2. Clarence.

3. Reeson.

4. Johnston correspondence.

Chapter Eighteen, Rescue: August 1945

1. Ann and Eddie Meanley are the sister-in-law and brother of Major William Meanley. They recorded the account of the rescue as told to them by Major Meanley. They shared this remarkable story with the author, and it is quoted here with their permission.

2. Bowman.

3. Reeson.

4. Johnston correspondence.

5. *Seattle Post-Intelligencer*, September 1, 1945.

6. Personnel file.

Chapter Nineteen, Return to the United States: September 1945

1. Following a diligent search on behalf of the author, Command Historian (retired) John Cloe gave her declassified military records pertaining to Foster Jones' disinterment directive. In a letter to Commanding General, Davis Air Force Base (Tucson, AZ), dated 27 April 1948:

FOR THE RECORD: *Two natives of Atka are cognizant of the whereabouts of the isolated grave of Mr. Jones…. This letter requests orders to be issued by CG, Adak, for these two persons when the Repatriation Program gets underway in Attu.*

1. It is requested that an invitation be extended to Mr. A. Prosoff and Mr. M. Lokanin, residents of Atka (formerly residents of Attu), to travel from Atka to Attu, for the purpose of rendering assistance to the Graves Registration Service in locating the remains of the late Mr. Foster Jones, formerly Indian teacher of Attu.

2. Upon acceptance, it is requested that appropriate travel orders be issued for travel to be performed by either or both Mr. Lokanin and Mr. Prosoff, from Atka to Attu and return, by either military air or water transportation.

3. It is necessary that Mr. Prosoff and Mr. Lokanin arrive at Attu during the period 1-15 July, at which time the GRS Repatriation Group will be engaged in disinterment activities at Attu. The specific date on which the presence of these two persons at Attu will be required will be furnished by the Commanding General, Davis Air Force Base, by Lt. Colonel Tony C. Frank, Graves Registration Officer, as soon as it is possible to set a definite date for the arrival of the Repatriation Group at Attu.

2. Simeon Oliver, who accompanied Lokanin and Prosoff, wrote on June 23, 1947:

WE FOUND THE SITE OF THE FORMER VILLAGE *of Attu completely bare of any remains of the village buildings. Two small Army huts stood on the site and [the] whole area leveled by the work of bulldozers. It took a few minutes for the men to find the outline of the foundation of their little church. From the northwest corner just a few paces they found the depression of the grave aligned with the mounds of two small graves in what was the tiny churchyard. Mike and Alfred then cleared the area and Colonel gave orders to a Lieutenant from the Attu base to exhume the body and on the next day remove it to the Army cemetery, Little Falls Cemetery, near the base on Massacre Bay."*

A declassified report from the Alaskan Operations Group, American Graves Registration Service in reference to

"...*examination of remains of Charles Foster Jones*," dated 15 July 1948 states, in part, "*The remains had been interred in a Japanese blanket. The body was clothed in trousers and a heavy blue coat. The clothing contained no markings or personal items. The skull of the remains revealed a small hole in the right frontal portion. The edges of the hole were slightly chipped indicating the force of impact. The only item of personal property found on the remains was a Masonic ring. The inside of the ring was inscribed CHAS. FOSTER JONES 8-13-23.*" Dated 3 August 1948. "*Mr. Jones is entitled to repatriation inasmuch as he was a citizen of the United States and whose home was in fact in the United States. His death outside of the continental limits thereof can be directly attributed to the war since he was employed or otherwise engaged in activities contributing to the prosecution of the war.*"

3. Lulu Fairbanks, "I've Been Thinking," *The Alaska Weekly*, September 28, 1945.
4. *San Francisco News*, September 12, 1945.
5. Elinor Christianson interview with the author.
6. Jones correspondence.
7. Personnel file.

Chapter Twenty, Home: 1945-1965

1. Department of the Interior, Office of the Secretary, December 7, 1945:

   DURING THE FIRST FEW MONTHS *of her captivity, she* [Etta] *was lodged at the Bund Hotel in Yokohama, and, thereafter, at a yacht club until she was transferred about a year ago to Totsuka. She had been evacuated, she said, because the Japs had correctly suspected that Yokohama would be bombed.*

   During her whole time as a prisoner, Mrs. Jones said, she was never once permitted to write or receive any private messages of any sort. She and the others interned with her were never even allowed to have a radio. They were permitted to buy the Nippon Times, an English language newspaper published in Tokyo. Naturally, all the news they got was to the effect that Japan was winning the war on all fronts.

'When the Americans retook the Philippines,' said Mrs. Jones, 'the *Nippon Times* saved face by saying the Japs had retreated from the Philippines, since they no longer had any strategic importance. Our capture of Okinawa was given similar news treatment.'

Mrs. Jones and her fellow internees used to spend considerable time at night trying to count the number of American bombers over Tokyo, where huge incendiary fires were plainly visible.

'In the morning,' she continued, 'when we would ask the guards what that was lighting up the Tokyo sky last night, they would invariably reply, 'Oh, that was American planes burning after being shot down by Japanese antiaircraft guns!'

'We would just smile. Of course, we knew better.'

In spite of being constantly fed with Jap-victory propaganda, Mrs. Jones said she never had a moment's despair over the final outcome or of her eventual rescue.

2. In *Pacific Motor Boat*, Etta wrote, "Foster did not broadcast long messages after the landing of the Japs. He could not. Nor had he trained the Natives as a fighting unit. There were no weapons. Neither did we hide in caves, or do any of the other spectacular things such as I have been reading since my return to the United States."

3. Newspaper accounts stated that Etta was treated by her captors with exceptional kindness, that she had her own state room when traveling to Japan. Actually, she was on a troop transport, was knocked down onto the deck, interrogated for hours then locked in a tiny room. While in Japan, she supposedly had her own personal maid at her beck and call and who tended to her every need. In fact, Etta was a Japanese POW, and she was treated as such—slapped, kicked, punched, threatened and systematically starved.

4. It was reported that after the war, Etta returned to Attu specifically to retrieve Native artifacts she had hidden in the caves. The fact is, Etta never returned to Alaska, the place that had brought her so much joy and such unimaginable despair.

5. Rose Curtice Butts, "Prisoners from Alaska," *The Alaska*

Sportsman, May 1948. The author states, "By their own choice, the surviving Aleuts did not return to the far island home, preferring to join their kinsmen at Atka instead." This contradicts Kohlhoff's report that when American troops freed the Aleuts, they were asked if they wanted to go home, and they all said yes.

Innokenty Golodoff declared, "We tried to go to Attu, but the Government wouldn't let us go." The Attu Natives said Interior officials told them there were insufficient numbers of Attu people to justify a hospital which would have to be built. "The Government told us to live with the Atka people." Alex Prossoff was also clear on this matter. "We wanted to go to Attu," he insisted, but were told "We must come to Atka" because Attu was occupied by soldiers and the village was destroyed. Interviews were held in January, 1979 "…intended for use by whosoever may be directed for fact-finding assignments as intended by the Executive director of the Aleutian/Pribilof Islands Association, Inc." When asked, "When you were being taken to Atka, how did you and your people feel about not being returned to Attu?" Innokenty Golodoff responded, "Everybody was homesick." Parascovia Lokanin's response to the same question was "We were sick about it."

6. *Muskegon* (Michigan) *Chronicle*, December 19, 1945.

7. *Kodiak* (Alaska) *Daily Mirror*, February 23, 1946.

8. After their release, the Australian POWs corresponded with Etta. Excerpts from their letters are included in this chapter.

9. Jones correspondence to Elinor Christianson, December 24, 1957.

Bibliography

Bowman, Alice M. *Not Now Tomorrow.* Australia: Daisy Press, 1996.

Christianson, Elinor (Smith). Communication with the author, December 3, 2003; January 15, 2005; March 30, 2005; July 12, 2005; May 7, 2006.

Clarence, Margaret. *Yield Not to the Wind.* Sydney: Management Development Publishers PTY Limited, 1982.

Fairbanks, Lulu. "I've Been Thinking." *Alaska Weekly.* September 28, 1945.

George, Otto. *Eskimo Medicine Man.* Portland: Oregon Historical Society, 1979.

Haugland, Vern. "Fate of Attu Couple Revealed." *Seattle Post-Intelligencer,* September 1, 1945.

Hrdlicka, Ales. *The Aleutian and Commodore Islands and Their Inhabitants.* Philadelphia: Wister Institute of Anatomy and Biology, 1945.

Jones, Etta. Unpublished manuscript, December 1945.

Jones, Etta. "I Am the Woman the Japs Captured in the Aleutians." *Pacific Motor Boat* (September 1946) 38–91.

Kenny, Catherine. *Captives: Australian Army Nurses in Japanese Prison Camps.* London: University of Queensland Press, 1987.

Lundin, Frank. Unpublished manuscript, 1967.

McDonald, Lucile. "Alaska Steam." *Alaska Geographic* 11 (1984).

Nelson, Hank. *POW Prisoners of War: Australians Under Nippon.* Sydney: ABC Enterprises, 1985.

Norman, Elizabeth. *We Band of Angels.* New York: Random House, 1999.

Petrivelli, Alice. Personal communication with the author, July 17, 2003.

"Priest, Surprised, Meets Widow

of Jap Victim." *Muskegon* (Michigan) *Chronicle*, December 12, 1945.

Reeson, Margaret. *Whereabouts Unknown*. Claremont, California: Albatross Books, 1993.

Richards, Eva Alvery. *Arctic Mood*. Caldwell, Idaho: Caxton Printers, 1949.

Snapp, Jeremy S. *Northwest Legacy: Sail, Steam and Motorships*. Lopez Island, Washington: Pacific Heritage Press, 1999.

Sugiyama, Masami. *Ichimai no shasin o ottte Aryushan o yuku*. Tokyo: Sugiyami, 1987.

"Woman Survivor of Attu Rescued," UPI, *San Francisco News*. September 12, 1945.

Index

About the Author

While growing up, Mary Breu knew that her great-aunt, Etta Jones, had lived an extraordinary life. At the conclusion of her teaching career, Mary set out to tell Etta's remarkable story. While doing research, she discovered that little, if anything, had been accurately written about Etta Jones's life story. To set the record straight, Mary began writing, using Etta's letters, saved by family members, and Etta's unpublished manuscript, written after her captivity. Mary's article "Pioneer and Prisoner: Etta Jones in Alaska" was published in the Spring/Fall 2003 issue of *Alaska History*, and then she wrote this book.

A Michigan native, with bachelor's and master's degrees, Mary taught elementary school for thirty-four years. She and her husband, Jerry, live in South Carolina and have two children, Jeff and Heather.

To learn more about Etta Jones and to contact Mary Breu, go to www.lastlettersfromattu.com.

About the Afterword Writer

Ray Hudson lived and worked as a teacher in the Aleutian Islands from 1964 to 1992. In addition to numerous articles on Aleutian history, he is the author of *Moments Rightly Placed: An Aleutian Memoir* and *Family After All: Alaska's Jesse Lee Home*, Vol. I, Unalaska, 1889–1925. He edited An *Aleutian Ethnography* by Lucien M. Turner. His poetry has appeared in *Ice Floe: Poetry of the Far North, The Comstock Review, World Order*, and other journals. A woodblock print artist, he has had one-person exhibitions at the Museum of Contemporary Art, Petropavlovsk-Kamchatsky, Russia, and the Museum of the Aleutians, Unalaska.

Printed in the USA
CPSIA information can be obtained
at www.ICGtesting.com
JSHW012020140824
68134JS00033B/2788

9 780882 408101